Goth

Dress, Body, Culture

Series Editor **Joanne B. Eicher**, *Regents' Professor, University of Minnesota*

Books in this provocative series seek to articulate the connections between culture and dress which is defined here in its broadest possible sense as any modification or supplement to the body. Interdisciplinary in approach, the series highlights the dialogue between identity and dress, cosmetics, coiffure, and body alterations as manifested in practices as varied as plastic surgery, tattooing, and ritual scarification. The series aims, in particular, to analyze the meaning of dress in relation to popular culture and gender issues and will include works grounded in anthropology, sociology, history, art history, literature, and folklore.

ISSN: 1360-466X

Previously published titles in the Series

Helen Bradley Foster, *"New Raiments of Self": African American Clothing in the Antebellum South*
Claudine Griggs, *S/he: Changing Sex and Changing Clothes*
Michaele Thurgood Haynes, *Dressing Up Debutantes: Pageantry and Glitz in Texas*
Anne Brydon and Sandra Niesson, *Consuming Fashion: Adorning the Transnational Body*
Dani Cavallaro and Alexandra Warwick, *Fashioning the Frame: Boundaries, Dress and the Body*
Judith Perani and Norma H. Wolff, *Cloth, Dress and Art Patronage in Africa*
Linda B. Arthur, *Religion, Dress and the Body*
Paul Jobling, *Fashion Spreads: Word and Image in Fashion Photography*
Fadwa El-Guindi, *Veil: Modesty, Privacy and Resistance*
Thomas S. Abler, *Hinterland Warriors and Military Dress: European Empires and Exotic Uniforms*
Linda Welters, *Folk Dress in Europe and Anatolia: Beliefs about Protection and Fertility*
Kim K.P. Johnson and Sharron J. Lennon, *Appearance and Power*
Barbara Burman, *The Culture of Sewing*
Annette Lynch, *Dress, Gender and Cultural Change*
Antonia Young, *Women Who Become Men*
David Muggleton, *Inside Subculture: The Postmodern Meaning of Style*
Nicola White, *Reconstructing Italian Fashion: America and the Development of the Italian Fashion Industry*
Brian J. McVeigh, *Wearing Ideology: The Uniformity of Self-Presentation in Japan*
Shaun Cole, *Don We Now Our Gay Apparel: Gay Men's Dress in the Twentieth Century*
Kate Ince, *Orlan: Millennial Female*
Nicola White and Ian Griffiths, *The Fashion Business: Theory, Practice, Image*
Ali Guy, Eileen Green and Maura Banim, *Through the Wardrobe: Women's Relationships with their Clothes*
Linda B. Arthur, *Undressing Religion: Commitment and Conversion from a Cross-Cultural Perspective*
William J.F. Keenan, *Dressed to Impress: Looking the Part*
Joanne Entwistle and Elizabeth Wilson, *Body Dressing*
Leigh Summers, *Bound to Please: A History of the Victorian Corset*

DRESS, BODY, CULTURE

Goth
Identity, Style and Subculture

Paul Hodkinson

Oxford • New York

LEARNING RESOURCES
CENTRE

Havering College
of Further and Higher Education

First published in 2002 by
Berg
Editorial offices:
150 Cowley Road, Oxford, OX4 1JJ, UK
838 Broadway, Third Floor, New York, NY 10003-4812, USA

Berg is an imprint of Oxford International Publishers Ltd.

Library of Congress Cataloging-in-Publication Data
Hodkinson, Paul.
    Goth : identity, style, and subculture / Paul Hodkinson.
        p. cm. – (Dress, body, culture, ISSN 1360-466X)
Includes bibliographical references.
    ISBN 1-85973-600-9 (Cloth) – ISBN 1-85973-605-X (Paper)
    1. Goth culture (Subculture)   2. Goth culture (Subculture) – Great
Britain.   I. Title.   II. Series.
    HQ796 .H62 2002
    306'.1–dc21

British Library Cataloguing-in-Publication Data
A catalogue record for this book is available from the British Library.

ISBN   1 85973 600 9 (Cloth)
       1 85973 605 X (Paper)

Contents

List of Illustrations

Acknowledgements

I am indebted in various ways to all manner of individuals both within and outside the two worlds crucial to the production of this book: academia and the goth scene.

First and foremost, I would like to thank my PhD supervisor Peter Symon for his knowledge, reliability, hard work and continual encouragement. Thanks are also due to Ann Gray and Angela McRobbie for their in-depth and insightful comments on my work and to the anonymous reader who reviewed my original thesis for Berg, for producing an invaluable set of ideas and suggestions on translating it to a book. For their interest and/or for providing valuable debate and discussion of the issues at the centre of this book, I also wish to mention by name Kathryn Earle, Andy Bennett, Mark Cieslik, Keith Harris, Chris Mann, Steve Miles, David Muggleton and Hillary Pilkington. More generally, I would like to thank, for support and advice, all the staff and postgraduates with whom I have spent time in the Department of Cultural Studies and Sociology, and the Centre for Urban and Regional Studies at the University of Birmingham. I am also grateful for the interest in my research shown by both staff and students in the School of Social Studies at University College Northampton.

Most of all, I wish to thank all those who took part in the research which led to this book, whether as interviewees, questionnaire respondents, photograph subjects, or merely providers of conversation, discussion or advice. In particular I am indebted to Jo Hampshire for her advice and help with the Whitby Festival Questionnaire, and to Greg Crighton, David McCullie, Nikki Brown and Leslie Morris for invaluable help, advice, company and free accommodation during my fieldwork. I would also like to give special mention to the subscribers of the Tainted mailing list, who have been an immediate source of advice, information and ideas on numerous occasions.

I am indebted also to the continual support and advice of my parents, Phil and Heather Hodkinson, and finally to Sarah Wainwright, not only for proofreading and full-time support, but for producing most of the photographic illustrations throughout the book.

1

From Participant to Researcher

A Weekend by the Sea

A car pulls up outside my home in the English city of Birmingham on a rainy Friday morning at the end of October 1998. The long black hair of its occupants informs me that this is my lift. I run outside toward the car, using my rucksack to shield my recently dyed and crimped purple and pink streaked hair from the rain. The tall, slim, male driver, wearing eye-liner and dressed up in tight black jeans and a purple velvet shirt, gets out and helps make space for my luggage in the back of the car, among numerous other bags and various pairs of large black boots. We get into the car, and I am greeted by the three female passengers, and immediately recognize the familiar sound of one of my favourite bands, The Mission, on the stereo. We are five goths on our way to spend a weekend with over a thousand other goths in a small North Yorkshire seaside town.

We have all received our tickets for the Whitby Gothic Weekend some months earlier, having sent a cheque to the organizer – a goth enthusiast turned entrepreneur – at the address specified in goth fanzines and web sites. We have been enthusing about the event ever since, both among friends at smaller goth events and, in my case, with a greater number of people on a national internet discussion group. The prospect of seeing old friends, meeting new ones and being in the presence of so many other goths from across the country creates an intense sense of excitement in the car. While listening to a variety of goth music, we eagerly discuss what to wear, how to do our hair, which of the live bands at the event are worth seeing, who else is going, and whether it will rain all weekend. We also engage in 'goth-spotting', a game which entails looking out for cars full of fellow enthusiasts heading for the same destination. We overtake and wave knowingly at two such groups during the journey, and spot several others at a motorway service station. Although a certain shyness seems to prohibit approaching and speaking to them, we communicate, with the exchange of glances, a clear sense of our shared identity, an amusement about the reactions of other travellers to our collective presence and a knowingness about our common destination. Although the style is diverse and somewhat malleable, goths rarely find it difficult to identify one another through appearance, and the destination of goths at a northbound motorway service station on this particular day is obvious.

A few hours later, as we drive into Whitby to find its streets full of goths, there is a desire immediately to abandon the car and join in this temporary occupation of a seaside town. Having checked into our bed and breakfast, we walk to The Elsinore, a pub which, like an increasing number of other businesses in the town, has recognized that their biannual goth visitors offer a potentially substantial increase in takings. On walking round the corner toward it, we are faced with a multitude of goths, lining the pavements and most of the road outside the pub, which displays an enormous 'Goths Welcome' banner on its wall. Although there are a variety of hairstyles, jewellery, types of make-up, clothing and boots among the crowds they are all relatively consistent with a distinctive range of tastes. Most obviously, the blues, pinks, purples, reds and greens among the crowd are offset by an excess of black. In addition, many males, as well as females, are wearing make-up and ear, nose, lip or eyebrow piercings. As we join them in what has become a ritual get-together, each of us gradually spots the familiar faces of other goths from Birmingham, and of friends from other parts of Britain, whom we had met at goth events in the past. As we mingle, throughout the weekend, we will all share these friends with one another, and will each broaden our base of goth contacts across the country. We shall also meet individuals who have travelled from abroad to attend the festival.

Toward the evening, we return to our bed and breakfast in order to get 'gothed up', which entails making our appearance as impressive as possible in relation to particular group tastes. Although ultimately geared toward attending the main event of the evening, this process is itself an important social event, involving the collective resolving of clothing dilemmas, mutual practical help with the back-combing, crimping or plaiting of hair and zipping up of the most awkward rubber or PVC tops or dresses, all accompanied by goth music. Going out, observing others, engaging with specialist media, visiting subcultural clothes retailers, and examining compact disc inlays for several years, have provided each of us with an in-depth knowledge about what clothes, hair and makeup are most likely to achieve the admiration of other goths. As we finally enter the event there is a keenness both to admire the appearances of friends and strangers from across the country, and to demonstrate our ability to hold our own among such a large crowd. At the same time as being a celebration of shared identity, this is something of a competition with a distinct, if complex set of rules.

As well as mingling with other goths, the evening event involves the live performance by bands from Britain, Scandinavia and the United States, which, though virtually unheard of outside the goth scene, are well known in countries across the world within it. In the absence of significant external interest, a global network of specialist record labels and retailers, with the help of mail-order, media and previous tours, have ensured that most of the audience is familiar with these, at best, semi-professional bands. Meanwhile, those not previously familiar, but impressed with the performances, are able to purchase CDs, T-shirts and posters and often even to meet members of the bands at the stalls run by each during the event.

As well as comprising the ultimate experience in taking part in the goth scene, then, this festival enables us to enhance our specialist knowledge and collections of artefacts for the future. Throughout the weekend, individuals give out flyers advertising goth events across the country and forthcoming CD releases. Others peddle goth fanzines containing national and international listings of events, interviews with goth bands, letters and specialist advertising. Those who do so know they will nowhere find a larger captive audience for their highly specialist products. The same is true for the specialist retailers, from across Britain, who have booked stalls at the Bizarre Bazaar, held during the second day of the event. While providing these retailers, who are often motivated as much by enthusiasm as by money, with an important boost in the quest to make ends meet, the Bazaar also provides festival-goers with the ultimate chance to enhance our goth clothes, makeup and music collections. Most of those I know at the festival have bought at least one item of clothing by the end of the day, and are preparing to wear it in the evening.

Two days on, my companions and I leave Whitby for another six months. In spite of the air of disappointment that this particular event is over, there is much to look forward to. Most of us have new fanzines to read, new CDs to listen to and clothes to show off to friends who didn't make the trip this time. We also have numerous experiences to recount of the performances of bands and of people's appearances and behaviour. As well as being recounted in local face-to-face situations, such personal 'reviews' of the weekend will flood into goth internet discussion groups, alongside invitations to look at photographs on freshly updated web sites. Finally, we have all enhanced the extent of our friendships with goths across the country, which involve mutual invitations to attend events in each other's localities. As well as providing the ultimate weekend of immediate fulfilment, then, the festival has provided us with renewed enthusiasm for the goth scene and enhanced our means to participate in the future.

Becoming a Critical Insider

'Gothic' has been used to describe various phenomena, from a historical tribe, to architecture and fashions of the past, to forms of contemporary literature and film. The Whitby Gothic Weekend, though, had its roots in a more particular subcultural grouping, which emerged in Britain in the early 1980s. Elements of punk, glam rock and new romantic, among other things, were gradually fused into a distinctive style of music and fashion. The music associated with what became known as the goth scene was most often described as 'dark', 'macabre' and 'sinister', and its associated styles of fashion most obviously, though not exclusively, consisted of black hair and clothes and distinctive styles of make-up for both genders. From the mid-1980s, the style and its associated practices and identities enjoyed international popularity for a few years, before surviving on a much smaller but equally widespread scale from the mid-1990s onward. I had been an enthusiastic participant in the goth scene since the beginning of that decade, but in 1996 my personal involvement became just one part of an extensive research project.

My aim was to conduct in-depth and thorough qualitative research on the goth scene in Britain for a number of years, in order to examine and account for the cultural form taken by the group. In particular, the focus was on the norms, meanings, motivations and social patterns of those involved, as well as the voluntary and commercial events, media and consumables which appeared to enable the goth scene to exist and survive on such a small scale. In order to achieve maximum depth and quality of information and understanding, I adopted a multi-method ethnographic approach, which included participant observation, in-depth interviews, media analysis and even a questionnaire. As Sara Cohen has pointed out, in the past rather too many studies on popular-music-related groupings have based their conclusions only on the textual analysis of styles or isolated interviews (Cohen 1993).

As important as the methodology I chose to adopt, in enhancing the process of doing research and the quality of my findings, was my relatively unambiguous position as a long-term genuine participant of the goth scene. Of course, it could be argued that the complexity and instability of contemporary identities and groupings makes the idea that a researcher can occupy the position of 'insider' a little hazardous (Song and Parker 1995: 243). Certainly, the goth scene is liable to have been experienced in different ways by different people and, by extension, such experiences and identities are liable to have been in continual movement according to time and context, making my own level of proximity or understanding unclear (Gillespie 1995: 67–73). It must also be recognized, of course, that an important additional point of difference was created, as soon as I adopted the role of social researcher.

It would be mistaken, though, to assume as a result of such complexities that all researchers would somehow have been equally well positioned to study goths. In spite of internal diversity, it will become clear throughout this book that distinctive shared norms, activities and identities tended to dominate the lifestyles of those involved, and the ways in which they viewed other people. In particular, the visual distinctiveness of the grouping meant that those who did not fit in were liable to be categorized as outsiders, regardless of the actual complexities of their identity. In contrast, my appearance, social patterns, consumer habits, subcultural knowledge and personal feelings of identity positioned me fairly clearly *within* the goth scene.

Indeed, in some respects my insider status was actually enhanced, as the project was built around an intensified attendance of clubs, gigs and festivals across Britain, including a concentrated focus on the cities of Birmingham, Plymouth and Leeds. Participation on internet discussion groups and other goth internet facilities widened the scope of my research within Britain, and was the main source of my more limited information and contacts outside the country. Whether off- or on-line, the authenticity of my participation greatly enhanced the process of acquiring contacts, interviewees and inform-ation. As well as having a suitable appearance, the manner in which I behaved in clubs – dancing, requesting songs from DJs and socializing – made meeting people, arranging interviews, taking photographs and gaining advice far easier than they might otherwise have been. After a while, I also learned to convey this insider status to the distinctive environment of goth on-line discussion groups (see Mann and Stewart 2000: 88–90; Hine 2000: 48). While appear-ance was initially out of the equation in this context, my affiliation was gradually revealed, through expressing informed opinions, advertising goth nights at which I DJed, publishing photographs of myself on the web and, eventually, meeting other members face to face.

As well as having practical value for gaining access to respondents, part-icipation in the goth scene was key to understanding the experiences and meanings of those involved (see Shutz 1964, 1970; Blumer 1969), and formed the basis of a more distanced, critical form of observation and analysis. Both of these were crucial to gaining a thorough picture, rather than being overly reliant upon the accounts of interviewees (Foster 1996: 59). Subcultural groupings such as the goth scene tend to be characterized by their own dom-inant discourses, values and assumptions, whose accuracy should not be taken for granted (Thornton 1995: 98). An argument by David Muggleton for a relatively uncritical foregrounding of the words of subcultural participants, then, may overrate the accuracy of their accounts (Muggleton 2000: 68). In contrast, ethnography offers the opportunity for first-hand verification (Gillespie 1995: 66).

Achieving maximum understanding of a grouping such as the goth scene, then, requires direct experience (Denzin 1989: 25; Cohen 1993: 124). In this respect, existing involvement made my participation, experiences and motivations more comparable to those of other goths than would have been the case had I been an outsider seeking temporarily to immerse myself for research purposes. Subjective experience and meanings, though, required critical interpretation in terms of research aims and theory, and were complemented by more distanced forms of observation and analysis. This required that I become a *critical insider*, continually taking mental steps back so as to observe, compare, contrast and question as well as to experience.

Direct experiences and observations functioned to complement and verify, but certainly not to eclipse the perceptions and meanings expressed to me by a total of seventy-two individuals in fifty-six separate open-ended interviews. As well as general participants, they included numerous DJs, event promoters, fanzine editors, bands, record label proprietors and specialist retailers. With the exceptions of four which were administered by post and five by e-mail, the interviews were conducted face to face. Being perceived as an insider was advantageous here too. As well as putting interviewees at ease to express themselves openly, my ability to recount genuine experiences and enthusiasms acted as an additional stimulus which was sometimes more effective than direct questioning (see Denzin 1989: 43). However, the open, flowing conversation which usually characterized face-to-face interviews was harder to achieve over e-mail, valuable though the medium was in enhancing the geographical breadth of my sample. In addition to the problems with conveying and gaining advantage from insider status, 'breaking the ice' was rather difficult on e-mail – arguably you might as well try to create rapport in the introduction to a postal questionnaire! Also, the length of time between each contribution and the difficulty of conveying meaningful tones or gestures meant that exchanges were often disjointed.

The final key method I employed, to which my insider status was rather less important, was a one-off self-completion questionnaire administered at the Whitby Gothic Weekend in October 1997. While for the most part my emphasis has been on in-depth, quality information, it was important to obtain some idea of typicality by gaining multi-choice answers and short additional comments from a wider range of goths. Importantly, the questionnaire sample of 112 was not large enough to allow generalizing confidently, and was not necessarily representative of the goth scene as a whole. Questionnaire data is, for the most part, treated as secondary relative to the other methods in the study. Nevertheless, it provided a number of useful quantitative estimates and some extremely valuable open-ended comments from goths, both of which are referred to from time to time throughout the book.

Outlining the Elements of a Subculture

The brief synopsis of a trip to the Whitby Gothic Weekend in the first section of this introductory chapter touches upon all the main elements of the British goth scene of the late 1990s. It gives a flavour of the strong sense of shared identity held between goths from across and beyond Britain, their relatively consistent adherence to an identifiable range of shared tastes, and their level of practical involvement in the goth scene through friendships, event attendance, consumption practices and even internet use. It also indicates the importance of specialist internal events, media and commercial operations to facilitating the goth scene from within – emphasizing the relative autonomy of the grouping. Such features are taken, by this book, to imply a level of cultural *substance*, which might distinguish the goth scene, as a *subculture*, from more fleeting, ephemeral amalgams of young people, music and style. The chapters that follow seek to conceptualize, explore and account for the level of substance of the goth scene in Britain, during the mid- to late 1990s.

Chapter 2 seeks to establish a revised conception of subculture in relation to a variety of popular cultural theories, including traditional subcultural theory, mass cultural theory, postmodern theories, notions of fluid collectivities and ethnographies of localized popular culture. In particular the chapter seeks to establish, contrary to the implications of many of these approaches, that media and commerce are wholly compatible with distinct, substantive groupings, as is the geographical dispersal of participants. Chapter 3 begins the analysis of extensive research data by exploring the relatively consistent stylistic values and tastes of the goth scene, and the ways in which they made its participants distinctive. Moving from external observation to subjective meanings, Chapter 4 links the distinct values of the goth scene to the sense of shared identity shared by subcultural members, and an equally strong feeling of collective distinction from perceived outsiders. Chapter 5 goes into greater detail on the themes of both its predecessors at the same time as beginning to analyse the infrastructure of the goth scene. Commitment and friendships are particularly focused upon, in the context of goth events, which are deemed the primary arena for everyday subcultural participation and as a crucial means of encouraging and facilitating future involvement.

In Chapters 6 and 7, the focus on infrastructure is developed in relation to the role of commerce in the goth scene. Chapter 6 focuses on the cultural producers responsible for the existence and availability of the consumables, media and events so crucial to the substantive form taken by the goth scene. In particular it distinguishes between the external commercially motivated producers and an internal DIY network of often culturally motivated participants. Meanwhile, Chapter 7 explores the selection and use of consumables for the participation of goths in their subculture and for the development of their version of its distinctive style. In the ensuing two chapters, I focus on the critical role of media in the facilitation and construction of the goth scene. Chapter 8 deals with the significance of 'traditional media', from tabloid moral panics to fanzines and flyers, as crucial forms of influence, knowledge and information to goths. This theme is developed further in Chapter 9, in relation to the increasingly important means of subcultural communication provided by the internet. Over these two chapters, it is emphasized that, during the late 1990s, small-scale specialist media – whether off-line or on-line – had become particularly significant in the translocal construction and facilitation of the goth scene. Finally, Chapter 10 provides a conclusion which, among other things, summarizes the main findings relating to the goth scene and re-emphasizes their wider theoretical significance.

Reworking Subculture

As indicated toward the end of the last chapter, this book seeks to concept-ualize the goth scene using a reworked and updated notion of subculture. While avoiding some of the term's previous implications, it will be used, essentially, to capture the relatively substantive, clearly bounded form taken by certain elective cultural groupings. This will be contrasted with an increasing tendency of late for theorists to emphasize that the saturation of society by media and commerce has led to the breakdown of collective boundaries. The following pages seek to justify and, eventually, to detail the proposed redefinition of subculture, in relation to the famous schools of theory with which the term is often associated and a variety of other key perspectives on popular culture and society. In different ways these contemporary theories all risk misrepresenting or excluding the substantive cultural features of group-ings such as the goth scene. In particular, the chapter will identify and seek to counter a tendency, across the theoretical spectrum, to assume that such substance can only exist in the absence of media and commerce.

Traditional Subcultural Theory

The beginnings of subcultural theory involved various theorists associated with what became known as the Chicago School (see Whyte 1943; Gordon 1947; A. Cohen 1955; Becker 1963; Irwin 1970). Though the emphasis of the theorists varies, the school is most famous for a conception of subcultures as deviant groups, whose emergence had to do with 'the interaction of people's perceptions of themselves with others' view of them' (Gelder and Thornton 1997: 11). This is, perhaps, best summarized in Albert Cohen's theoretical introduction to a study of 'Delinquent Boys' (1955). For Cohen, subcultures consisted of individuals collectively resolving societal status problems by developing new values which rendered status-worthy the characteristics they shared:

> One solution [to status problems] is for individuals who share such problems to gravitate towards one another and jointly to establish new norms, new criteria of

status which define as meritorious the characteristics they do possess, the kinds of conduct of which they are capable. (1955: 65–6)

Acquisition of status within the subculture entailed being labelled and, hence, excluded from the rest of society, something the group would respond to through its own hostility to outsiders, to the extent that non-conformity with dominant norms often became virtuous. As the subculture became more substantive, distinctive and independent, members would become increasingly dependent on each other for social contact and validation of their beliefs and way of life.

The themes of labelling and subcultural dislike of 'normal' society are also emphasized in Howard Becker's work which, among other things, is notable for its emphasis on the boundaries drawn by jazz musicians between themselves and their values as 'hip' and their audience as 'squares' (Becker 1963: 79–100). The notion of increasing polarization between subculture and the rest of society, as a result of outside labelling, is developed further in relation to drug-takers in Britain by Jock Young (1971) and in relation to media moral panics surrounding mods and rockers by Stan Cohen. For Cohen, the generalized negative images of subcultures in the mass media both reinforced dominant values and constructed the future form of such groupings (S. Cohen 1972: 166).

The work associated with Birmingham University's Centre for Contemporary Cultural Studies (CCCS) was most responsible for the association of subculture with groupings based around spectacular styles (teds, mods, punks, skins, motorbike boys and so on). Rather than individual problems of status, The Birmingham School, from a neo-Marxist perspective, regarded subcultures as a reflection of the position of mainly working-class young people in relation to the particular societal conditions of 1960s and 1970s Britain (P. Cohen 1972; J. Clarke et al. 1977; Hebdige 1977, 1979; Willis 1978). Spectacular youth subcultures, it is argued, functioned to resolve the contradictory societal position of working-class young people between the traditional values of a working-class 'parent culture' and a modern hegemonic culture of mass consumption dominated by media and commerce (J. Clarke et al. 1977: 16; P. Cohen 1972: 23).

Essentially, by forming subcultures characterized by argot and ritual, young people retained aspects of working-class culture, while their embrace of hedonistic consumption and emphasis on taste and style reflected their position within dominant capitalist society. Crucially though, their consumption, unlike that of the general public, was deemed to be characterized by active selection and appropriation – assigning to everyday objects new subversive meanings in their subcultural context (Hebdige 1979). Semiological interpretation of the overall styles and the subcultural norms with which they were deemed to be homologically aligned (see Willis 1978), suggested that, as a whole, they functioned 'magically' to resolve contradictions and symbolically to subvert the dominant meanings of consumer culture (P. Cohen 1972; Hebdige 1979). Hebdige sums up this perspective in relation to mods:

> Thus the scooter, a formerly ultra-respectable means of transport was appropriated and converted into a weapon and a symbol of solidarity. Thus pills, medically diagnosed for the treatment of neurosis, were appropriated and used as an end-in-themselves . . . The style they created, therefore, constituted a parody of the consumer society in which they were situated. The mod dealt his blows by inverting and distorting the images (of neatness, short hair) so cherished by his employers and parents . . . The mod triumphed with symbolic victories . . . (Hebdige 1977: 93)

Consistent with materialist perceptions of the futility of resistance on a cultural level, however, the dominant forces of mass media and commerce, in Hebdige's account, eventually would incorporate subcultural styles, strip them of any subversive meanings and sell them back to the general public (1979: 96).

There are numerous well-recounted criticisms of the Chicago School and, particularly, the Birmingham School approaches, of which I shall recount those that are most significant to this book. First, through their theoretical emphasis on the solving of status problems in one case, and on symbolic structural resistance in the other, both traditions present an overly simplistic opposition between subculture and dominant culture. There is a relative neglect of features such as internal diversity, external overlaps, individual movement between subcultures, the instability of the groups themselves and the large numbers of relatively uncommitted 'hangers-on' (G. Clarke 1981: 82–3). While Albert Cohen assumes that subcultures solved the same status problems for all members, Birmingham theorists presuppose the existence of singular, subversive meanings of subcultural styles which, ultimately, reflected the shared class position of participants.

Furthermore, there is a tendency to imply, without detail or evidence, that subcultures somehow originated through large numbers of disparate individuals all simultaneously and spontaneously reacting in the same way to ascribed social conditions. Albert Cohen (1955) indicates vaguely that a process of 'mutual gravitation' of disaffected individuals (ibid.: 70) and their 'effective interaction with one another' led to the creation of subcultures (ibid.: 59). Meanwhile, the Birmingham School's neo-Marxist view of subcultures as spontaneous responses to structural contradictions (e.g. P. Cohen 1972; J. Clarke et al. 1977) precludes any kind of agency, choice or diversity on the part of subculturalists and, more importantly, underestimates the positive role of factors such as media and commerce in the construction of such groupings (Thornton 1995: 119). The structuralist assumption of subcultural authenticity reflects not just Marxist theoretical preoccupations, as David Muggleton (2000: 14) would have it, but also an uncritical acceptance of the more exaggerated claims to authenticity of subcultural participants themselves (Thornton 1995: 119). Meanwhile, even Stan Cohen (1972), who usefully details the role of negative mass-media coverage in the shaping of already existing formations, provides rather less in the way of documentation of their initial emergence.

The tendency to locate both media and commerce in an oppositional relationship to subcultures is a particularly problematic element of most subcultural theory (Thornton 1995: 116; McRobbie 1989: 36, 1994: 161). Their role is restricted, in Jock Young and Stan Cohen's accounts, to the inadvertent labelling and strengthening of existing subcultures. Meanwhile, for Hebdige, everyday consumables merely provide raw materials for creative subcultural subversion. The notion of incorporation suggests that media and commerce only become self-consciously involved in the marketing of subcultural styles *after* they have been established for a time, and Hebdige emphasizes that this involvement effectively spells the demise of subcultures (Hebdige 1979: 96). In contrast, Thornton suggests that subcultures are liable to involve a variety of both positive and negative forms of direct media involvement right from their beginnings:

> subcultures do not germinate from a seed and grow by force of their own energy into mysterious movements, only to be belatedly digested by the media. Rather, media, and other cultural industries are there and effective right from the start. (Thornton 1995: 117)

Similarly Angela McRobbie indicates a neglect of the role of small-scale moneymaking – sometimes by subcultural participants themselves – in the development and survival of subcultures:

> The point at which subcultures offered a career through the magical change of the commodity have warranted as little attention as the network of small-scale entrepreneurial activities which financed the counter culture. (McRobbie 1989: 36)

While many of these criticisms of subcultural theory reflect genuine flaws, there is also a sense, in contemporary writing on the subject, that significant changes in popular culture since the 1960s and 1970s have rendered the theory increasingly irrelevant. Most notably, theoretical accounts of the increased saturation of all corners of society by media and commerce usually imply that subculture, with its implications of substance, authenticity, distinctiveness and meaning, has become out-of-date. Thus, Dick Hebdige himself has suggested that:

> Theoretical models are as tied to their own times as the human bodies that produce them. The idea of subculture-as-negation grew up alongside punk, remained inextricably linked to it, and died when it died. (Hebdige 1988: 8)

We shall now look in turn at the two theoretical approaches which most emphasize the media- and commerce-induced erosion of cultural boundaries and, hence, most reject the notion of subculture and, indeed, substantive communities in general. With more in common with one another than may first appear, these take the form of mass cultural and postmodern approaches to popular culture.

Mass Culture and Pseudo-individuation

Theories of mass culture, whose most famous proponents, perhaps, are the Neo-Marxist Frankfurt School (e.g. Adorno 1941; Adorno and Horkheimer 1944; Marcuse 1964), suggest that large-scale concentrated culture industries marketing standardized popular cultural products have created a passive, uncreative and essentially homogenous 'mass culture'. Thus, in the first half of the twentieth century, popular films, novels or pieces of music were deemed by Theador Adorno to be replacing thought-provoking, meaningful, critical and complex forms of art with standardized commercial formulas designed to maximize sales by appealing to individuals' baser senses (Adorno 1941). The predictability and rigidity of such forms, it was argued, encouraged passive consumption, homogeneity and escapism rather than intellectual fulfilment or diversity. There is little room in such notions of mass culture, whether from the Frankfurt School or from theorists from different traditions (e.g. MacDonald 1957), for the kind of substantive or meaningful deviations or appropriations implied by subcultural theory. Such apparent instances of creativity or originality would surely have been regarded by Adorno not as symbolic resistance, but as a form of pseudo- or sensuous individuation – an ideological mask for the, in fact, superficial and standardized form of every facet of popular culture:

> The sensuous individuation of the work, to which mass culture must continue to lay claim precisely if it is to be able to perform its complementary function profitably in a standardized society, contradicts the abstractness and self-sameness to which the world has shrunk (Adorno 1944: 57).

In the late twentieth century, notions of mass culture resurfaced in the form of theories of homogenization on a global scale. The focus is on hyper-concentrated culture industries, in the form of a handful of transnational corporations, expanding massively into new markets across the globe. This situation, it is suggested, has resulted in an intensification and expansion to global proportions of the cultural standardization described by Adorno, Marcuse and others (Peet 1982, 1989; Schiller 1985, 1991, 1992). It is argued that the one-way flow of Western commercialized cultural products through-out the world, most obviously in the form of pop stars, TV shows, films and fast-food outlets, has had a direct cultural effect on their audiences (Dorfman and Mattelart 1991). As a consequence, distinctive, independent peripheral cultures are being swamped and destroyed by a passive, escapist, shallow and ideological mass-consumer culture, characterized by:

> standardised, programmed ways of thinking with little room for regional variation. Global capitalism evolves as a single way of life gradually incorporating into its social relations, ways of producing and styles of consumption, the majority of the world's population (Peet 1989: 193).

Wallis and Malm (1984: 299–303, 1992: 214) have produced a somewhat more sophisticated theorization of this situation. They outline a complex set of interactions between global and local popular-music technologies and styles in the ongoing production of an international 'transculture', composed of the most universally accessible elements appropriated from music styles throughout the world. In a circular process, the ever-developing transculture interacts again and again with local cultures, creating a new set of hybrids each time which, in turn, feed back into it. While the process is more complex, the eventual result is surely the same as for Peet and Schiller: the transculture gradually becomes more universal, shallow and meaningless than the original local cultures, which gradually lose more and more of their distinctiveness. Consistent with this notion of multi-directional cultural flows leading to homogenization, Dirlik argues that the 'guerrilla marketing tactics' of world capitalism, in the form of media and commercial forces, function to appro-priate, standardize and mass-market elements of locally specific cultures (Dirlik 1996: 32). Miyoshi describes such behaviour by transnationals as colonialism, asserting that the return to authentic, distinctive cultures 'is a closed route' (Miyoshi 1996: 95).

Although, in the case of the theories immediately above, the emphasis is on place rather than on rootless groupings based around style, their view of media and commerce, like that of the Frankfurt School, is clearly at odds with notions of deviant, subversive or merely substantive consumer subcultures.

The implication from Adorno is that there can be no meaningful or substantive styles of music or art except those entirely detached from the workings of the culture industries. Meanwhile, for Dirlik and others, any semblance of difference or substantive community that surfaces is liable immediately to lose its depth, authenticity and meaning as part of a process of appropriation, standardization and mass-marketing. Interestingly, while Dick Hebdige is optimistic about the substance and subversiveness of subcultures during their initial moments of spontaneity, his description of the appropriation of such styles at a later point shares Dirlik's view that media and marketing function essentially to water down and render insignificant (Hebdige 1979: 96).

The notion that the concentration and expansion of the culture industries entails an all-inclusive process of massification can be criticized from various angles. First, it tends to assume an inevitable influence on culture, largely on the basis of an assessment of commercial motives and a critique of the content of particular cultural forms (Tomlinson 1991: 38). Even Hebdige falls into this trap, contrasting the active creativity and imagination of a small number of innovative subculturalists with an apparently passive, manipulated societal majority or 'mainstream', including those who adopted subcultural styles after the moment of incorporation. One consequence of this is a wholesale neglect of the significance of the cultural practices of young women, many of whom, according to McRobbie, were confined to indoor activities and, hence, reliant upon the fashionable products of 'teenybopper' culture (McRobbie and Garber 1977; McRobbie 1980: 29). The 'on the streets' focus of subcultural theory meant that such girls were effectively dismissed as part of the generalized cultural mainstream. Seeking to move beyond such unsubstantiated assumptions about the passivity of the majority, McRobbie and others have taken notions of active consumption beyond spectacular subcultures, illustrating the self-empowerment of various individuals and groups, through distinct creative use of mass media and commercial products (e.g. McRobbie and Garber 1977; McRobbie 1989, 1994; Willis 1990). In a similar vein, but this time in direct response to notions of global homogenization, audience research relating to some of the most criticized media products (e.g. Ang 1985; Liebes and Katz 1993) has revealed complex, active processes of negotiation rather than an inevitable replacement of authentic local culture with global mass culture. Therefore, while CCCS claims of subcultural resistance may have been exaggerated, the implication of total passivity implied in notions of mass culture seems equally problematic.

Mass-culture theorists also share with the Birmingham School an assumption that commerce and media inevitably lead to the production of standardized, superficial cultural products (Strinati 1995: 40). The almost total dismissal of differences between products and consumers, using notions such as pseudo-individuation, appropriation and incorporation, underestimates the cultural significance of the commercial targeting of specialist markets (Curtin 1996). It will become clear in this book that, as well as broadly defined audience groupings based around age, class, marital status or general social outlook (Chaney, 1996: 25–42; Curtin, 1996), such marketing can include small-scale, highly specialist and substantive segments. Furthermore, the reduction of media and commerce to *mass* media and commerce, as a result of the greater market share of the latter, neglects the independence and creativity involved in smaller-scale, more specialized entrepreneurial and communicative practices (see Atton 2002). One particularly unfortunate effect of this, on which I shall elaborate later, is that notions of local, spontaneous, face-to-face culture become regarded as the only alternative to a mediated, homogenous, commercial mass (Strinati 1995: 43). The reality and potential for relatively distinct, or independent *translocal* cultural groupings, to whom small-scale specialist media and commerce are integral, seem seldom considered. The importance of such small-scale 'DIY' commerce, particularly in relation to youth cultures, has been usefully emphasized by McRobbie (1989: 25, 1999: 10), and will be an important theme later in the book in relation to the goth scene.

From Sameness to 'Similarity of Difference'

Interestingly, the exaggerated implication, in theories of mass homogenization, that media and commerce function to erode the kind of substantive subcultural groupings in which we are interested is also the conclusion of an at-first-glance contrasting set of theories, associated with the notion of post-modernism. Like theorists of mass culture, postmodernists have tended to emphasize that, as part of a change of emphasis in the economy from manufactured goods to commercial services, more and more aspects of culture are becoming inseparable from communications technologies and commercial processes of production and consumption (Harvey 1989; Lash and Urry 1987). However, rather than focusing on organized mass-marketing of standardized products by transnationals, they outline an increasingly rapid and disorganized proliferation of products and images around the globe as a result of a ceaseless search by competing flexible businesses for something different to sell, in a saturated market (Harvey 1989: 287–9; Lash and Urry 1987).

As part of a process labelled 'the end of organized capitalism', this expansion and speed-up of production and consumption processes has, it is argued, led to continually accelerating cycles of consumer fashion (Lash and Urry 1987). Rather than standardization, Jameson suggests, commerce is embracing innovation and experimentation in an intense drive to produce 'ever more novel-seeming goods . . . at ever greater rates of turnover' (Jameson 1991: 4). The speed and intensity of the production and distribution of 'images' in the form of objects and media content, according to Jean Baudrillard (1983, 1988), is such that none of them is any longer attached to any real or concrete meaning. Rather, the depthless, infinitely adaptable commodities begin to interact, mix with and refer to one another: 'It is no longer a question of imitation, nor of reduplication, nor even of parody. It is rather a question of substituting signs of the real for the real itself' (Baudrillard 1988: 167).

Aspects of what Baudrillard calls 'hyperreality' have been illustrated by a number of theorists with relation to examples of commercial popular culture (Jameson 1982, 1991; Chambers 1985, 1988; Hebdige 1988). For example, Chambers (1985, 1988) draws attention to the tendency of emerging genres of popular music to mix together existing styles and, in the process, to strip them of any previous cultural contexts so that they represent only 'their own transitory practice' (Chambers 1985: 199). Meanwhile, Hebdige (1988: 212), moving away from his earlier subcultural interpretations, describes the 'raiding and pasting together of rhythms, images and sounds from multiple sources'. Importantly, he also indicates a consequent mixing together of the consumers of such sounds:

> It no longer appears adequate to confine the appeal of these forms . . . to the ghetto of discrete, numerically small subcultures. For they permeate and help to organise a much broader, less bounded territory whose cultures, subjectivities, identities impinge upon each other. (ibid.)

The cultural implications of saturation by simulacra, then, are that consumers become free from coherent, distinctive or meaningful cultural ties. They choose from and mix diverse and fleeting points of identification from the immense range of images on offer. The coherent individual subject, as a result, is deemed to have fragmented into multiple, disparate points of identity (Jameson 1991: 15). Traditional points of collective identification, such as class, gender, race and indeed place, are gradually replaced by elective, build-your-own, consumer identities (Muggleton 1997: 189). The popular cultural sphere cannot be conceived in terms of subcultures opposed to the mainstream or, indeed, to one another. There is no place for 'us and them', minority versus majority or even minority versus minority in a mixed up, all-encompassing culture of the postmodern:

> modernity was an era of clearly differentiated, yet internally homogenous, collectivities. Postmodernity, however, appears to entail the inverse of this process:

internal fragmentation has reached such proportions that the boundaries between established cultural collectivities appear to be breaking down . . . (Muggleton 1997: 191).

Some theorists have taken up such notions of multiple identities, the break-down of distinct social categories and confusion between reality and simulation, in relation to the specific context of the internet (Turkle 1995; Poster 1995). The blurring of distinctions of real/virtual, human/machine and self/other, as well as the ability to occupy endless different ephemeral positions of identity simultaneously and to access any site at the touch of a button in a potentially anonymous world are often emphasized. Explored a little further in Chapter 9, this notion of the replacement of collective identities, meanings and distinctions by an ever-changing plurality of virtual selves is consistent with that in postmodern approaches to popular culture in general – summed up enthusiastically by Polhemous: 'While fashion celebrated change and sub-cultural style celebrated group identity, the inhabitants of Styleworld celebrate the truth of falsehood, the authenticity of simulation, the meaningfulness of gibberish' (Polhemus 1997: 149–50).

There is surely some value in postmodern theory's recognition of the disorganized character of the proliferation of products and images in late capitalism, and in its emphasis on the increasing ties between social identities and an ever-changing array of diverse and hybrid consumables. It follows from this that some identities are liable to become fragmented and malle-able, and that certain cultural boundaries, including those related to style, may become less clear and permanent. However, it would be mistaken to generalize such useful observations into a universal theory by suggesting that *all* cultural boundaries are, or will soon be, entirely eroded, or that group belonging, collective identity and cultural meaning are becoming irrelevant. As Hetherington has argued, we should avoid 'trying to get social theory to work holistically and represent the world as a single, simple picture' (Hetherington 1998a: 9).

It should be remembered, then, that the more exaggerated descriptions of proliferation of difference tend, too often, to be backed up by references to the textual content of those popular cultural forms or hypothetical situations which best fit the theoretical picture (Goodwin 1991: 181; Featherstone 1991: 5). The problem is not only one of generalization, but also a lack of empirical data about the everyday meanings, identifications and collectivities which revolve around the use of such products (S. Cohen 1993: 127). This applies as much to postmodern interpretations of the internet as it does to those who focus on off-line examples. Turkle's fascinating account, for example, is much more interested in the play of identities involved in the on-line transfer of texts in multi-user domains than in the many aspects of cyberspace more consistent with existing identities, or, indeed, the location of most net-use within the context of predominantly off-line lives (Kendall 1999).

Like theories of mass culture, then, postmodern approaches tend to rely heavily on theoretical presuppositions and selected textual analysis. And this is not the only similarity between the two. Although the one laments the manipulative power of big business and the other seems more prone to celebrate the endless choice of fluid postmodern consumers, they both describe a de-differentiation of society as a result of saturation by media and commerce. While Peet and Schiller theorize the homogenization of culture through the mass-marketing of standardized products, Baudrillard and Jameson predict the blurring of boundaries as a result of the disconnection of an increasing range of cultural forms from substantive meanings. The postmodern 'similarity of difference' referred to by Muggleton (1997: 192) and the homogenous mass-consumer culture described by theorists of cultural imperialism are not so far opposed as it may first appear. Most importantly from the point of view of this book, both theories regard media and commercial saturation as incompatible with substantive or distinctive cultural groupings and, hence, are liable either to exclude or to misrepresent the relative stability and boundedness of groupings such as the goth scene.

Fluid Collectivities

A number of recent contributions to the study of lifestyles have sought to blend elements of postmodern theory with a focus on identifiable affinity groups of one kind or another. While rather more realistic and, in some cases, more empirically grounded than some of the more generalized postmodern proclamations, acknowledgements of distinctiveness and shared identity tend, in most examples of such work, still to be somewhat overshadowed by an emphasis upon fluidity and ephemerality. More specifically, the desire to put some distance between themselves and traditional subcultural theory has been partially responsible for the coining of a rather confusing plethora of new terms to replace subculture, some of which we shall examine here.

The most popular 'replacement' for subculture appears currently to be the notion of *neo-tribe*, as theorized by Maffesoli (1996) and Bauman (1992a, 1992b). Maffesoli emphasizes that consumer neo-tribes comprise the expression of group identity through rituals and, sometimes, a sense of distinction from other groups. While rejecting their conceptualization as directly oppositional, he outlines the energy and commitment of members, and the neo-tribes' importance as a source of emotional attachment and identity within a wider sociality (Maffesoli 1996: 96). Furthermore, neo-tribal member-ship, for Maffesoli, constitutes the retention by individuals of a degree of control and independence from forces of normalization such as the mass media, the fashion industry and fast-food outlets (ibid. 1996: 41). This 'reappropriation of one's existence' or 'explosion of life' (ibid.: 51) is deemed part of a general trend toward the replacement of individualism with a re-emergence of sociality and, specifically, puissance – an underground people power based on a sensual 'will to live' (ibid.: 31–55). At the same time, however, Maffesoli is at pains to emphasize the crucial relationship of neo-tribes with elective consumption practices. As a result of their consequent lack of structural anchorage, bound-aries are deemed fluid and the consequent ease with which one can opt in or out makes attachment to the groupings highly ephemeral and partial: 'It is less a question of belonging to a gang, a family or a community, than of switching from one group to another' (ibid.: 76).

The ultimate fluidity and, indeed, superficiality of neo-tribes is emphasized even more strongly in Zygmunt Bauman's account, which replaces Maffesoli's emphasis on sociality with an individualistic interpretation. Instead of com-prising a revival of the communal or the social, neo-tribes reflect a desperate and ill-fated search for lost community, which results only in greater fragment-ation (Bauman 1992a, 1992b). The ease of joining and leaving neo-tribes encourages consumers continually to find new solutions to their personal 'problems of survival' by negotiating ongoing privatized routes through a postmodern world of choices:

> The tribe-forming and dismantling sociality is not a symptom of declining individuality but a most powerful factor in its perpetuation. Neo-tribes are fickle, ephemeral and elusive products of life under conditions of privatised survival (Bauman 1992b: 25).

Writing more recently, Bennett (1999, 2000) specifically advocates the replacement of the term *subculture* with that of *neo-tribe* in order to reflect the dynamic pluralistic relationship between contemporary young consumers and popular culture. Drawing on fieldwork carried out on dance cultures, he argues that music consumption has more to do with continually developing and changing individual repertoires of taste than with conformity to rigid subcultural genres (1999: 610). As well as failing to capture the complexity of such individual patterns of taste and identity, subculture was deemed in the late 1990s, to have become a vague and hence unhelpful 'catch-all' descriptor (Bennett 1999: 603).

A somewhat similar set of themes predominates in the work of those who prefer to use the general term *lifestyle* rather than to focus on particular subcultural groupings (e.g. Jenkins 1983; Chaney 1996). Richard Jenkins (1983) used this term as a descriptor for the activities and affiliations of early 1980s working-class youth in Belfast. Explicitly rejecting the term 'subculture' because of its implications of a simplistic opposition to a dominant culture and its inability to account for overlaps between groupings of young people, he proposed that 'lifestyle' allows for both differences and commonalities and recognition of change as well as stability (ibid.: 41–2). More recently, David Chaney has compiled a comprehensive rationale behind the use of lifestyles to describe the variety of 'patterns of action that differentiate people' (Chaney 1996: 5). In an approach perhaps reminiscent of Maffesoli's, for Chaney lifestyles involve the relation between consumption and 'communities within which a competent use of commodities is taken to be a display of membership' (ibid.: 45). Chaney focuses particularly on the importance of shared sensibilities, which imply 'a distinctive form of cultural affiliation' and provide profane elements to individual lives (ibid.: 129). At the same time, however, he seeks to embrace postmodern interpretations of commercial saturation, emphasizing the ultimate instabilities and overlaps which characterize all such groupings:

> The social groups identified or collected by their lifestyles are not distinct and stable entities. It is rather than the need for a vocabulary of lifestyles indicates a process of change towards the prevalence of more fluid and ambiguous structures of social identification. (ibid.: 94)

Rob Shields (1992a, 1992b) entertains the notion of lifestyles and, indeed, that of neo-tribes, in relation to the commercial colonization of culture. He emphasizes that such groupings retain certain characteristics associated with subculture, notably shared symbols, value systems, tastes and subjectivities. However, the sheer range of objects, images and identities presented by the media and the shopping mall are deemed to result in the development, by individuals, of a plurality of self-presentations or masks (Shields 1992a: 14–17, 1992b: 107). Rather than placing all their eggs in one basket and adopting a consistent affiliation with a particular subculture, then, consumers negotiate their way between a series of sometimes contradictory performances.

Kevin Hetherington (1992, 1998a, 1998b) adopts what seems a slightly more substantive notion of social groupings which, while similar to elements of Maffesoli's theorizing, prompts the use of yet another different term. *Bunde* is an intermediate category between forms of community based on tradition (Gemeinschaft) and those based on instrumental rational action (Gesellschaft) (Tonnies 1955). It refers to elective and often short-lived forms of collective identity motivated by a desire for an affective sense of belonging. Hetherington applies the term to various contemporary groupings, including new age travellers and various 'new social movements', involvement in which is often deemed to reflect individual desire for emotional security as much as external political motives (Hetherington 1998a: 99, 146). While this account appears to allow greater scope for group substance than some of the other explanations described here, Hetherington is at pains to emphasize that the basis of bunde in the affective and expressive makes them 'heterogenous, multiple and diverse assemblages of practice' characterized by inconsistencies, instabilities and mutations (ibid.: 158–9).

Another important contribution to cultural theory which adopts a position somewhere between Baudrillard's visions of meaningless consumer chaos and traditional subcultural theory, is Willis's account of 'common culture' (Willis 1990). Replacing his earlier emphasis on particular fixed subcultural groupings of youth (1978) with a focus on 'everyday cultures', he too acknowledges the centrality of consumption to the practices and identities of young people. As a result, 'organic communications', based on physical proximity, are breaking down, replaced by superficial community walls which 'zigzag wildly around the urban mass' (Willis 1990: 141). At the same time, Willis rejects theories of postmodernism and of mass manipulation, insisting that young people produce their own collective meanings through selective, creative use of the range of cultural goods on offer. 'Organic communities' then, are replaced by *proto-communities*, which involve shared consumer interests or tastes, but are deemed more akin to an unstable and disorganized 'spaced out queue of people' than an intense 'talking circle' (ibid.).

In the sphere of popular-music studies, developing academic conceptions of the term *scene* – a word commonly used by music fans themselves – have been developed in order to describe loosely knit categories based around particular music genres. Harris, who focuses upon the plethora of semi-autonomous local and translocal scenes surrounding the umbrella genre of extreme metal, defends the word 'scene' by emphasizing that, beyond an implication that music is inseparable from social processes, it is infinitely malleable and universal: 'The implication is that scenes include everything, from tight-knit local music communities to isolated musicians and occasional fans, since all contribute to and feed off a larger space(s) of musical practice' (Harris 2000: 25). It is also emphasized that scenes are fluid and hence shift toward and away from one another, and that individuals continually negotiate pathways within and between them (ibid.). Harris's writing draws upon an earlier discussion by Straw (1991) who also emphasized the term's potential flexibility, arguing that it usefully described the diverse yet partially unified amalgam of genres, styles and practices (including goth, it should be noted) which coexisted for a number of years in the late 1980s under the umbrella term 'alternative rock'.

David Muggleton, cited earlier in full support of postmodern theory, has subsequently produced a more in-depth and cautious approach to the subject, based on interview research (Muggleton 2000). Rather than suggesting, as he had done previously, that subcultures were a phenomenon of the past, he proposes that they still exist, but in somewhat postmodern form. Although the terminology is different, the implied notion of *postmodern subculture* appears to involve a mixture of substance and fluidity similar to those of many other theorists covered in this section. Thus the commitment of sub-cultural participants and the strength of their sense of distinction from outsiders are cited as characteristics which quell 'excessive postmodernist claims'. Nevertheless, Muggleton concludes with a 'qualified acknowledge-ment of a postmodern sensibility' as a result of what he deems the hybridity, diversity and fluidity of subcultures. As he puts it:

> Subculturalists are postmodern in that they demonstrate a fragmented, heterogenous and individualistic stylistic identification. This is a liminal sensibility that manifests itself as an expression of freedom from structure, control and restraint, ensuring that stasis is rejected in favour of movement and fluidity. (Muggleton 2000: 158)

It is not readily apparent what to make of this remarkable plethora of concepts and explanations. Most of the accounts described come across as more realistic and useful than either over-generalized postmodernist proclam-ations of loss of meaning or neo-Frankfurt-School notions of massification. They offer more productive alternatives to traditional subcultural theory and, as will become clear, present various observations applicable to the case of the goth scene. For a number of reasons, however, I have opted not to utilize any of the suggested replacements for subculture. Most obviously, the exces-sive number of different proposals as to how we conceptualize elective groupings creates a problem in itself. This is especially the case since, apart from a common avoidance of traditional subcultural theory, few of the theorists clearly explain how their preferred term differs from the other proposals in the offing. For example, the apparent compatibility of Hetherington's compelling account of affective affinity groupings with much of Maffesoli's account of the sociality of neo-tribes makes it a little unclear why he was not content to adapt the same term. Meanwhile Shields refers to lifestyles, tribes, bunde and even subcultures fairly interchangeably and without any clear differentiation or explanation over the course of his own otherwise thought-provoking and useful contributions to *Lifestyle Shopping* (Shields, 1992a, 1992b). The imprecise way in which subculture has sometimes been used is certainly a cause for concern, but the current enthusiasm for coining more and more alternatives seems liable only to further complicate things.

More importantly, perhaps, a number of the individual explanations, because of the range of substantive and fluid groupings they seek to include under a single term, are themselves unclear. The term 'scene' is openly lauded by Harris (2000: 25) for its catch-all qualities, but the attempt to allow for the fixities and fluidities of virtually any music-related practices or affiliations, surely risks limiting the term's theoretical value. Similarly, Chaney, while insisting, on the one hand, that shared sensibilities 'will be why lifestyles matter' and that they imply 'a distinctive form of cultural affiliation' (1996: 129), at the same time wants to reject the notion of groupings as 'distinct and stable entities' (ibid.: 94). The recognition, here, of elements of both stability and instability in popular culture as a whole is a valuable one, and I would have little hesitation in advocating the use of *lifestyle* as an umbrella term, applicable to patterns of popular cultural practices and identities in general. However, there is also a need for terminology of greater precision in order to reflect the contrasting levels of substance or fluidity which characterize different lifestyles and lifestyle groupings.

At the same time as attempting to provide the breadth of definition to encompass elements of substance, commitment and meaning, however, most of the explanations described leave us in little doubt that the most important feature of the affiliations and groupings described is their partiality and instability. While such ultimate emphasis on fluidity may be justified in some cases, overgeneralization will result in exclusion or misrepresentation of those individuals or groupings which do not fit the picture. To his credit, Hetherington specifically avoids the pitfall of overgeneralizing his explanation, emphasizing that: 'It is important that we do not try and find one term or one concept to understand this set of phenomena, but retain some sense of multiplicity of terms and concepts' (Hetherington 1998: 3). Although excessive multiplicity of terms creates confusion, especially where they are not clearly differentiated, it would seem to make sense to replace attempts to apply single concepts across the board with the use of a limited number of clearly defined terms which are narrower in scope. In particular, this would enable us to differentiate those groupings which are predominantly ephemeral from those which entail far greater levels of commitment, continuity, distinctiveness or, to put it in general terms, substance. It will become clear throughout this book that the goth scene belonged fairly clearly in the latter category.

Local or Translocal?

In contrast to much of the theory described in the previous two sections, cultural substance of the kind in which we are interested has been emphasized fairly consistently by ethnographies of popular cultural practices and identities focused on particular towns or cities. An empirical focus on the relationship between local physical proximity and relatively stable, committed and autonomous lifestyles has provided a challenge to some of the more exaggerated claims of theories of global mass culture and postmodern fluidity. Indeed, even for Andy Bennett, the otherwise fluid cultural expressions of young music fans are given certain roots by their local setting:

> If, however, such neo-tribal forms of musicalised expression represent highly fluid and transient modes of collective identity, at the same time they are not so fluid and transient as to cancel out any form of meaningful interaction with the local environments from which they emerge. (Bennett 2000: 84)

Consistent with Bennett's emphasis on locality are a series of ethnographic studies of local music-related practices and identities which emerged in the late twentieth century, most notably perhaps those by Ruth Finnegan (1989) and Sara Cohen (1991, 1993, 1994) on the English cities Milton Keynes and Liverpool, and Barry Shank (1994) on Austin, Texas. While different in their precise emphasis, all draw attention to the geographical and economic history of the cities concerned – implying a relationship between that history and the substantive nature of local musical culture (Finnegan 1989: 22–7; Cohen 1991: 9–19; Shank 1994: 7–8). Furthermore, Cohen and Shank specifically establish a continuity between the internal *musical* history of their respective cities and local styles and practices of the present. Cohen (1991, 1994), for example, suggests that aspects of Liverpool's musical past, such as The Beatles and The Cavern Club, were key to a strong sense of local identity held by musicians and fans, many of whom perceived and sought to reproduce a distinctive 'Liverpool Sound' (Cohen 1994). For his part, Shank (1994) suggests that some of the styles and attitudes associated with traditional local sounds such as Rhythm and Blues and Honky Tonk were traceable as clear local inflections upon certain contemporary national genres. In addition to this historical focus, local cultural substance is implied in the general impression, throughout all three texts in question, of a somewhat self-generated, coherent and substantive music culture of the present, comprised of infrastructural elements rooted within the locality. In other words, the emphasis is very much upon local bands performing to local fans in local pubs, and upon their practising, recording and associating with other local bands in local studios, and advertising their gigs or tapes in local record and music shops or local newspapers.

At times, such small-scale, relatively autonomous, rooted and committed forms of music culture are explicitly contrasted with exaggerated notions of saturation by placeless, timeless and meaningless commercial images. Finnegan attacks Adornian versions of commercial mass music culture, contrasting them with the 'local, grassroots bands' and 'face to face' audiences she describes (Finnegan 1989: 121–2). Meanwhile, Cohen contrasts what she argues are strong attachments of Liverpool's musicians and fans to distinctive forms of local culture with theories claiming to document the irrelevance of place to a postmodern world (Cohen 1994: 133). Through their in-depth, localized and ethnographically informed approaches, then, such studies provide clear evidence of popular-music-related lifestyles which contrast markedly with theoretical visions of superficiality, fluidity and mean-inglessness. However, the emphasis on regional history, localized infrastructure and face-to-face interactions as primary facilitators for such substance may underemphasize those aspects of the popular-music industry which do not revolve around anywhere in particular.

In particular, there is rather a shortage of attention to non-place-specific influences on the local cultures described, notably in the form of media and commerce. Indeed, Sarah Thornton has likened Finnegan and Cohen's neglect of the media to that of Birmingham School subcultural theory: 'They depict internally generated culture, disclose local creativity and give positive valuation to the culture of the people, but only at the cost of removing the media from their pictures of the cultural process' (Thornton 1995: 120). While the media are not, in fact, entirely 'removed', there does seem insufficient room in the detailed accounts of local pubs, recording studios and even independent music stores for an in-depth focus on the impact of national or international radio, press or television on local music practices and identities. Similarly, the interaction of musicians and audiences with mass-produced recorded music from around the world seems, particularly for Finnegan and Cohen, a peripheral concern. More specifically, in relation to this book's concerns, the extent of the focus on localized culture results in an under-emphasis on small, substantive music-related groupings, such as this book's case study, the goth scene, which – partly by virtue of their links with media and commerce – operate *translocally* (Kruse 1993: 38).

At the same time as offering an effective rebuke to mass cultural and post-modern theories, then, this localized approach largely shares the dichotomy they both present between global media and commerce – deemed to degrade substantive cultural groupings – and localized face-to-face interactions – which are implied to be their only truly effective means of fruition. What is often unrecognized across most perspectives in the great local/global debate is that, as Hannerz (1996: 98) has put it: 'What is personal, primary, and small-scale, is not necessarily narrowly confined in space, and what spans continents need not be large scale in any other way' (Hannerz 1996: 98). We should also add, here, that 'what is personal, primary and small-scale' is also not necessarily unmediated or independent of the process of buying and selling.

In fairness, just as media and commerce come into the equation at times, there is the occasional hint, among the generally localized emphasis of Cohen, Shank and Finnegan, about translocal genres or groupings. Notably, Shank (1994: 91–117) draws attention to the national and global connections relating to punk, and Finnegan (1989: 61, 93) focuses now and again on the national networks of Milton Keynes's country and western and folk music worlds. While such references are useful, a greater emphasis on the translocal has been recognized elsewhere. Jon Stratton's categorization of subcultures such as surfies and bikers as 'commercial subcultures' emphasizes that an implication with consumer culture and corporate marketing strategies can make distinctive coherent sets of cultural values highly transferable between capitalist countries (Stratton 1985: 184). More recently, Keith Harris's work on extreme metal has involved a fascinating focus on the global distribution of such specialist music and fashion and the transnational institutions and forms of identity which accompany them (Harris 2000). Similarly, Marion Leonard (1998) has described the transnational, but highly participatory micro-media network of physical and electronic fanzines which make up the Riot Grrrl movement, emphasizing that 'whilst the zines may reach people in other countries, their content and scale of production give the impression of conversing with a small group of friends' (Leonard 1998: 108).

While Leonard opts to conceptualize Riot Grrrl as a somewhat disorganized and rhizomic network, a slightly more coherent and substantive form of translocal identity appears to be implied by Mark Slobin, who coins the term 'affinity interculture' to describe the tendency for certain forms of music to "call out" to geographically dispersed audiences (Slobin 1993: 68). Slobin goes into disappointingly little detail as to the characteristics or makeup of such groupings, but the kind of translocal shared identity he alludes to is illustrated by an observation from Simon Reynolds: 'A noise band in Manchester can have more in common with a peer group in Austin, Texas than one of its "neighbours" two blocks away' (Reynolds 1990, cited in Kruse 1993: 34). This comment is used by Holly Kruse to illustrate the way in which 'alternative' music scenes across the United States and Britain are connected with one another through shared tastes and through networks of communication and commerce (Kruse 1993: 34). Her recognition that – even in the relatively loose genre of 'alternative' music – local identities and traditions interact with relatively coherent translocal frames of reference resonates somewhat with the way in which I seek to characterize the even greater levels of translocal consistency, distinctiveness and shared identity which were evident in the case of the goth scene.

A later-1990s body of work on 'computer-mediated community' has also provided useful material on translocal forms of affiliation. In contrast to the more postmodernist approaches described earlier, emphasis is placed on the role of the internet in facilitating substantive communities based around discussion groups. Such studies have frequently noted that, in spite of being geographically dispersed and reliant upon electronic media, participants tend to share common interests, hold feelings of commitment and identity towards one another and collectively defend their electronic boundaries (Baym 1995, 1997; Watson 1997; McLaughlin et al. 1997; Fernback 1999). Wellman and Gulia sum up the potential of the technology for the creation of the most widespread yet small-scale of communities by pointing out, in relation to Marshall McLuhan's famous slogan, that although the world is not a global village, 'one's "village" could span the globe' (Wellman and Gulia 1999: 169). While it will be shown that, for the goth scene, internet discussion groups were only one part of a predominantly off-line 'community', this body of work is useful in its recognition of the potential role of the internet as medium for the facilitation of non-locally-specific forms of collective identity.

Consistent with elements of the material covered in recent pages, this book is at pains to emphasize the translocal form taken by the goth scene and, by inference, comparable groupings. Geographically separated goths shared both a translocal sense of identity and a relatively consistent and distinctive set of tastes and values. It will also become clear, consistent with Kruse, that both of these 'abstract' characteristics were enabled by concrete translocal connections in the form of media, commerce, and travel (Kruse 1993). Crucially, then, the argument is not merely that certain elements of styles such as goth find their way to a variety of geographically disparate countries, towns and cities – though this may well be the case. Rather, the suggestion is of the translocal and, potentially, transnational existence of such lifestyles as relatively interconnected wholes. While greater depth of research would be required in order to ascertain levels of similarity and connection from country to country, it is clear that the British goth scene took the form of a unified translocal amalgam of distinctive style, identity, values and practices, complete with an associated infrastructure. Contrary to postmodernist emphasis on the fluidity of consumer culture, then, the intention here is to theorize and illustrate a notion of translocal cultural groupings of substance.

Four Indicators of (Sub)Cultural Substance

Importantly, conceptualizing such cultural substance does not entail a return to the traditional forms of subcultural theory on which the chapter started.

Contrary to the implications of Chicago and Birmingham versions of subculture, participation in the goth scene did not appear to entail the same 'problem-solving' function for all members and neither did it signify any specific or all-important subversion of consumer culture. The style encapsulated significant elements of diversity and dynamism, its boundaries were not absolute, and levels of commitment varied from one individual to another. Furthermore, rather than owing itself entirely to the automatic gravitation or spontaneous creative practices of participants, the goth scene's initial construction and subsequent survival rested upon external and internal networks of information and organization, often in the form of media and commerce. But in spite of overlaps and complexities, the initial temptation to describe goths using a term such as *neo-tribe* or *lifestyle* was gradually tempered by the realization that such a move would have over-inflated the diversity and instability of their grouping. Crucially, fluidity and substance are not matters of binary opposition, but of degree. In this particular case, the observation that the goth scene involved elements of movement, overlap and change does not somehow obfuscate the remarkable levels of commitment, identity, distinctiveness and autonomy which were evident.

Rather than attempting to capture such elements of cultural substance by means of yet another new term, I have opted to do so via the development of what I regard as a more relevant, workable and up-to-date conception of *subculture*. The term is a familiar one and the revision seeks, largely, to remove overly problematic elements of the theories with which it has been associated and clarify a number of further connotations, rather than to redefine fundamentally. Essentially, the task is to combine useful general aspects of the Birmingham and Chicago School approaches, with a more flexible approach to contemporary identities and recognition of the roles of media and commerce in the construction of popular cultural groupings. The scope of the term is broadened through severing its automatic link with resistance, problem-solving, class conflict or spontaneity. At the same time, however, the reworking proposes limits to its use by replacing these specific criteria with the general defining theme of cultural substance.

This theme has been broken down into the four indicative criteria of *identity, commitment, consistent distinctiveness* and *autonomy*. Rather than these four comprising a definitive blueprint, each of them should be regarded as a contributory feature which, taken cumulatively with the others, increases the appropriateness of the term *subculture*, in the relative degree to which each is applicable. The combination of this degree of malleability with a set of specific criteria should maximize the potential for meaningful use of the concept at the same time as recognizing the greater relevance of alternative terminology – in the form of Maffesoli's notion of neo-tribe perhaps – to describe more fleeting or superficial forms of affiliation. What follows is an introduction to each indicator, briefly illustrated by references to the detailed exploration of the goth scene which is to come.

Consistent Distinctiveness

In spite of their potential problems, it would be an over-generalization to seek the absolute removal of notions of symbolic resistance, homology and the collective resolving of structural contradictions from the analysis of popular culture. However, none of these features should be regarded as an essential defining characteristic of the term subculture. For the most part, the functions, meanings and symbols of subcultural involvement are liable to vary between participants and to reflect complex processes of cultural choice and coincidence rather than an automatic shared reaction to circumstances. However, this does not mean that there is no distinctiveness or consistency to the styles and values of contemporary groupings, or that, where present, such features are not socially significant. While accepting the inevitability of a degree of internal difference and change over time, then, the first indicator of subcultural substance comprises the existence of a set of shared tastes and values which is distinctive from those of other groups and reasonably consistent, from one participant to the next, one place to the next and one year to the next.

In spite of internal diversity, then, it will become clear in the following chapter that the goth scene was characterized by a relatively clear set of ideals and tastes. Even in its least spectacular manifestations, the visual style of goths tended to enable them to identify one another with ease and to result in reactions ranging from captivation to ridicule and even alarm from outsiders. It will also be shown that the relative consistency of the goth style was enforced by means of equally consistent systems of subcultural rewards and penalties. Namely, gaining acceptance, popularity and status was often dependent upon making oneself sufficiently compatible with the distinctive tastes of the subculture. It is important that such clear evidence of *relative* consistency and distinctiveness is not obscured by an overemphasis on diversity and dynamism.

Identity

Widdicombe and Wooffitt (1995: 22–8) and Muggleton (2000: 11) have rightly emphasized that Birmingham School subcultural theory tended to take insufficient account of the views of young people themselves. The second indicator of subcultural substance seeks to redress this problem by focusing on the extent to which participants hold a perception that they are involved in a distinct cultural grouping and share feelings of identity with one another. Leaving aside the importance of evaluating consistent distinctiveness from a distance, a clear and sustained subjective sense of group identity, in itself, begins to establish a grouping as substantive rather than ephemeral. In the case of the goth scene, while the precise importance of subcultural identity relative to other aspects of life differed between them, we shall see that a sense of like-mindedness with other goths – regardless of their geographical location – was often regarded by participants as the single most important part of their identity.

As important as a sense of affiliation with perceived insiders, here, are feelings of distinction from those regarded as outsiders, an emphasis clearly present in some of the subcultural theory from Birmingham and, particularly, Chicago, as well as the more recent work of Thornton (1995). While the notion of subjective identity and distinction is also present in the explanations of many who seek to move beyond the term subculture (e.g. Chaney 1996; Hetherington 1998a; Maffesoli 1996) the partial, ephemeral character of the affinities they seek to infer contrasts somewhat with the rather more one-dimensional sense of 'us' and 'them' in which we are interested.

Commitment

It is also proposed that subcultures are liable to influence extensively the everyday lives of participants in practice, and that, more often than not, this concentrated involvement will last years rather than months. Depending upon the nature of the group in question, subcultures are liable to account for a considerable proportion of free time, friendship patterns, shopping routes, collections of commodities, going-out habits and even internet use. Turning again to our case study, it will become clear that, even for those goths who were reluctant to explicitly locate themselves as members, the subculture often dominated their lifestyle in practice. Consistent with the operation of social pressures relating to tastes and norms, such intense levels of participation among goths can also be explained, in part, by the potential benefits of displays of commitment to one's personal standing. In contrast, those who flirted around the goth scene's boundaries tended to receive fewer social rewards. A tendency for concentrated and continuous practical involvement among participants, then, may also distinguish subcultures from more fleeting, partial forms of affiliation, in which the energies of participants are shared more equally across a variety of groups.

Autonomy

We have already emphasized the perspective of McRobbie, Thornton and others that notions of subculture as spontaneous and authentic unjustifiably exclude media and commerce from their analysis (McRobbie 1989, 1999; Thornton 1995). Throughout the chapter I have consistently raised questions over a number of perspectives which assume that media and commerce act as catalysts for the breakdown of substantive groupings. In contrast, my reworked notion of subculture regards both these crucial elements of contemporary Western societies as critical to the construction and facilitation of subcultures. Thus, behind the identities, practices and values of the goth scene lay a complex infrastructure of events, consumer goods and communications, all of which were thoroughly implicated in media and commerce.

In spite of the consequent implication that we should avoid notions of escaping or subverting 'the system', though, it would be mistaken to assume all groupings are equally lacking in autonomy. Rather, there is a need to distinguish between different scales and types of media and commerce and, hence, different kinds of grouping. Independent, enthusiasm-driven specialist record labels are entirely different from transnational conglomerates, and widely read niche-style magazines ought not to be pigeonholed alongside home-made fanzines with a three-figure readership. In the same way, small-scale specialist events promoted and DJed by subcultural enthusiasts should not be bracketed with those which are professionally promoted for a more socially diverse clientele. It should also be recognized that the implication of a grouping with certain profit-making activities does not somehow remove the significance of any voluntary activities which also contribute to its survival and development.

The final indicator of subculture, then, is that the grouping concerned, while inevitably connected to the society and politico-economic system of which it is a part, retains a *relatively* high level of autonomy. Most notably, a good proportion of the productive or organizational activities which underpin it are liable to be undertaken by and for enthusiasts. Furthermore, in some cases, profit-making operations will run alongside extensive semi-commercial and voluntary activities, indicating particularly high levels of grass-roots insider participation in cultural production. Therefore, while the exchange of money for goods and services and the use of media technologies had always been integral to participation in the goth scene, we shall see that in Britain in the late 1990s, the record labels, bands, DJs, promoters and producers of fanzines and websites involved were often subcultural participants providing exclusive services for their fellow enthusiasts and, frequently, making little or no money from doing so.

Clearly, an assessment of the extent to which groupings operate autonomously requires a means to distinguish between the scales and levels of independence of different productive activities. Useful as a starting point here is Sarah Thornton's identification of the role of three different types of medium

– micro, niche and mass – in the construction of late-1980s club cultures in Britain. Thornton's focus, though, is more on the general size and scale of media rather than on their level of independence or specialism, and in any case there is a sense in which her distinctions get a little overshadowed by her central assertion that, in one form or another, media construct subcultures. In contrast, our specific interest here is in distinguishing between internal or *subcultural* forms of media and commerce – which operate mostly within the networks of a particular grouping – and external or *non-subcultural* products and services, produced by larger-scale commercial interests for a broader consumer base. Such categories are inevitably imperfect: there will always be a considerable grey area between the two and a diversity within each. However, the distinction enables an assessment of extent to which groupings operate autonomously, and the degree to which they are facilitated and constructed from within. Most elements of the British goth scene during my research period did fall reasonably clearly into one category or the other. While non-subcultural products and producers were heavily implicated, specialist subcultural events, consumables and media were playing an unusually significant role in the generation of the grouping.

Conclusion

Subcultures, then, can be seen as distinguishable from more fluid elective collectivities by their level of substance, something indicated by the *relative* satisfaction by a given grouping of the criteria outlined. It remains important to recognize that even the most substantive of subcultures will retain elements of diversity, that some individuals will adopt elements of their values without any particular commitment, and that even the most committed participants are not somehow isolated from other interests or priorities. At the same time as emphasizing these elements of fluidity, though, this book seeks – by focusing in relative terms on levels of identity, commitment, coherence and autonomy – to infer that subcultures are more notable for their substance than for their ephemerality. The chapters which follow illustrate the ways in which the late-1990s British goth scene fitted the criteria outlined and seek to provide explanations for its levels of translocal substance.

3

Goth as a Subcultural Style

The reworking outlined in the previous chapter suggests that, in most cases, groupings for which the term subculture is appropriate should involve a set of tastes and norms which has a significant degree of distinctiveness and internal consistency. In contrast, a more diverse, fluctuating array of values or behaviours might indicate a more fluid, transitory amalgamation, for whom neo-tribe or one of the other 'alternative' terms outlined might prove more suitable. In the case of the goth scene, shared tastes and norms manifested themselves primarily in the arena of style. In Chapter 4 it will be suggested that, in spite of its importance, the identification of an 'objectively' distinctive and consistent style does not necessarily carry as much overall weight as an indicator of subcultural substance as do the subjective perceptions of identity or practical commitment of participants. However, in order to give the non-familiar reader a clear sense of the characteristics of the goth scene, it makes sense to deal with issues of style at the outset. While the main focus of this book is the British goth scene during the late 1990s, we will begin with a brief descriptive history of the subculture, focused particularly upon the looks and sounds of the bands who did so much to set the tone for the distinctive subcultural tastes adopted and developed by fans in the years which followed.

The Emergence of a Style

Prior to and during the first half of the 1980s, certain mostly British-based sounds and images of the immediate post-punk climate became crystallized into an identifiable movement. While various factors were involved, some of which will be discussed at greater length elsewhere, there is little doubt that music and its performers were most directly responsible for the emergence of the stylistic characteristics of goth. The androgynous glamour and deep-voiced vocals of 1970s David Bowie provided an important precursor to goth, as did the sombre, depressing angst of Joy Division toward the 1980s.[1] More directly, though, the 'darker' direction in which Siouxsie and the Banshees began to take some of the themes of punk around the turn of the decade provided both a general mood and particular sounds and images from which others would draw for the following two decades and beyond. Most notable, perhaps, were the sinister jangling guitars and wailing sombre lyrics which characterized albums such as *Ju Ju* (1981), and even more so, vocalist Siouxsie Sioux's appearance, which had shifted from its early focus on reappropriation of Nazi imagery and the like to a somewhat less politically provocative 'darker' theme, characterized most obviously by black back-combed hair and distinctively styled heavy dark make-up accentuating the eyes, cheekbones and lips. This look would be imitated, in part or in full, by female and sometimes male goths for the following two decades. The most important starting point of goth, however, was probably provided by the images and sounds of Bauhaus – notably the single, 'Bela Lugosi's Dead', released in 1979 (Thompson and Greene, Alternative Press 1994). The performance of this song, and indeed much of the band's set, contained most of the distinctive themes which still pervade the goth scene, from macabre funereal musical tone and tempo, to lyrical references to the undead, to deep-voiced eerie vocals, to a dark twisted form of androgyny in the appearance of the band and most of its following.

In the period following these early signs, a cluster of emerging bands, many of whom played gigs alongside one another from time to time, found themselves placed by the music press into a scene temporarily labelled post- or sometimes positive-punk and, eventually, goth (Scathe 2000). In addition to the continual relatively high-profile presence of Siouxsie and the Banshees and their acquaintances The Cure, the most important acts included Bauhaus, Southern Death Cult (later known as Death Cult and finally as The Cult), Play Dead, The Birthday Party, Alien Sex Fiend, U.K. Decay, Sex Gang Children, Virgin Prunes and Specimen. From 1982, the last of these were heavily involved in a London-based nightclub known as The Batcave, which ended up acting as an initial melting pot for many of the bands and fans associated with the fledgling style. Most notable, perhaps, was the further development and establishment among performers and their following of variants of the dark femininity pioneered by Bauhaus and Siouxsie and the Banshees. A particularly important and lasting addition to the style was Specimen's use of ripped fishnet and other see-through fabrics, in the form of tops as well as tights. The club also acted as a magnet for the music press, keen in the wake of punk to find, report and, ultimately, construct any possible successors. It would appear that the term 'goth' was mentioned in passing by a number of those involved, including Tony Wilson, producer of Joy Division and members of both Southern Death Cult and U.K. Decay (Thompson and Greene, Alternative Press 1994; Scathe 2000). However, there is little doubt that it was publicized and made to stick as a label for the new scene by music journalists, perhaps most notably David Dorrell of the *New Musical Express* (Scathe 2000).

As the music and style spread across and beyond Britain via the music press, radio and occasional television performances, record distribution and live tours, more and more nightclubs accommodated the numerous teenagers adopting the sounds and styles of what was soon to become widely known as the goth scene. Toward the mid-1980s a Leeds band called The Sisters of Mercy, who had come together in 1981, began to emerge as the most high-profile and, indeed, influential band associated with goth. Consistently catchy jangly guitar riffs, powerful base lines and deep-voiced vocals, together with the crispness of beat provided by an electronic drum machine, contributed to a sound consistent with but somewhat more accessible than that of many of the earlier positive-punk bands. While their visual image was stylistically less extreme and innovative than that of the likes of Specimen or Alien Sex Fiend, it had the effect of solidifying many of the themes of goth in its heyday – notably the dark hair, pointed boots, tight black jeans and shades often worn by members of the band. The clarity and effectiveness of image and sound, together with the enthusiasm of the music press for a band which seemed so perfectly placed to pick up the goth mantle, led quickly to indie chart success and a contract with WEA in 1984. From the mid-1980s to the early 1990s, this more accessible yet highly distinctive form of goth, termed 'gothic rock' in two influential books by journalist Mick Mercer (1988, 1991), acted as a clear central focus for the greater and greater numbers of teenagers adopting the style, buying the now widely available music, attending relevant nightclubs and sharing an associated sense of distinctiveness and identity. Radio, press and television coverage graced not only the Sisters of Mercy, but the band's acrimonious offshoot The Mission, as well as Fields of the Nephilim, All About Eve and The Cult. An equally high profile was afforded to continual new material from the veritable veterans, Siouxsie and the Banshees and The Cure.

By the mid-1990s, however, the goth style had seemingly used up its time in the media and commercial spotlight and all but disappeared from public view. The intense attachment of many participants to the style of the goth scene, though, ensured its small-scale survival. From across and beyond Britain there emerged a new generation of bands who were reliant upon small-scale specialist labels, media and clubs, and who were motivated more by their own enthusiasm than by any realistic hope of breaking into public view or making significant money. A combination of these ever-emerging new bands and the enduring appeal of the music and images of 1980s goth ensured that while its details would diversify and change, the central themes survived relatively intact. It is with the consistency and distinctiveness of the goth scene during my research in the late 1990s, that the remainder of this chapter will concern itself.

Individuality or Conformity?

In Chapter 2, we explored the argument proposed by numerous theorists that distinctive, identifiable cultural groupings have fallen by the wayside as part of the increasing tendency for boundaries to crumble in the midst of a postmodern proliferation of diversity. The pastiche and cross-fertilization of previously distinct styles is a central feature of such theory. The implication is that, rather than being clearly organized into a limited number of mutually distinct predictable patterns, different types of clothing, make-up, sounds and accessories float freely, available for appropriation into any number of different individualized concoctions (Polhemous 1997, Muggleton 1997). As a result, individuals are no longer constrained – in their appearance, their music or any other tastes – by any particular cultural affiliation. Instead, it is argued that we each continually develop our own unique pick 'n' mix of artefacts from a veritable supermarket of style, where everything is available to anyone in combination with anything else. Acceptance of the validity of this theoretical position clearly suggests abandonment of the notion of distinctiveness which this chapter seeks to develop, and invites a denial of any predictable connection between the different elements of an individual's appearance or music tastes. As Muggleton has put it, '"appearance perception" becomes a hazardous undertaking, an ever-increasing number of interpretations being possible' (1997: 192).

An acceptance of this notion of the breakdown of clear distinct styles pervades the reasoning of some of those who seek to replace the notion of subculture with terms such as *neo-tribe*, *scene* and *lifestyle*. While acknowledging some kind of stylistic organization to the range of floating artefacts, such descriptors seek to move away from the fixed, consistent and clearly bounded sets of looks and sounds implied by traditional subcultural theory. Bennett, for example, argues that music tastes tend to have as much to do with individualized processes of selection and meaning as with the collective normative systems:

> Sifting through various types of music, artists and sounds, consumers characteristically choose songs and instrumental pieces which appeal to *them* with the effect that the stylistic boundaries existing between the latter become rather less important than the meaning which the chosen body of music as a whole assumes for the listener. (Bennett 1999: 610)

Muggleton has also argued that style and taste are essentially individualized, playing down the importance of distinct collective styles on the basis of the testimonies of participants themselves. Even in those cases where his interview respondents cautiously accepted an involvement with a particular genre or grouping, he reports a strong perception that their tastes and those of fellow participants were individual and distinctive to themselves rather than determined by group norms (Muggleton 2000: 55–80). This is consistent with the observation of Sarah Thornton (1995: 99) that participants of early 1990s British club culture tended to play up the heterogeneity of the 'crowd' with which they associated themselves. On the basis of such apparent evidence of internal diversity, Muggleton concludes that contemporary subcultures are essentially liminal and, as such, 'characterised as much by ambiguity and diversity as by coherence and definition' (Muggleton 2000: 75).

Many of my own open-ended interview respondents were also keen to emphasize their individuality rather than talking about their conformity to a clear and consistent set of group-specific symbols, as in the case of the following respondent from Plymouth:

G1 (*male*):   You can do what you want and you can get away with it, and not actually give a shit what anyone thinks of you.[2]

This finding was replicated in some responses to the questionnaire I conducted at the Whitby Gothic Weekend.

WQ5b: In your own words, please explain what the goth scene is all about.
43 (*male*):   Having the absolute freedom to dress as you want and to express yourself as you want.[3]

As alluded to in the introduction to this book, though, an over-reliance upon the ways in which subcultural participants choose to respond to direct questioning can sometimes result in debatable conclusions. Although individuality did manifest itself to some degree, as we shall see, a careful comparative analysis of the behaviour, appearance and testimonies of goths over a substantial period of time and in various places indicated that many interviewees exaggerated the extent of their stylistic difference from other goths and underplayed the internal consistency of the style. In Chapter 4, this tendency to exaggerate one's individuality will be explained with reference to social pressures induced by subcultural received wisdom, or ideology. For now, though, we are concerned with the actual levels of consistency of the stylistic practices of goths.

As alluded to above, it should be emphasized that, to a degree, the style *was* flexible, changeable and diverse, and that it overlapped in places with the styles of certain other groupings. While the following pages will in relative terms illustrate an overall consistency and distinctiveness, we are *not* talking here about the exhaustive, absolute level of distinctiveness or internal same-ness spoken of, for example, by purist theorists of community (e.g. Tonnies 1955; Redfield 1955). Indeed, rather than conceiving of the goth scene's values as forming a wholly exclusive singular subcultural way of being, it would be preferable to regard participants as engaging in a limited sort of pick 'n' mix, in which the vast majority of selections have to be drawn from a relat-ively clear subcultural range of acceptable possibilities. Therefore, although we have cautioned against overestimation of the role of individuality, it *did* manifest itself to a limited degree. Goths wishing to gain the respect of their peers usually sought to select their own individual concoction from the range of acceptable artefacts and themes and also to make subtle additions and adaptations from beyond the established stylistic boundaries. There was a need for a mixture of conformity and innovation, as explained by the follow-ing interviewee:

> B6 (*male*): I think you have to conform to a certain extent and then just take bits from everywhere until you see things that you like and eventually you have your own look because of it.

Meanwhile, although it clearly placed one within the boundaries of the subculture, adopting 'standard' goth artefacts and modes of behaviour over-predictably sometimes resulted in accusations of pretentiousness or 'trying too hard'. An element of individuality, then, guaranteed a degree of overall diversity and helped ensure the dynamism of the style as a whole.

Nevertheless, both individual variations and general changes tended to occur in the context of an overall consistency with the strict general stylistic regulations of the group. Significant transgressions also tended to be the privilege of initially established and respected participants, due to the safety net of their existing reputation and their possession of an in-depth under-standing of what kinds of stylistic encroachments might be suitable. It tended to be more difficult for newcomers to the goth scene successfully to deviate:

> S3 (*female*): You don't really know much about gothic clothing at the beginning so you don't know much about the scene to have developed your own style of gothdom (laughs).

Important though it was, then, the tendency for certain types of trans-gression to take place was less notable than the overall levels of commitment to the subculture's distinctive range of aesthetic features. We shall see through-out the book that the range from which individuals would select was relatively consistent from time to time and place to place and, usually, distinctive to the subculture, even in non-extreme cases. While there were overlaps with various elements of external culture, then, goths were usually able to identify one another in the street on the basis of appearance, regardless of where they were, as alluded to by the following interviewee from Birmingham:

J12 (*male*): Like I go down to Cambridge to stay with friends of mine and I saw – like everywhere I've gone – I wouldn't have noticed them before but I've noticed them now – the goths, in all the different areas. I point them out. Its like 'one of our boys!'

PH: Does it feel like that then?

J12 (*male*): Yeah, it feels like that in Birmingham too. If I'm walking . . . and I'll see someone from the Toreador [Birmingham goth pub] or some general goth, I'll walk past and think, 'that's one of our lot that is' and I'll give them a nod or something like that.

Indeed, goths I spent time with often made use of their ability to recognize fellow participants. For example, if unable to find their way to an event, it was an established strategy to identify other goths and follow them, with considerable confidence, from their appearance, as to where they were going.

There is insufficient space, here, to cover every single artefact valued within the goth scene, or to detail all the complex ways in which individual goths selected from, combined and subtly transgressed them. I merely attempt to outline the most important stylistic features of the subculture, in relation to particularly prominent and consistent general themes. Entitled 'the sombre and the macabre', 'femininity and ambiguity' and 'fragments of related styles', these are clearly artificial umbrella categories and, as such, inevitably characterized by diversity and overlap. It should also be emphasized, again, that individuals assembled their own style by selecting from the elements I describe and that as a consequence few, if any, adopted all of them. The value of the categories is that they allow a demonstration of the general stylistic consistencies of the goth scene, without glossing over elements of diversity and dynamism.

The Sombre and the Macabre

Most obviously perhaps, the goth style revolved around a general emphasis on artefacts, appearances and music deemed suitably dark, sombre and, sometimes, macabre. The following questionnaire respondent indicated some of the ways in which such themes manifested themselves:

Figure 3.1 (Photograph: S. L. Wainwright)

WQ5b: In your own words, please explain what is the goth scene all about?
107 (*female*): The music (dark, depressing), the look – lots of black, white faces, black eyeliner, crucifixes, churches, graveyards.

Most obvious and important, was an overwhelming and consistent emphasis on the colour black, whether in terms of clothing, hair, lipstick, household decoration or even pet cats! In terms of personal appearance, the theme was also implicit in a tendency for many goths to wear white foundation on their faces to offset thick, usually extended black eyeliner, cheekbone accentuating blusher and dark lipstick (see Figure 3.1), all of which can be traced right

Figure 3.2 (See p. 44. Photograph: S. L. Wainwright)

back to a number of the early 1980s bands. Rather ironically, given the amount of time most of them spent on their appearance, goths also tended to expect their pubs or clubs to be particularly darkened, often with stage smoke for added atmosphere.

While significant numbers of early elements, such as those mentioned above, were evidently alive and well, the general theme of the sombre and the macabre had also developed in various ways. Fashions emerged, within the scene, for items which were relatively marginal to the style of the original generation but nevertheless consistent with the general themes their images

Figure 3.3 (See p. 45. Photograph: S. L. Wainwright)

and sounds were associated with. For example, once the general goth theme had been established for a time, many elaborated on its logical association with horror by drawing upon various images originating in macabre fiction such as crucifixes, bats and vampires (see Figure 3.2), sometimes in a tongue-in-cheek self-conscious manner, sometimes not. At times, such progressions were linked to the clear and direct influence of media products. The profile

Figure 3.4 (See p. 46. Photograph: S. L. Wainwright)

of vampire and horror fiction, for example, was raised particularly high in the early 1990s by Hollywood films such as *Bram Stoker's Dracula* (American Zoetrobe/Columbia Pictures/Osiris Films 1992) and *Interview with the Vampire* (Geffen Pictures/Warner Brothers 1994). The appearance of the vampire protagonists in such films reinforced the existing enthusiasm among goth males for whitened faces, long dark hair and shades (see Figure 3.3).

Meanwhile, for females, the general representations of elements of eighteenth- and nineteenth-century fashion in such fiction further encouraged the adoption of certain styles of clothing associated with the gothic revival of those times and with the Victorian period which followed it. While already established as acceptable due to the original influence of elements of punk fashion, and further encouraged by late 1980s artists such as Patricia Morrison and Julianne Regan, the wearing of dark-coloured corsets, bodices and lacy or velvet tops and dresses was undoubtedly encouraged though the development of a more direct link between goth participants and vampire fiction (see Figure 3.4).

Among a somewhat smaller minority, particularly taken by the vampire theme, status-bestowing personal decorations also came to include fake fangs, coloured contact lenses and elaborate 'horror'-style make-up. Indeed, there was something of a loosely bounded subgroup, in which a direct emphasis on vampire fiction – via appearance, conversation, collections of literature and even role-playing games – was particularly noticeable. As part of the British goth scene as a whole, however, those deemed over-obsessed with or over-serious about such themes were sometimes looked down upon. The majority, whose interest was essentially in a melancholic sombre set of music- and fashion-related themes in more general terms, valued a more subtle, or at least humorous, appropriation of horror imagery, and tended to regard extreme embrace of vampirism as a crude confirmation of popular stereo-types. The following view, although unusual in its directness, reflected the sentiments of many:

D3 (*male*): The vampires – you know, the ones that play masquerade [vampire role-playing game] and so on and they dress up as goths and they have really bad horrendous make-up and so on and it invariably involves fake blood running down their faces and things like that – they turn up at goth clubs, and they fail to fit in completely, because they've completely missed the point.

As well as manifesting itself in a greater variety of ways compared with practice in the early 1980s, there were also, by the late 1990s, more obvious transgressions of the emphasis on dark imagery than there had been in the 1980s. Most notably, although black remained predominant, brighter colours had clearly become more acceptable in terms of hair, clothing and make-up. What began as a somewhat humorous and deliberate transgression by certain individuals had resulted in the growing translocal acceptance of the previously detested colour pink, as a complement to black, among goths in Britain. This was followed by a similar relaxing of rules relating to other bright colours.

Crucially, though, they were usually juxtaposed with hair, make-up or other clothes more consistent with the sinister theme we are describing. Black, then, remained the most prominent colour for the vast majority of goths and, similarly, most retained a variety of other specific features relating to the theme, which could be traced back to the bands of the 1980s. For example, even the small minority for whom dark colours seemed of marginal significance tended to wear their make-up in a tell-tale goth style, notably with excessive extended eye-liner, accentuated cheekbones and pale foundation.

In general terms, the music associated with the goth scene during the late 1990s was more diverse than the fashion. Nevertheless, from the early 1980s up to and including the time of my research, a significant proportion of the play-lists at most goth-oriented clubs could be reasonably accurately described using one or more of the adjectives 'dark', 'sinister', 'deep' and 'sombre'. Such related themes, though, applied to a considerable variety of music, with deep-voiced male vocalists, high-pitched female vocalists, both slow and fast tempos, various styles of guitar from tuneful and jangly to aggressive and thrash-style, real and electronically simulated drums and, increasingly, in the 1990s, both atmospheric keyboard chords and more upbeat electronic sequences. In particular, there is little doubt that newer bands associated with the goth scene were producing a considerable diversity of styles, ranging from those focused on early and particularly late 1980s guitar-based goth sounds to those who sought to merge such sounds with electronic chords, sequences and dance beats, to others who largely resisted such technology in favour of what they regarded as an up-to-date tuneful, catchy 'indie' style of goth.[5] In spite of their variety, however, there were few bands associated with the goth scene which had no connection whatever with the themes of gloom and darkness we have been describing. Even the most thoroughly dance-oriented bands which attracted a consistent goth following, such as Apoptygma Berzerk, Covenant and VNV Nation, retained deep, harsh vocals, sombre metaphorical lyrics and powerful atmospheric chords.

While their consistent manifestation in fashion and music were clear, the importance of the sombre and the macabre in terms of behaviour, attitude and outlook was more ambiguous. Excessive grumpiness and depression *did* appear to be exhibited by certain individuals, but the majority had become resistant to such traits, regarding them, as with excessive displays of interest in vampirism, as a misplaced negative stereotype of goths held by outsiders. Therefore, while some goths did claim that membership of their subculture entailed holding particular 'attitudes', most played down the importance of negative or miserable outlooks on life, preferring to emphasize a positive enthusiasm towards goth styles of music and fashion. This came across particularly clearly in the Whitby Festival Questionnaire.

WQ5b: In your own words, please explain what is the goth scene all about.

32 (*male*): Rejoicing in a high-spirited view of the darker side of life, pushing the frontiers of style and sound.

40 (*female*): To me it is about being able to dress how I feel – it is NOT about being miserable and dull.

Femininity and Ambiguity

Social constructionist approaches to gender suggest that due to the constructed and, hence, malleable nature of sexual categories, they might – in the right discursive and cultural circumstance – become disconnected from the series of repeated stylistic and behavioural performances which actually produce and reproduce gendered identities. Judith Butler, among other 'queer theorists', seeks the undermining of and *dei*dentification from essentialized gender categories, via a number of possible strategies including the proliferation of drag and camp. The parodic transgression of gender roles is deemed to have the potential to expose the constructed and performative nature of the dominant notions of male and female which form their target (e.g. Butler 1990, 1991, 1993; Meyer, 1994). Albeit without the parody or the overt political ends, the goth scene's distinctive normative environment consistently loosened the links between stylistic facets of gender and the fixed sex categories of male and female. More specifically, without actually rendering such categories insignificant, goth had from its very beginnings been characterized by the predominance, for both males and females, of particular kinds of style which would normally be associated with femininity. One of my e-mail interviewees provides a useful introduction to these:

> J1 (*female*): I think that the nature of 'goth culture' in itself is conducive to 'femininity' ... in that sexual ambiguity is expressed within the clothes, make-up and music of the scene.

Most importantly, particular styles of make-up, which had been common-place ever since the days of Bauhaus and The Batcave, remained popular for both males and females during the late 1990s (see Figure 3.5). Equally, goths of both genders had always worn considerable amounts of silver jewellery, notably earrings, nose rings, bracelets and necklaces. The main change which had occurred by the 1990s was that piercings, for both genders, had also spread to lips, eyebrows, tongues and belly buttons and that jewellery was more likely to be coloured. In addition to jewellery and make-up, numerous examples of relatively feminine styles of clothes – many of which also consistent with the emphasis on sombreness – had been important for both sexes from the scene's conception. Relatively long-established examples included the Victorian items described in the last section for women, alongside frilly shirts and velvet jackets for both sexes (see Figure 3.6).

However, by the late 1990s, the long-term emphasis on femininity had intensified in both popularity and extremity compared with its importance a decade earlier. While the wearing, by males and females, of fishnet tights and mesh tops had been a part of the goth style since the days of Specimen,

Figure 3.5 (See p. 48. Photograph: S. L. Wainwright)

it had become much more commonplace by the mid- to late 1990s (see Figure 3.7). Even more notably, via a gradual process of individual transgressions, the wearing of long and short skirts, by male as well as female goths, had become unexceptional (see Figure 3.8).

There were also further diversifications of the way in which femininity manifested itself. Many of the 1980s styles of clothes described, now associated with 'trad goths', were often either combined with or rejected in favour of newer influences. In a move which in some ways harked back to

Figure 3.6 (See p. 49. Photograph: S. L. Wainwright)

some of the original influences of punk, aspects of the 1990s fetish scene and, indeed, the sex industry generally became popular. Goths of both sexes were increasingly likely to be seen in black and sometimes coloured PVC and rubber trousers, skirts, leggings, corsets, tops and dog collars (see Figure 3.9).

Importantly, in the context of the goth scene, all but the most extreme examples of such attire were often valued more in terms of their subcultural aesthetic qualities than for their sexual connotations. The differential symbolic

Figure 3.7 (See p. 50. Photograph: S. L. Wainwright)

Figure 3.8 (See p. 50. Photograph: S. L. Wainwright)

value of fetish clothing in subcultural and non-subcultural environments was demonstrated by the fact that, while entirely comfortable wearing such clothes at goth clubs, many female goths were nervous about the possible reaction to them in environments they regarded as more mainstream:

R1 (*female*): Say I went into a trendy club wearing what I wore to the last Dust to Dust [goth band] gig – which comprised several layers of ripped fishnets, platform boots, hot pants and quite a low-cut corset – I would have had the hell hassled out of me and probably have ended up being raped at the end of the night or something.

Returning to the theme more generally, femininity manifested itself not just in controllable factors such as clothing, make-up and jewellery, but also in the physical appearance of individuals' faces and bodies. Hence, right from the days of Bauhaus, the most venerated and fancied males in the goth scene, in terms of appearance, tended to have slim bodies and faces, and minimum body hair. The following respondent explained that, for him, a key appeal of the goth scene was that, in this distinctive cultural climate, his somewhat effeminate body became a positive, rather than a negative characteristic:

Figure 3.9 (See p. 51. Photograph: S. L. Wainwright)

G4 (*male*): It's basically that I can feel comfortable that I can be a skinny, weedy bloke who, like, is a bit emotional sometimes. It's almost a bonus in fact.

Slimness of body and face, were, on the whole, also valued for females – consistent with more dominant fashion – although the ability to show off an ample chest with the help of a basque or other suitable low-cut top often seemed to more than compensate for those with larger general proportions.

Respondent G4's reference to being able to be 'a bit emotional sometimes', in addition to his slimness, accurately indicates that the display by males of certain behavioural characteristics and attitudes associated with femininity was also more common in the goth scene than most elements of society outside it. This was certainly reflected strongly in some examples of goth music, where the stereotype of emotional, self-indulgent and angst-ridden themes – all of which tend to be associated with femininity rather than masculinity – was a generalization, but not an entirely inaccurate one. Although certainly not a prominent theme among the positive-punk scene of the early 1980s, or indeed some of the harder industrial music played at some goth clubs toward the mid-1990s, some of the most popular goth music frequently exhibited such characteristics. Notably, the atmospheric guitars, keyboards, slow tempo, wailing vocals and angst-ridden lyrics which characterized much of The Cure's music serve as a consistent example, as do certain ballads by The Mission, Fields of the Nephilim, All About Eve and others.[6] Toward the mid- to late 1990s, although the influence of industrial music had resulted in more incorporation of dance-oriented and sometimes heavy guitar-based sounds into some goth music, lyrical themes and the use of emotional, atmospheric tones meant that it often retained elements of emotional self-indulgence.

The manifestation of this emphasis on being emotional in the behaviour of male goths, from time to time, was connected by one female participant to what she perceived as a greater tendency for them to engage in same-sex tactility:

D6 (*female*): They [male goths] can actually get closer to another male. They wouldn't feel ashamed of hugging another man or crying on his shoulder or something like that whereas if they were more macho then perhaps 'huh, you poof, you can't hold my hand', or you know.

The emphasis, for both males and females, on a feminine appearance was also linked with a general acceptance and, sometimes, even veneration of sexual ambiguity. While the majority of goths behaved in accordance with

heterosexual norms throughout wider society, there was little if any disapproval or surprise, in goth clubs, at the occasional sight of people of the
same sex holding hands, cuddling or kissing. In addition, many male and
female goths, in the course of informal conversations and occasional on-line
forum discussions throughout my research, keenly indicated that they were
attracted to goths of both sexes. There was at times a distinct impression
that non-hetero sexualities, while certainly not the norm, were a transgression
to be admired.

Such unusually high incidence and acceptance, outside of the gay or fetish
scenes, of same-sex behaviour may have involved a number of factors, notably
the way in which gender and sexual ambiguity tend to be conflated with one
another by the media, the direct influence of apparently bisexual musicians
related to the scene – most notably, perhaps, goth's glam-rock ancestor David
Bowie (see Hebdige 1979: 60–2), the general experimentalism and transgression, sexual and otherwise, associated with the much-renowned early
1980s Batcave club and the degree of overlap between goth and fetishism.
However, it seems highly likely that it also involved a slightly more gradual,
grass-roots-level response, on the part of some goths, to regularly being in a
cultural environment in which the division between males and females was
significantly blurred by subcultural style. As bisexual theorist Heather Came
has put it, 'The difference between a heterosexual future and a bisexual or
lesbian one lies in the absence of rigid gender roles' (Came 1996: 28). Thus,
one respondent could explain to me that she regarded gender and sexual
ambiguity in the goth scene as thoroughly intertwined:

> A9 (*female*): ... with the way we dress ... there's always been that element of
> bisexuality – I mean you get very feminine-looking men don't you?

She went on to elaborate on the point in relation to her own sexuality, explaining that she was attracted to particular forms of femininity, which, in the
specific context of the goth scene, she might find in both males and females.
While virtually impossible to prove, it seems plausible that a female attracted
to a particularly feminine goth appearance in men may move toward finding
similar characteristics equally attractive when they are exhibited by a woman.
Similarly, from the point of view of a goth male, the gap between being
attracted to subcultural forms of femininity in goth women and being
attracted to similar features in goth men seems more bridgeable in such an
androgynous environment.

Having become established, open expressions of bisexuality in goth clubs
and pubs are likely to have reproduced themselves more directly, in the same
way that other behavioural or stylistic fashions do. This is not necessarily to

suggest that sexual desires can be consciously manipulated, but merely that, as Came has put it, 'visibility creates chances for others' (Came 1996: 27). Whether the subcultural environment effected a change in the sexuality of previously straight participants, or merely enabled individuals already pre-disposed to same-sex attraction to realize this in practice, seems a conundrum which would require considerably more discussion than we have space for here. Either interpretation, though, serves to emphasize the key general point that in respect of gender and by extension sexuality the goth scene involved a highly distinctive stylistic and normative environment.

Fragments of Related Styles

While, the goth scene's range of styles had a considerable degree of consistency and distinctiveness, as I have been arguing, a number of elements reflected overlaps with other music or fashion scenes. Thus, in addition to selecting more unique 'goth' items, participants engaging in their subcultural stylistic pick 'n' mix often tended to select one or two items of clothing or accessories associated with related scenes or subcultures. We have already referred to the importance of elements of punk and fetish as influences because of the ways in which the items described fitted under the first two stylistic sections. This final 'theme' consists of a number of more miscellaneous items shared between goths and other groupings. Most notable here was the popularity among goths of certain items associated with the somewhat diverse range of genres collectively known as 'alternative culture'. Will Straw explains that in the 1980s, 'alternative' functioned as something of an umbrella term for a mixture of styles deemed non-mainstream:

> the capacity of this culture to cater to the most specific of taste formations is accompanied by the sense that no particular stylistic exercise may be held up as emblematic of a collective, forward movement on the part of this terrain as a whole . . . (Straw 1991: 375)

Alongside punks, indie fans, crusties and others, during the 1980s and also the early 1990s goths often regarded their grouping to be one of the specific taste formations under this umbrella. While the use of this term and the physical association of goths with punks, crusties and indie rock fans was rather less common by the time of my research, selected music and artefacts associated with the latter had been retained by the goth scene. Most notably perhaps, some goths' enthusiasm for fluorescent-coloured hair dyes, braided hair, various kinds of body piercing and combat trousers were shared with some other 'alternative' groupings. A liking for certain bands or songs associated with indie, punk and crusty scenes was also fairly common among goths. Importantly, in both appearance and music tastes, only certain 'external' elements were visible, and these tended to take their place alongside more distinctive subcultural tastes.

There were also overlaps with rock culture more generally, in that many goths wore T-shirts of their favourite bands which, while containing subcult-urally distinctive bands and designs, resembled those worn by rock fans of varying stylistic persuasions. In addition, increasing numbers of goths wore tops which in their general shape and style resembled such rock band T-shirts, but whose text consisted of a self-conscious, light-hearted reference to the individual's involvement in the goth scene per se. Examples of the slogans on such T-shirts, which were usually produced and sold by enthusiasts turned entrepreneurs, included 'SAD OLD GOTH', 'GOTH TART' and, even, 'SPICE GOTH' (see Figure 3.10). Whilst such overt statements of subcultural self-consciousness were not a part of the early goth scene, their consistency with it is clear, as is their distinctiveness. Quite simply, who but a goth would wear such a T-shirt? The implications of such overt statements of identity will be explored in greater depth in Chapter 4.

Due to certain stylistic crossovers toward the late 1990s, there was also an increasing, though not unanimous, acceptance in the goth scene of limited examples of music associated with extreme or death metal. While far more aggressive, masculine and thrash guitar-based on the whole, these genres had by then taken on some of the features of goth – particularly the prominence of black hair and clothes, and the wearing of horror-style make-up. Because of this and the resulting media descriptions of such music and style, elements of such harder sounds and images had influenced the music and fashion tastes of some goths. Importantly, however, others overtly excluded anything they regarded as 'metal' from their music collections and appearances, and explicitly objected to such influences in others. In addition to these 'alternative' and rock styles, the goth scene's criteria of status favoured certain examples of other styles of music and fashion. We have already mentioned the important influence of certain clothes and accessories associated with the fetish scene. In addition to this, the origins of the goth scene, and the location of the early lives of many current participants in the 1980s, had induced a nostalgic enjoyment of listening and dancing to some of the new romantic pop music of that period – which also fitted with the femininity of goth style in general. Nostalgia for new romantic also encouraged a tendency to wear frilly shirts, military jackets of various kinds, morning coats and other items associated with bands such as Adam and the Ants (see Figure 3.11). As one interviewee put it:

Figure 3.10 (See p. 57. Photograph: S. L. Wainwright)

K1 (*male*): As soon as you paint Adam Ant black he's a goth isn't he!

Finally, a gradual incorporation of particular aspects of dance-club fashions into goth appearances was taking place during my research – notably in the form of tops, skirts and trousers featuring reflective or ultraviolet sensitive designs, braided hair and fluorescent make-up. Those who embraced such influences particularly enthusiastically were sometimes known as 'cyber goths' (see Figure 3.12).

Figure 3.11 (See p. 57. Photograph: S. L. Wainwright)

Symbolizing Identity

Crucially, the selected elements of what I have called 'related' styles, which became acceptable for goths, did not necessarily reflect any inherent homological fit between them and the other themes of the subculture. Similarly, while it may certainly be possible to outline certain overlaps and links, I am not attempting here to underline a 'natural' or inherent homology within or between the two core themes of sombreness and femininity. While I have

Figure 3.12 (See p. 58. Photograph: S. L. Wainwright)

emphasized the linkage between current and past manifestations of the themes in order to establish consistency over time, the overall range of styles should be regarded as having come together through a mixture of coincidences, logical associations, individual innovations and, most importantly, considerable construction and consolidation through events, commerce and media (dealt with in detail later in the book). It should again be emphasized, therefore, that my reference to stylistic consistency pertains to the extent to which, in spite of its consisting of numerous elements cobbled together from different sources at different stages, there was a discernible distinctive goth style, which manifested itself consistently from one individual to the next, one place to the next and one year to the next.

Crucially, the notion of homology indicates the existence of an underlying essential meaning directly symbolized by all the stylistic and behavioural elements. This book will specifically resist such reductionism. In particular, we should not treat the goth style, or any particular elements of it, as symbolic of any particular structural, psychological or political circumstances or goals. As has been pointed out by Gary Clarke, such analysis mistakenly treats style as an 'objective category to be measured' and privileges the interpretation of theoretically driven semiotician, with little regard for the experience of participants themselves (G. Clarke 1981: 87; also see Muggleton 2000: 9–14). Such attempts to 'make sense' of youth styles often consist of little more than speculation and, at times, have imposed rather than extracted meanings. In spite of the criticism afforded to the likes of Hebdige on this score, more recent attempts to discern meaning from a textual analysis of style and behaviour have suffered similar problems. Albeit in the context of an otherwise insightful discussion of dance culture and femininity, Angela McRobbie's interpretation of dummies, ice lollies and whistles as a symbolic means by which young women insulated their bodies from sexual invasion has to be seen as a case in point (McRobbie 1994: 169). Equally, Richard and Kruger's 'revelation' of an important symbolic link between ravers dancing in warehouses and the industrial labour more traditionally associated with such spaces comes across as more than a little forced (Richard and Kruger 1998: 163). There can be little doubt, surely, that had they been discussed with the majority of participants of such groupings, these explanations would have been met with bemusement. Without wanting to endorse an uncritical reliance upon the accounts of insiders, we should surely be wary of interpretations which seem to take little account of them at all.

Some readers, however, might regard the symbolic significance of the goth scene as rather more obvious and apparent than the examples of academic interpretation I have cited above. They may have expected a book on goth to interpret and structurally or even psychoanalytically account for the apparent fascination of goths with such themes as horror, death, misery and gender ambiguity. Quite simply, though, the pursuit of such underlying links and causalities, through an attempt to read meaning from style, would have entailed a process far more characterized by construction than by revelation. As well as glossing over the diversity and complexity of the process of discovering, liking, becoming involved in and taking part in the goth scene, such an approach would mistakenly assume that all the facts of the goth scene and its participants' lives were somehow reflected transparently in the clothes, hairstyles and make-up they preferred. Years of ethnographic research as an insider have confirmed for me that there was no underlying shared structural, psychological or political meaning to be discerned from the style. Many participants themselves were sceptical as to whether the aesthetic details of the goth scene were intrinsically connected with particular attitudes or goals. Indeed, there was a particular tendency for hostility toward the suggestion that their dark hair or clothes said anything about their character, outlook or behaviour. The most noticeable general point that came across, from both interviews and general ethnographic experience, was that style was held to be significant in and of itself as a set of enthusiastic preferences located within, and not beyond, the sphere of the aesthetic.

It should not be inferred from this, however, that the goth style was meaningless or that it was experienced as such by its subscribers. While its aesthetic features were not homologically connected to any distinctive social problems or political viewpoints, there is little doubt that they were enough, in themselves, to represent the strong sense of affiliation that participants shared with one another and their collective sense of distinction and superiority over a perceived 'mainstream' society. Many participants felt there was some sort of link between their style and certain general qualities they shared with other goths, including individuality, creativity, open-mindedness and commitment, which will be discussed in Chapter 4. Crucially, however, these traits were not intrinsically linked to or discernible from the distinctive features of their style, but rather to the fact that, as a whole, it served to make goths feel collectively distinctive. What was of utmost importance, then, was the belonging and status which were signified by the styles described – something to which consistent distinctiveness was crucial.

Conclusion

In summary then, there *was* a diversity of style within the goth scene, but any flexibility in terms of individual interpretations and subtle transgressions took place in the context of overall commitment to a complex but generally consistent and identifiable set of tastes. This relative consistent distinctiveness constituted an externally observable difference between the goth scene and society outside it – something which satisfies the first of our criteria for the delineation of the group as a subculture. It also begins to give us an idea of the level of practical subcultural commitment exhibited by subcultural participants, discussed at greater length at various points later in the book. Furthermore, the style both symbolized the strong subjective subcultural identity held by most goths and acted as the practical basis for the distinctions they drew between insiders and outsiders. It is to these subjective issues of identity and difference that we shall now turn.

Notes

1. Please note that examples of music released by all the bands mentioned in the main text or the endnotes throughout can be found in the discography on pp. 211–3 at the back of this book.

2. Interviewees are referred to throughout the book using a letter and a number, followed by an indication of their gender in brackets. Where questions or comments from the questioner are included in the extract, these are referred to using my own initials, PH. While giving pseudonyms to respondents might have provided the most reader-friendly means of referring to respondents, those whom I consulted on the matter were not happy to be referred to under pseudonyms. In addition, it was decided that such names would have affected the authenticity of the book, especially in the case of high-profile individuals within the goth scene. Although some respondents expressed a preference for being referred to by their real names, this option was not acceptable, since it would have compromised the anonymity of any who preferred to remain anonymous. This left the compromise option of using a code and indicating gender as clearly the most ethical and effective way to proceed.

3. Respondents to the Whitby Festival Questionnaire are referred to by a single number from 1 to 112 and their gender is indicated in brackets. Each extract of questionnaire responses begins with the question which prompted it, preceded by the initials WQ and the question number.

4. Captions are not used for the photographs in this chapter as it was decided that there was sufficient introduction to them in the text and that descriptive captions would merely be stating the obvious. Nevertheless, the reader should bear in mind that, as one might expect, few of the photographs perfectly illustrate in full every single element of the text with which they are associated.

5. The number of small-scale 1990s goth bands makes picking out individual examples difficult. Inclusion here does not reflect any particular level of importance to the goth scene as compared to the numerous other bands I could have picked – it's merely that in their style they happen to illustrate the point in question. Examples of bands whose material was often relatively faithful to the dominant 1980s sounds included Nosferatu, Merry Thoughts, Die Laughing, Funhouse. Examples of bands merging more traditional goth sounds with electronic or dance sequences included Nekromantik, Suspiria, Apoptygma Berzerk and VNV Nation. Examples of bands producing what might be described as an indie version of the goth sound included Manuskript and The Horatii.

6. Examples of releases characterized by an emotional feel which might generally be regarded as 'feminine' rather than masculine, include The Mission's single, 'Butterfly on a Wheel', All About Eve's debut album 'All About Eve', The Cure's 'Disintegration' album and Fields of the Nephilim's 'Elizium' album. On the other

hand, examples of aggressive-sounding music, which fits rather less comfortably with the general theme of femininity, included Nine Inch Nails' tracks such as 'Closer' and Front Line Assembly's 'Plasticity'. The latter are often regarded as 'industrial' music, but were popular among goths.

4

Insiders and Outsiders

Toward the end of Chapter 3, we noted the tendency for some goths to wear slogan T-shirts containing the word 'goth', which quite literally spelled out their conscious subcultural affiliation to onlookers. At the time, we were concerned with the role of such garments as part of the relatively consistent and distinctive range of tastes held by goths. This chapter, though, will focus in detail on the strong *perception* of subcultural identity and collective distinction to which such overt examples of self-labelling draw our attention. In other words, we are changing tack, from a relatively objectivist examination of exhibited tastes to an emphasis on the subjective understandings and meanings of participants (Thornton 1995: 106). This is because, however distinct they may look or sound, the visible styles of a given grouping do not in themselves demonstrate cultural substance. According to the definition of subculture we have outlined, in most cases the exhibition of such distinctive tastes and norms will be linked to a strong perception of collective belonging among those involved.

Anthony Cohen goes so far as to argue that such subjective feelings and imaginings ought actually to take precedence over observable traits or behaviours in the delineation of a given grouping: '. . . culture – the community as experienced by its members – does not consist in social structure or in "the doing" of social behaviour. It inheres, rather, in "the thinking" about it . . . Community exists in the minds of its members' (A. Cohen 1985: 98). To a degree, this book accepts Cohen's stance on the importance of consciousness and perception and, as a result, regards shared identity as probably the single most important of the indicators of subculture outlined in Chapter Two. 'The thinking' about social behaviour, though, must not be emphasized to the point of excluding 'the doing' of it. It is not just that the observable, physical characteristics we have outlined provided in themselves a partial indication of the substantive cultural form taken by the goth scene. Later in the chapter we shall see that this observable consistent distinctiveness was directly related to the sense of identity shared by goths. More specifically, it formed the basis of the conscious distinctions and boundaries they drew between insiders and outsiders. Distinctiveness and identity, then, were inextricably linked with one another.

Perceptions of Affiliation

Prior to examining evidence of collective identity in the goth scene, I would emphasize that some recent studies have questioned the importance of group-belonging to those involved in contemporary music or style groupings. As we have seen, for example, David Muggleton's apparently punk-, goth- or mod-oriented interviewees were keener to emphasize their individuality rather than conformity to particular group norms. As well as regarding this as evidence of stylistic fluidity and cross-fertilization, Muggleton specifically argues that such accounts illustrate the receding importance to young people of subjective group identifications or labels (Muggleton 2000: 55–80). The seemingly subcultural interviewees in a study by Widdicombe and Wooffitt also sought, through evasive conversational strategies, to resist what they regarded as invitations to explain their appearance in terms of a subcultural affiliation. On the basis of this apparent lack of collective identity, the authors criticize the 'over-committed' picture of subcultural identity presented by subcultural theory (Widdicombe and Wooffitt 1995: 94–115).

To a critical insider, this kind of outward resistance to labels, among apparently affiliated young people, seems relatively unsurprising. More open to question, however, is the rather uncritical approach to such data taken by the authors. Neither Widdicombe and Wooffitt nor Muggleton raise sufficient questions as to the accuracy of their interviewee's statements as a reflection of the way in which they really felt. The possibility, for example, that rejection of group labels may have reflected a desire to defy outside expectations or, indeed, to comply with received wisdom within a subcultural grouping, is given insufficient consideration. In Muggleton's case, a relativist position is adopted whereby 'truth' is deemed synonymous with the subjective lived experience of subculturalists and invulnerable to deconstruction from 'outside': 'To claim from the outside as it were, that people's indigenous meanings are contradictory is to ignore how such apparent contradictions can make perfect, logical sense to those involved, given their own definition of the situation' (Muggleton 2000: 59). The implication that the words of subcultural participants are beyond 'external' critique rather trustingly assumes that the way they choose to present themselves is an infallible representation of their experiences or those of their compatriots. After all, what if the 'apparent contradictions' in the accounts of individuals do not reflect some impenetrable insider logic, but merely the fact that they have not properly thought an issue through, or that they are overly keen to present themselves in a particular way? As many insiders would (in the right social circumstances) surely concede, goths, punks, mods and the like are every bit as capable of inaccuracies and exaggerations as anyone else in society.

A well-articulated self-critique from one of my interviewees illustrates that proclamations of 'individuality' on the part of goths were a very well estab-lished yet highly questionable 'common sense' response to questions relating to style and identity:

PH: So what you're kind of saying is that it is important to be different?
T3 (*female*): Yeah, although you always say that like, you're all individuals, but
               everyone's got the same boots on! Do you know what I mean – 'oh
               aren't we individual with all our ripped fishnets and our New Rocks
               [make of boot]'.

Indeed, while outright or hostile rejections of subcultural identity were actually quite rare in the interviews I conducted, this desire to emphasize individuality was sometimes linked with a degree of hesitancy about directly describing oneself as 'a goth'. Nevertheless, it is clear from the aforementioned self-conscious slogans on T-shirts and badges that some individuals *were* keen to associate themselves directly and openly with goth as a label, something in no way diluted by the self-conscious humour which often characterized such attire. Consistent with this, although some were more cautious than others, all those who took part in my open-ended, unstructured interviews eventually indicated a strong sense of group affiliation. Indeed, in some cases, participants were positively enthusiastic to identify themselves as members of the goth scene:

J6 (*female*): If someone goes 'goth!', I go, 'yes, I've been recognized!'

Meanwhile, others disclosed a conscious identification with a perceived goth scene in the course of placing themselves in relation to a number of perceived different 'types' of goth, and some even described their own internal movement over time, from one to another:

C2 (*male*): I started off as a sort of tail-coaty goth and went more and more
             vampiry, and then I switched colours to beige – and I was sort of
             Nephilimy beige goth for a while – I had a beige tail-coat, beige leather
             trousers and beige boots.

For the most part, even those who were initially resistant tended to become more relaxed about disclosing their sense of affiliation as discussions progressed. At the very least, most became happy to talk about being involved in the goth scene or goth stuff, or to associate themselves explicitly with music, clothes, events and fanzines they chose to describe as goth. Most importantly, regardless of whether they initially described themselves as a goth, with or without prefix, virtually every respondent, at some point in his or her interview, emphasized feelings of identification, similarity and community, with others perceived to share their tastes in fashion and music. Here is one example of many such comments:

> M2 (*male*): Goth is a tribe . . . it's just a group of people that get together and say . . . 'we have something in common – we have how we dress, how we look, how we feel and the kind of people we're interested in or music we're interested in, in common.'

In contrast to traditional conceptions of place-centred community and to the recent academic emphasis on localized music scenes, as described in Chapter 2, goths' sense of identity extended every bit as far as their stylistic preferences. Therefore, interviewees indicated strong identifications with strangers perceived to share their subcultural affiliation in countries across the globe. Many spoke of a particular enjoyment of the geographical breadth of their identity, and emphasized the value of being able to take part in the goth scene outside their locality or country. I asked the following respondent whether it would matter to him if the goth scene was confined to his home city of York:

> C2 (*male*): It would be harder because if you went anywhere else people would think 'ohhhh, what's that?', whereas you know you've always got some people who you've got something in common with – you've got a point of contact, anywhere in the world more or less.

It should not be inferred, though, that place had no importance for any participants of the goth scene. Although my research did not entirely uphold their views, some believed the goth scene was different from locality to locality within Britain. Occasionally, I even came across regional or local rivalries within the bounds of the translocal goth scene, illustrated by the following description of a letter in a goth fanzine:

> L1 (*female*): This lad had wrote in and said – 'we've got people from Leeds coming to our nightclub' . . . he was like [imitates] 'we're Bradford goths and people from Leeds are coming to our nightclub!'

Such animosity also emerged, occasionally, between those regarding themselves as northerners and southerners in Britain. The annoyance of one respondent from Leeds about the perceived 'complacency' and 'apathy' of

London goths prompted him to produce and distribute stickers in the capital's goth clubs which read as follows: 'NEWSFLASH . . . travelling outside the M25 does not make your hair extensions fall out or your piercings turn septic . . . wake up to the bigger picture!' (McCullie 1999). In addition to these local or regional loyalties, some interviewees indicated a clear sense of British national identity within the goth scene, as in the following espousal of British-based goth music over its foreign equivalents.

> M5 (*male*): I think all foreign goth is shit. It was invented in Northampton in 1979 by Bauhaus and no one else knows how to do it apart from us lot.

While such regional or national identifications were *not* especially common, they show that place had a degree of significance to some goths' sense of themselves.

Even in the strongest cases, though, whereabouts remained secondary to goths' sense of shared identification with one other. After all, the fact that such national or local identifications always seemed to be expressed in the form of comparisons with goths from elsewhere serves only further to demonstrate the primary importance of subcultural identity. This was illustrated particularly effectively when interviewees were given the hypothetical choice of spending time with goths from a foreign country or non-goths from closer to home. They unanimously selected the former, as in the following comments by interviewees from Birmingham and Leeds:

> T3 (*female*): I would feel more comfortable with goths. I would just think 'cool, goths', I wouldn't think of them as foreign, I'd just feel totally comfortable straight away, rather than with the English people sitting there and, I don't know, just feeling totally uncomfortable.
>
> L1 (*female*): I'd identify more with the goths definitely – because like they probably know bands that you like, and you'd have more to discuss wouldn't you? Rather than like 'oh, I come from Leeds', 'where abouts in Leeds?' blah blah – that'd probably be it – where if it were a bunch of goths you'd say 'oh, I like this and that' and they'd tell you where to go out on a night.

Therefore, in contrast to its importance to musicians and audiences in local studies such as those of Finnegan (1989), Cohen (1991) and Shank (1994), it was clear that, for my subculturally affiliated respondents, place-related identities were at best a secondary consideration.

The Primacy of Subcultural Identity

Other traditional markers of social identity such as class, occupation, ethnicity and gender also tended to take a secondary position of importance relative to subcultural affiliation. Although not statistically representative, due to its reliance upon a sample of 112 individuals who happened to have travelled to attend a particular event, the Whitby Festival Questionnaire provided some idea of the social make-up of the goth scene in regard of such criteria, which I shall briefly summarize for the general information of the reader.[1] In respect of age, answers indicated that the largest number of goths were in the '21–25' category, with sizeable minorities in the categories '16–20' and '26–30'. In terms of lifestyle, a majority of approximately two to one indicated they did not live with a partner or spouse, although almost one in ten said they had children. While there was an equal gender split, a much greater discrepancy was indicated in regard of class and ethnicity, with most respondents either in middle-class occupations or in further or higher education, and an overwhelming ninety-seven per cent identifying themselves as white (see Appendix Table 1, p. 199).

As we have seen in the Chapter 3, the androgynous features of the goth style meant that attachment to gender categories may have been loosened somewhat, but it was certainly not undermined. As one would expect in the overall context of a gendered society, being male or female remained important in the overall sense of self of participants, both within context of the goth scene and, of course, in the general context of family, education and work. However, extensive ethnographic experience leaves little doubt that had I reworked the aforementioned geographical hypothetical situation, so as to compare interviewees' feelings of sameness based on gender with those based on subcultural identity, the responses would have been just as clearly in favour of the latter. Notably, in the same way that comments about place tended to involve the observation of differences within the goth scene, gender tended to be discussed by goths in relation to the primary context of the subculture.

In terms of class and ethnicity, the prominence of subcultural over structural forms of consciousness was probably even greater. This can be partially explained by the high proportion in the goth scene of young people in their late teens to mid-twenties, many of whom were students. It has often been argued that during such a period of 'youth', individuals occupy a liminal, self-exploratory position, between the more fixed markers of structural identity which characterize both childhood dependence and adulthood responsibility (Lury, 1996: 195–6; Thornton, 1995: 102–3). In addition, we have seen that the subculture was dominated by white, middle-class individuals, a socio-economic grouping well known for being rather less conscious of their class or ethnic status than members of minority or subordinate social groups (Dyer 1997). This too, may help to explain the relative significance to goths of their elective subcultural identity.

For the minority of goths with backgrounds in subordinate social groups, though, subcultural identity seemed every bit as prominent. I asked the following respondent whether he felt he had more in common with goths, or with other members of the localized, working-class community in which he had lived most of his life. There was a clear sense that, while it remained important, the class identity was something he identified with his past, while his current sense of affiliation was based primarily on the sharing of stylistic preferences.

> J12 (*male*): Oh, the goths! . . . its not so much to do with where you're from, its to do with what you're into. My taste in music is probably the same as their [goths'] taste in music, my taste in clothes is probably the same as theirs or whatever.

Later on in the interview, like most other respondents, he conveyed strongly, the primacy of the goth scene to his sense of identity:

> J12 (*male*): I've got a very camaraderie type attitude: 'that's one of our boys' type attitude even though I don't know them. They're still goth so they're alright by me.

Consistent with this, none of the minority of working-class or non-white individuals who took part in the research provided any indication that the importance of their subcultural identity was any less than in the case of their white middle-class counterparts. While a subordinate class or ethnic identity may have made the initial jump into subcultural involvement a more considerable one, it appears that, once this step had been taken, the new elective identity was liable to take precedence for a time.

Equally, while non-heterosexual practices or orientations tend rapidly in much of society to take central place in the sense of self of individuals (Plummer 1995: 85), this too was less certain in the goth scene. First, the majority of non-heterosexual goths I came across either identified as bisexual or rejected all sexual categories rather than taking on an exclusive gay identity. Secondly, identification and association with others on the basis of shared sexuality seemed often to be less important to individuals than taking part in the goth scene. This can be regarded as logical since, as we have seen, non-heterosexuals in the goth scene tended already to have a relatively safe space as well as the respect of their peers. There was less need to legitimize one's same-sex orientation or practices through seeking exclusive gay space or community, and probably less pressure than there would have been in the context of the gay scene to reject any lingering opposite-sex desires (Came 1996: 27; Eadie 1996: 17). Finally, while many goth clubs tended to be regarded as *relatively* safe spaces for discrete non-heterosexual activity, the gay scene was not always regarded as equally tolerant of goths' tastes in music or fashion. As the following interviewee put it:

> T4 (*female*): Anything alternative as far as music and dress goes is totally out [in gay clubs] ... you do get many dirty looks for it ... they just look you up and down as if, you know, 'get out of our club, you're just one of those lipstick lesbians'.

As with the other social markers we have looked at, then, non-heterosexual orientations often seemed to have a lower overall importance to identity than subcultural attachment to the goth scene.

Finally, in relation to age, although many did gradually drop out of the goth scene as they became older, increasing numbers appeared to remain involved up to and beyond their thirties. Those I came across who had done so appeared still to regard it as of considerable importance to their overall sense of self, in spite of full-time careers, mortgages, long-term partners and even, in some cases, children. The following respondent, in his late twenties, insisted that although career commitments meant he couldn't go out as much as he used to, his sense of affiliation for the goth scene remained as strong as ever:

> B6 (*male*): If you're a student ... you've got less responsibilities ... whereas I don't really have as much time ... I mean I'm still into it as much as I ever was, but maybe not so proactively involved in the whole thing of it, but that's only because of time and responsibility.

The intention, here, is not to argue that subcultural identity undermined every other part of goth participants' lives, twenty-four hours a day. However, there is a clear contrast between the relatively central place of this single affiliation in the identities of goths and the thoroughly ephemeral multi-affiliated individuals referred to in postmodern theory and, to a lesser degree, in the use of notions such as neo-tribalism (Maffesoli 1996; Bauman 1992a, 1992b; Bennett 1999; Shields 1992a), scene (Harris 2000) and postmodern subculture (Muggleton 2000). As well as tending to take precedence over place, gender, class and other structural foci for identity, the goth scene tended to be its participants' most important leisure or consumer-related affiliation. Rather than having to share their identities equally with several other interests or hobbies, the goth scene was one of those lifestyle groupings which demanded a considerable proportion of one's sense of self. The following statement as to its centrality was not untypical:

> W1 (*male*): It is the most important thing in my life, there's no doubt about it, it is the most important thing in my life – I couldn't fathom existing without it at all.

Without rendering observations of cultural superficiality and multiplicity inaccurate in general terms, then, the case of the goth scene certainly raises questions about attempts to apply such models across the board.

'Trendies'

The danger of theoretical overemphasis on multiplicity and ephemerality is illustrated even more clearly, perhaps, by the connection between goths' translocal affiliation with one another and an equally strong sense of collective distinction from those whose appearance or lifestyles were deemed antithetical to those of the subculture. This usually involved a generalized conception of 'normal' culture, 'the mainstream' or 'trendies'. The importance of this sense of distinctiveness was demonstrated by the tendency for many goths to resort to such denigration of 'trendies' in response to questioning concerning the characteristics of the goth scene itself, as with the following comment in response to the Whitby Festival Questionnaire:

> WQ5b: In your own words, please explain what is the goth scene is all about.
> 109 (*female*): Being different to all the mindless, brain-dead clones that walk around small town England.

The practice of distinguishing one's own tastes from those of a perceived 'other' in order to legitimize them is referred to by Pierre Bourdieu as part of his study of classification and cultural tastes:

> Tastes (i.e. manifested preferences) are the practical affirmation of an inevitable difference. It is no accident that, when they have to be justified, they are asserted purely negatively, by the refusal of others' tastes . . . all tastes are perhaps first and foremost, distastes. (Bourdieu 1984: 56)

The specific importance of a single point of collective subcultural identity and distinction among goths, though, is particularly consistent with Sarah Thornton's account (1995: 99), inspired by Bourdieu, of the negative construction by British clubbers of a similar 'mainstream', against which they defined and strengthened their own sense of identity. David Locher makes a similar point in the context of a study of a subculture based around 'industrial' music, arguing that in order to be an insider:

> it is not enough to like that which the other members like, one must also dislike what the other members do not like . . . it is the exclusionary nature of such groups that reinforces cohesion among the members (Locher 1998: 101).

This emphasis is broadly consistent, of course, with Howard Becker's discussion, some decades ago, of the significance of a derision of 'squares' for the strength of distinctive identity and indeed superiority or 'hipness' held by jazz musicians (Becker 1963). The relationship between identity and difference in contemporary elective affiliations is also discussed in detail by theorists of more fluid unstable forms of collective identity, notably Chaney (1996) and Hetherington (1998a). As well as a general sense of the importance of distinction, though, what Thornton's and Locher's perspectives point to is the primacy to some individuals of relatively one-dimensional 'us' and 'them' distinctions revolving around a single affiliation. This can be contrasted with the emphasis on numerous cross-cutting and ever changing systems of tastes and distastes, identifications and disidentifications focused on by more postmodern-oriented approaches.

Among goths, the strength of the distinction from perceived outsiders was particularly intensive as a result of the prejudice and occasional violence goths were prone to receive in light of their unconventional appearance. Many interviewees keenly recounted experiences of such abuse or assault, as in this example from a Leeds-based interviewee:

> N1 (*female*): Me and [friend] were walking past Berlins and these couple of lasses were like going 'ere you tarts, vampire bitches' . . . you go in city pubs and all the lads are like 'what have you got that in your lip for, what else you got done?'

The perception among goths that such incidents reflected the narrow-minded characteristics of a societal majority is illustrated by the way the same interviewee used such experiences to justify her own dislike of 'trendies':

> N1 (*female*): When you get treated like that why should you have respect for someone else from their type of group?

Similarly, a Birmingham respondent regarded 'trendies' with considerable caution as a result of past experience of abuse, in spite of placing some of his friends within this category:

> J12 (*male*): I had a discussion with a trendy mate . . . and I said 'well how many times have you been at a bus stop and had a goth shouting abuse at you and starting a fight on you? . . . it's happened to me with your lot – we're the ones that get trouble off you'.

The way the receipt of such hostility strengthened goths' reciprocal dislike of a perceived homogenous group of 'trendies' has a clear resemblance to Albert Cohen's circle of increasing subcultural delinquency (A. Cohen 1955). For Cohen, as subcultural members earn contempt or aggression from society outside, they collectively come to devalue 'the good will and respect of those whose good will and respect are forfeit anyway' and the subculture 'comes to include hostile and contemptuous images of those groups whose enmity they have earned' (ibid.: 68). The final part of the circular process is that the shared identity of subcultural insiders is thoroughly intensified by the process: 'The hostility of the "out-group", thus engendered or aggravated may serve to protect the "in-group" from mixed feelings about its way of life' (ibid.: 69). Although Cohen's account, like those of Jock Young (1971) and Stan Cohen (1972), may overestimate and oversimplify the importance of outside hostility to the construction of subcultural identities, a circular process along the lines of that described certainly appears to have fed and intensified goths' sense of 'us' and 'them', as here:

> J12 (*male*): The way I see it . . . all us goths should be mates because we've all got the one common factor and that's the trendies taking the piss out of us all.

However, it was clear that goths' dislike of the mainstream also tended to reflect a positive and necessary enjoyment on their part of feeling collectively different and, more specifically, superior to 'outsiders'. Not surprisingly, perhaps, when it was put to interviewees that the sense of subcultural identity they so cherished was often reliant upon a rather elitist differentiation of themselves from outsiders, the instant reaction was often to disagree. The following response was typical:

> T3 (*female*): I think it's not what you are *not* into, it's what you *are* into. It's what goth *is*.

The questionable accuracy of the first part of this sentiment, though, was indicated when respondents were asked how they would feel if goth music and style were prominent in the mass media and highly popular throughout society. In response, the same interviewee articulated the link between shared identity and collective distinction extremely honestly and clearly:

T3 (*female*): If every single person in the UK was a goth then a lot of goths wouldn't like it . . . I think I'd still be one, but I wouldn't like everyone else being one.
S7 (*female*): I wouldn't like it.
PH: Why?
T3: It's not like you're a goth because you want to stand out, but you do like sort of being different from everyone else, although when you're with a load of goths you blend in, but you're all different, if you know what I mean, from everyone else.

As well as re-emphasizing the somewhat one-dimensional sense of identity and distinction held by many, the way in which goths so frequently positioned themselves against those they perceived as 'trendies' is significant in that it implies they also shared a set of moral assumptions about their lifestyle which allowed many of them to understand it as culturally superior. These I shall refer to as the *ideals* of the subculture.

Subcultural Ideals

Importantly, unlike so-called 'new social movements', the goth scene involved no external political objectives. Rather, its ideals concerned the character and survival of the group as such (Maffesoli 1996: 96), and the basis of its cultural superiority over other sections of society. As has been indicated by Sarah Thornton (1995), as well as sometimes being expressed openly, the self-perceptions of subcultural participants can often be revealed by the ways in which they negatively characterize outsiders. In the case of the goth scene, a careful analysis of what goths said their group stood both for and against revealed the central importance of two themes – individuality and commitment.

The most common basis on which goths distinguished themselves from 'trendies' was a perception that the latter mindlessly followed mass-media fashions in dress and music, rather than exercising individual discrimination or taste:

K1 (*male*): They have no defined style, their style is to go with what is selling in the shops rather than sifting through, people just go with what's in Top Man currently or stuff like that.

Due to their supposed indiscriminate adherence to passing commercial fads, 'trendies' were perceived as a homogenous group, something which goths usually contrasted with the relative diversity of their own subculture:

C2 (*male*): If you look at a group of goths, there are similarities there but there's a lot more differences than if you had a group of normal people.

As we have already seen, goths, consistent with the subcultural interviewees of Thornton (1995: 99) and Muggleton (2000: 55–79), tended to perceive that their subculture encapsulated diversity, creativity and individuality. This can be illustrated by another Whitby Festival Questionnaire response:

WQ5b: In your own words, please explain what is the goth scene all about.
30 (*male*): Complete freedom of expression, diversity.

In particular, it was often stated by interviewees that the goth scene entailed an open-minded environment which encouraged people to do their own thing, free from the kinds of social pressures to conform which characterized mainstream society. As one Plymouth-based interviewee succinctly put it:

J5 (*female*): There's no peer pressure within goth.

In addition, the goth scene was often perceived as being characterized by open-mindedness and tolerance in respect of social characteristics such as gender, race and sexuality, in contrast to perceptions of trendies who, as well as often being regarded as violent, tended to be associated with prejudice:

S3 (female): I've never met a goth that's been sexist or homophobic or anything. All the trendies I've met seem to have something like that – like they don't like black people or gay people or something . . . but every goth is very open-minded because they've been taken the piss out of and they know what it feels like.

As well as a disapproval of the 'sheepishness', narrow-mindedness and intolerance to difference of those 'taken in' by dominant music and fashion trends, there was among goths a specific dislike of the commercialism associated with 'trendy' clothes and music. In a familiar viewpoint associated with rock music generally (see Frith 1981; Cohen 1991), the involvement of commercial motives was deemed to clash with the ideal of authentic individual expression. Thus, many bands, promoters, record labels and other small businesses connected with the goth scene were keen to emphasize their artistic motivations and to make it clear that money was a marginal consideration. The vocalist of American goth band Faith and the Muse perceived a direct contradiction between the two:

> M7 (*female*): I recently had a talk with another singer who just wants to 'make it' in the music business, which is not a smart thing to do, unless you have no soul . . . there are numerous successful artists out there who have made their name on 'Bubble-gum . . . music': that which has no real substance or meaning!

In contrast to notions of the mainstream as dominated by commercial interests and a mass narrow-minded culture, then, goths tended to regard their own subculture as encapsulating authentic artistic expression by musicians, and the exercise of equally instinctive discriminating tastes in music and clothing by a diverse and open-minded set of individual fans.

The second subcultural ideal, fairly consistently alluded to by goths, was commitment. Whether in terms of the intensity or longevity of individual participation, depth of knowledge and understanding, or even involvement in production and organizational activities, goths tended to regard themselves as strongly committed to their preferred styles of music and fashion and to the lifestyle with which it was connected. Conversely, as well as being deemed to lack individuality, 'trendies' and the kinds of music and fashion with which they were associated were often derided as fickle and superficial. Furthermore, those who regarded themselves as goths but were deemed not to be taking part in the subculture with sufficient conviction were in danger of being labelled 'part-timers' (Muggleton 2000: 82–7). In the following example a Birmingham interviewee describes his dislike, during the 1980s, of those deemed only to take part in the goth scene for individual nights out and hence to lack a permanent subcultural appearance:

> C4 (*male*): There was the stiffs wasn't there, that used to come down the clubs. Stiffs . . . had daytime jobs and had say just short hair that they spiked for the weekend who thought they were really cool they were being really different, but to us . . . they were just . . . part-timers . . . because we were doing it full-on.

Although not engaged in by all goths, such derision of part-timers seemed just as prominent among contemporary participants as a whole. In the next example, the age of participants and their lack of stylistic extremity or of in-depth subcultural knowledge are taken as evidence of insufficient commitment. Notably, the display of interest in a commercially successful and externally well-known band and of what is deemed a temporary or superficial subcultural appearance are taken to suggest that the individuals concerned have only scratched the surface of the subculture:

S7 (*female*): Yeah, like the baby goths. I think that's probably Marilyn Manson's fault.

T3 (*female*): It's like when you go to Edwards [Birmingham goth club] and there's all these fifteen-year-olds jumping about with their Marilyn Manson T-shirts.

S7: They've got short hair, and they've just got a little bit of eye-liner, a little bit of lipstick and they think, 'oh I'm a goth'.

As indicated already, the distinction drawn by goths between themselves as committed and individual and the mainstream as commercial, shallow and homogenous was shared with many other music-related amalgams, notably those described by Thornton (1995) and Muggleton (2000). In addition, many of the elements which make up the ideals can be traced to a general emphasis on artistic authenticity that goes far beyond contemporary popular music or fashion. Notably, it resides in the way proponents of 'legit-imate' discerning bourgeois culture distinguish themselves from the 'vulgar' tastes of mass society, as described in Bourdieu's famous work, *Distinction* (1984). It is also directly promoted by some of the most well known of cultural theories – most notably, perhaps, the contrast drawn by Adorno (1941) between standardized 'popular music' and artistic 'serious music'. A similar emphasis on authenticity is present in the moral elevation, by CCCS subcultural theorists, of innovative and spontaneous subcultural 'resistance' above a passive, media-manipulated general public. Indeed, Hebdige's account actually contains a theoretical reference to part-timers, in the form of a distinction between self-conscious, innovative 'originals' and media-induced, trend-following 'hangers-on' (Hebdige 1979: 122).

In the same way that Bourdieu subjects the discourse of dominant bourgeois culture to rigorous deconstruction, the appeals to authenticity and individ-uality of contemporary subcultural participants ought not to be accepted at face value. For this reason, Sarah Thornton makes use of the term *subcultural ideology* to refer to the production and circulation of shared 'common-sense' understandings and ideals within particular groupings (Thornton 1995: 98, 115). Without dismissing the value of what subcultural participants say, the use of 'ideology' here establishes that their verbalized understandings, rather than being taken as gospel, should be subject to the critical spotlight. It acknowledges that goths, punks, clubbers and others have tended to share certain well-established, value-laden assumptions which may not always be entirely accurate or coherent when applied to the actual workings of their group or, indeed, of those they contrast themselves with.

In the case of the goth scene, while the degree of consistency of the ideals described from one goth to the next and one place to the next was significant in itself as a subcultural trait, it does not take a great deal of analysis to discern fairly clear flaws in some of their assumptions, particularly in respect of the notion of individuality. Most importantly, it is clear that this ideal does not sit comfortably with that of subcultural commitment. On the one hand, many goths understood their subculture as superior to the mainstream on the basis of its encouragement of diversity, creativity and self-expression, while on the other they valued and demanded, as membership criteria, significant devotion to something in particular. Of course, if commitment to the ideal of being individual in its general sense would have sufficed, then there would be no contradiction. However, having examined the denigrations of part-timers and trendies by goths, I find it clear that, in practice, commitment was nearly always judged against a rather more distinctive set of criteria, including specific hairstyles, clothing, make-up and exhibited music tastes.

As well as general factors such as frequency of participation and contribution to the well-being of the subculture, then, gaining inclusion and respect required that individuals demonstrate commitment and in-depth understanding of the specific range of tastes and norms which made the subculture distinctive. As we have seen in Chapter 3, it was important to demonstrate a degree of individual innovation, but only in the context of a general display of commitment to the range of tastes which symbolized the goth scene. Without wanting to diminish the significance of individuals developing their own version of the goth style, it is clear that what was substantively 'individual' was less the behaviour and appearance of one goth compared to another than the overall range of collective stylistic criteria which they shared. It was these specific shared tastes which usually formed the basis of distinctions and judgements drawn by goths between insiders, outsiders and part-timers.

'Gother than Thou Syndrome'

The styles described in the Chapter 3, then, were not merely symbolic of subcultural identity, important though this was. They also functioned as a shared and translocally consistent system of classification whereby goths collectively distinguished themselves from outsiders and, by extension, created hierarchies of status among themselves. Sarah Thornton (1995) has theorized such classifications and distinctions among subcultural participants through further adaptation of the writings of Bourdieu. She adapts – for discussion of the specific classificatory systems of subcultures – the term *cultural capital*, which essentially refers to knowledges, cultural goods or modes of behaviour which bestow status and social advantages on individuals in relation to dominant systems of taste (Bourdieu 1984). Therefore *subcultural capital* should be taken to involve the degree of status-inducing properties one holds in relation to the particular tastes or values of a given subcultural grouping. Thornton provides examples from club culture to illustrate the adaptation of the term: 'Just as books and paintings display cultural capital in the family home, so subcultural capital is objectified in the form of fashionable haircuts and well assembled record collections' (Thornton 1995: 11).

The recognition that subcultural participants tend to classify and judge others by means of a conscious and mutually agreed set of standards is what makes this pluralization of cultural capital useful to our discussion of the goth scene here. It fits with our emphasis on the way the classificatory practices of goths somewhat undermined the credibility of their verbal espousals of individuality, open-mindedness and freedom of expression. Of course, the notion of subcultural capital resurrects some valuable aspects of Chicago School approaches to subculture, notably Albert Cohen's emphasis on alternative 'group standards' and subcultural 'criteria of status' (1955) and Becker's notion of 'hipness' (1963). The term subcultural capital is particularly useful though, since as well as referring to levels of status at the level of perception and consciousness, it allows us to capture the practical rewards liable to be afforded to those who achieve it and the lack of social opportunities for those who do not. We shall begin to see in Chapter 5 that in the case of the goth scene, such rewards most obviously took the form of attention, friendships and romantic opportunities.

Subcultural capital is also useful since, as well as explaining the basis for divisions between insiders and outsiders, it alludes to differential levels of status and rewards *within* both outsider or insider groups. Therefore, although they were all outsiders, goths objected less to punks, crusties and fetishists than they did to trendies. Similarly, as in the denigration of perceived 'part-timers', it is clear that, even having satisfied the basic criteria for subcultural membership, individuals were not free from the classification or judgement of their fellow insiders. While few were keen to acknowledge that they engaged in it themselves, many respondents complained about the judgemental side of the goth scene and the resulting competitiveness among insiders, which was commonly known as 'gother than thou syndrome'. The following exchange summed this up splendidly:

J8 (*female*): I think some goths get off on that. They have to be the weirdest, the most mysterious, the most facial piercings.

L1 (*female*): Those are the pretentious people that stand there and say 'I'm more gothier than you are, my clothes are better than yours'.

J8: Those are the people that sleep in coffins on a night and not only do they do it but they tell everyone that they do it (laughter).

Of course, what this exchange does not recognize is that, while it may have varied in extent, such competitiveness, alongside the continual tendency to classify and judge others, was actually engaged in by most if not all goths. As the following respondent explains, newcomers to the goth scene tended to be particularly aware of the hierarchies it created, and their own position at the bottom thereof. Again, the importance of having the right appearance, as primary exhibitor of subcultural capital, is clear:

B6 (*male*): You know what you're like when you're wearing your first pair of black jeans and a black shirt and short hair, and . . . you're just in awe of everyone and you feel ever so humble buying your first pair of boots and you feel like you shouldn't because you're not worthy sort of thing (*laughter*) . . . there were all these glowering, towering pale forlorn-looking gothic type people and you're just like some seventeen-year-old with your Sisters of Mercy T-shirt.

Gaining and maintaining subcultural capital, and the social rewards it entailed, then, was a key concern and motivation for most goths. When it offered the prospect of such rewards, the system of classification we have been describing induced considerable encouragement for individuals to collect, learn about and exhibit examples of established subcultural style and behaviour. While effective innovations sometimes resulted in particularly high social rewards and over-predictable imitations were often frowned upon, the bread and butter of subcultural capital usually revolved around one's overall commitment to existing shared systems of taste.

Conclusion

Understanding the importance to goths of an ability to distinguish between insiders and outsiders, then, has enabled us to create a linkage between the distinctive stylistic features of the goth scene, described in Chapter 3, and the sense of identity which has concerned us in this chapter. As well as being important in their own right, the range of styles functioned as key everyday criteria in the delineation of subcultural capital and hence in the ability of goths to discern differential status levels among themselves and to establish boundaries between themselves and outsiders. Consistent distinctiveness, therefore, played a crucial role in the subjective perceptions of identity on which this chapter began. Subcultural capital, though, manifested itself not only in the way individuals looked but also in other indications of practical commitment, notably the depth of their subcultural knowledge, the size and appropriateness of their collections of records, fanzines, posters and other artefacts and the frequency and exclusivity of their practical participation. The high rewards for commitment meant that the strong consciousness of identity focused on in this chapter tended to run alongside the subculture's dominance of friendship patterns, going-out habits, shopping routes, cultural possessions and even internet use. All of these will be addressed in the chapters which follow.

Notes

1. Selected quantitative findings from the Whitby Festival Questionnaire are referred to at various points in the remainder of the book. For more detail on the quantitative results of the questionnaire, please see the tables in the Appendix, pp. 199–202.

5

Events, Friendships and Commitment

There is little doubt that for goths the most important practical activities were going out to events and socializing with other members of the subculture. Some 66 per cent of respondents to the Whitby Festival Questionnaire selected 'nightclubs and pubs' among the three most important aspects of the goth scene for them, and 43 per cent indicated that 'socializing' was *the* single most important activity (see Appendix, Table 4, p. 201). The significance of going out to goth events to properly participating in the goth scene was also demonstrated qualitatively in the accounts of interviewees. For the following respondent from a small isolated town, an ability to keep up with the goth scene via specialist media failed to compensate for his inability regularly to attend goth events.

> D4 (*male*): Well, in small towns and villages there tends to be no goth scene to be involved in . . . being able to hang out with your 'crowd', listening to a goth band or at a goth disco without having to travel hundreds of miles has to be better than knowing what's going on but not being able to participate.

Consistent with these sentiments, another respondent, who had plenty of events to attend in his home city of Leeds, suggested that if the subculture were to die, it would be going out to events that he would miss most of all:

> M2 (*male*): I doubt if I'd actually change how I dress . . . I *would* get bothered if there were no more gigs or clubs to go to.

In addition to emphasizing their importance from the subjective point of view of participants, this chapter focuses on events as a key element, alongside commodities and media, of the subcultural infrastructure that lay behind and facilitated the identities, styles and commitments which characterized the goth scene. At the end of Chapter 2, a subcultural/non-subcultural distinction was outlined, in order for us to distinguish between those elements of this infrastructure which could be regarded as largely internal and autonomous and those which overlapped considerably with society outside. Consistent with this general distinction, we will distinguish in this chapter between specialist *subcultural* events, largely oriented toward the goth scene, and external *non-subcultural* events, where goths formed a small part of a more diverse clientele. As we shall see, the night-life of most goths tended to be dominated by the former, something consistent with two key indicators of subcultural substance: the practical commitment to the goth scene among its participants and the relative autonomy of the grouping as a whole.

Mixed Events and Recruitment

Before we address the importance of specifically goth-oriented or subcultural events, there is a need to examine the role played by more mixed events attended by goths. During the late 1980s and early 1990s, it was not uncommon for goths to form a reasonable proportion of the clientele for general 'alternative' events, which also accommodated punks, indie fans, crusties and others. Toward the early 1990s, however, the stylistic emphasis of many such events had moved away from goth, in favour of less extreme forms of British indie guitar rock and grunge music from the United States. During my research, I came across only one or two events which included goth music alongside various other 'alternative' styles. One of these was the Saturday night event at a venue known as The Phono in Leeds, described by the following respondent:

> C1 (*female*): Saturday night you get the weirdest collection. You get like a hip-hop spot, you get an indie spot, you get a goth slot, and then an indie spot. They all somehow meld together and it works.

While the inclusion of goth in such alternative events was rare by the late 1990s, 'goth-friendly' non-subcultural events were also provided in the form of the one-off gigs of such 'cross-over' bands as Garbage and Placebo which, as a result of their incorporation of elements of femininity and sombreness, appealed to goths as well as to certain indie music fans. Also, general rock clubs had, for the most part, taken up the previous role of alternative nights, in terms of providing a regular non-exclusive space for goths. Despite their being in a minority, and lucky to hear two or three specialist goth songs played all night, goths sometimes found that rock clubs offered a relatively safe environment in relation to the their unconventional appearance and a play-list which was preferable to chart- or dance-oriented clubs. Both factors were accentuated as a result of the increasing use of goth imagery and sounds in certain strains of death and black metal, notably Type O Negative and Marilyn Manson, which had facilitated an interest in and sympathy for the goth scene among some of their fans. Attendance by goths at such events was often inversely proportionate to the local availability of more exclusive spaces. In particular, those who lived in smallish towns and cities sometimes had to settle for general rock nights because of the insufficient number of goths to support anything more exclusive. In the city of Plymouth, where the only predominantly goth night was held on Mondays, respondents begrudgingly attended a general rock club at weekends. Even in Birmingham, where there were a greater number of specialist goth events, the lack of one after pub-closing time on Saturdays prompted many to attend a large general rock night.

The presence of small numbers of goths and the playing of occasional examples of goth music at alternative and rock pubs, clubs or gigs created important points of cultural contact between the music, fashion and individual participants of this otherwise fairly insular subculture and those of other music scenes. The mixture of styles and affiliations within such spaces created the potential for individuals to move *between* different specialist groups (see Malbon 1998: 280). Indeed, for some individuals, they probably resulted in continual movement and fluctuation *between* different styles and affiliations in the manner described by Bennett (1999) and others who have emphasized the prevalence of ephemerality in contemporary youth culture. Attendance at non-subcultural events may also have prompted certain long-term partic-ipants of substantive subcultures like the goth scene to begin to diversify their tastes or even to transfer their commitment to other groupings. I came across a group of goths in Birmingham, for example, who, having attended some hard-core dance-oriented events out of curiosity, appeared to become more interested in the general culture of which they were a part, and to spend less of their time at goth events. In spite of such possibilities, however, mixed events were of greatest significance – for our purposes – as a cultural route for individuals *into* a relatively long-term, committed involvement with the goth scene's exclusive subcultural networks of events, commerce and media.

Numerous goths explained to me that the inter-style contact in such spaces was responsible for their initial discovery of goth music, fashion, clubs and friends. Respondent T3, quoted here, became interested as a result of a goth-oriented room which happened to form the upstairs section of an Birmingham indie club she had attended for some time:

T3 (*female*): Basically one day we were downstairs in Edwards – I was about seventeen – and she [*indicates friend*] said 'oh come upstairs' and I said 'what's up there?' and she said 'all these vampire people' and I went up there and said 'wow' and I loved it.

Having been initially attracted to goth music, style or individuals as a result of mixed pubs and clubs, would-be recruits often ended up deliberately seeking out and attending exclusive goth events, and as a result gradually making more and more subcultural friends, something which opened the doors to subcultural networks of influence and information. The following respondent explained that a liking for the appearance of a minority of goths at 'alternative' nights had prompted him to attend a new, more goth-specific night, a move which opened the door to greater involvement in the subculture:

> K1 (*male*): I went to a club called The Studio [alternative club] in Plymouth. The only people who were dressing up were the goths – and that was when Charlies [goth-oriented club] opened up as well and that was more of a goth thing. It [becoming involved in the goth scene] was through mixing with people.

Claiming Subcultural Space

Specialist goth pub and club nights had emerged in greater numbers from the early to mid-1990s, partly as a result of the increasing exclusion of goth music from 'alternative' events. In spite of the willingness of some to attend mixed events rather than staying at home, goths wherever possible attended nights oriented largely toward their own subculture. Respondent W1's practical commitment was typical in this respect:

> W1 (*male*): When I go out, I like to go out to goth clubs, or to see a goth band. It doesn't mean that I won't go anywhere else, but I really won't go anywhere else on a regular basis.

Such subcultural events, then, were targeted at – and hence attended by – goths, and were relatively obscure outside the subculture's networks of communication. In addition to its diverse Saturday night event, described earlier, The Phono, in Leeds, ran a Sunday night goth club, which was far more popular among goths. One interviewee describes its level of exclusiveness:

> C1 (*female*): One of the mainstays of the Phono was always the Sunday night goth club . . . in some ways it was closed off from the rest of the world.

Although the kind of direct selection and exclusion through door policies characteristic of some clubs (Thornton 1995: 113) was relatively uncommon in the goth scene, the relative exclusivity of its events was maintained through their means of promotion, the decor of the venue and the type of entertainment inside. Whether in the form of flyers, posters, websites or adverts in fanzines or on-line discussion groups, information making clear the generic orientation of the night would be placed in actual and virtual spaces frequented by the intended subcultural audience. Meanwhile, at the events themselves, music and venue decor were made consistent with the tastes of the goth scene as perceived by promoters and DJs, most of whom were also enthusiasts.

The Mercat, a Birmingham market pub with a Saturday goth night, was characterized by features typical of many goth events. On entering, one immediately noticed a dark smoky atmosphere, a large screen exhibiting goth music videos, and posters on the walls for past and future goth events. Loud music was played throughout the night, and a particularly darkened smoke-filled corner was set aside for dancing. The music included a range of goth tracks – from early 1980s Bauhaus to the more contemporary and dance-oriented Apoptygma Berzerk – alongside occasional examples of related genres deemed sufficiently consistent with the tastes of the subculture. This specialist range of music, alongside the dark smoky atmosphere of the pub, served to provide appeal to the goths themselves as well as a somewhat intimidating atmosphere for any outsiders not filtered out by the event's means of promotion.

Of even greater importance to the subcultural status of the event or venue, though, was the appearance and behaviour of the goth-oriented clientele. Though in general he presents clubs as more fluid than the goth spaces I observed, Ben Malbon's observation about the ways particular forms of behaviour can serve to claim spaces for affinity groupings is relevant here:

> Acting out certain roles, dressing in a similar manner, dancing in a certain way, even drinking similar beers are all ways in which the affinity of the group can be reinforced, the territory of the club experience claimed (Malbon 1998: 176).

Most importantly, no insider or outsider to the goth scene could have failed to note the clear and relatively consistent exhibition of subcultural appearances by the majority of those present at goth events. More than anything else, such a demonstration of visual distinctiveness functioned to claim the space inhabited by goths as their own.

While much of the behaviour at goth events overlapped with rock pub, club and gig culture generally (see Finnegan 1989; Cohen 1991), certain rituals were more specific. There were a particular range of ways in which goths tended to dance, for example. While relatively diverse and neither exclusive to the group nor particularly difficult to pick up, these loose dance-floor conventions were revealed on occasion by the laughing, scoffing or disapproving stares which resulted from unwitting transgressions. On more than one occasion, for example, I witnessed disapproval of heavy-metal-style head-banging, for example. Various behavioural manifestations of the goth scene's general feminine stylistic theme also served to mark out its subcultural spaces. Thus, the tendency at goth events for activities in gents' toilets to be dominated by the touching-up of make-up in front of the mirror surely had the potential to disorientate those more used to experiencing such spaces as havens of concentrated homophobia. They might also have found themselves somewhat disturbed by the greater likelihood in goth clubs than in most other non-gay spaces, of same-sex embracing, flirting and kissing by both males and females.

The subcultural nature of goth events was further strengthened by the contrasting behaviour of the goth clientele toward those whom they classified as insiders and toward those whom they considered outsiders. During one goth night I attended in Leeds, I noticed that the entry of two short-haired males dressed in blue jeans and brightly coloured shirts prompted resentful stares and mutterings to the effect of 'what are those trendies doing here?' among a group of goths sitting nearby. While not everyone reacted so directly, my long-term experience of the goth scene enables a confident assertion that most would have noted the presence of these individuals, demarcated them as outsiders, and set out to avoid contact with them, as indeed I did myself. In rare instances where direct verbal or physical contact with strangers perceived as outsiders did take place, most goths tended to disengage as quickly as possible, while in contrast they were often quick to befriend unfamiliar individuals with sufficient subcultural capital.

Nevertheless, the tendency of occasional punks, metallers and others to be accepted, if not always warmly welcomed, in goth spaces, emphasized that not all outsiders were equally excluded. Such differentiation between outsiders was illustrated clearly on a goth e-mail list discussion, when one subscriber expressed worries about the implications of a new membership policy in a local goth club for individuals such as herself who weren't obviously affiliated. The reply, reproduced here, reassured her that only obvious or unfriendly outsiders should be excluded, and specified the particular stylistic characteristics of such individuals.

Subject: Re: Torrie info
hatty wrote:
>And does this mean that I won't be able to get a card? . . .
No, but they can now keep the people who are obviously not goth (or goth-friendly) out – the kind of people with designer shoes/jeans/shirts/hairstyles/all of the above.

As for not being a Goth – you're obviously not a trendy, and you've been there before, so they wouldn't have a problem with letting you in.
(MurkyGoth 1999)[1]

Note also, in this example, that the individual was demarcated as acceptable through being regarded as a regular. Frequent attendance or acquaintance with insiders were sometimes key sources of subcultural capital for those who did not obviously look the part.

In addition to their selective means of promotion, then, the decor, music and particularly the appearance and behaviour of clientele at goth-specific events served to police their relative exclusivity. Contrasting with descriptions of some clubs as fluid spaces inhabited by fickle or multi-affiliated individuals (e.g. Bennett 1999, 2000; Malbon 1998), the importance of such specialist events to going-out patterns indicates the relatively high levels of commitment and autonomy which characterized the goth scene. While outsiders tended to stand out markedly, such spaces were key sources of safety, belonging and friendships for goths themselves.

Accumulating Status and Friendships

WQ5b: In your own words, please explain what is the goth scene all about.
44 (*female*): It's about dressing up in your best stuff, socializing and making new friends and listening to great music.

As well as having subcultural functions, goth events had certain commonalities with other kinds of clubbing, and hence, theories of 'club culture' (Redhead 1997a, 1997b; Malbon 1998, 1999). For example, they included instantaneous physical and social fulfilment in the form of dancing, flirting, drinking and, in a minority of cases, drug-taking. In addition, goth club experiences involved something of a displacement of everyday inhibitions, a degree of 'losing oneself' while dancing, with or without drugs, and for some a degree of escape from more stressful elements of life. However, the experiences and functions of regular attendance at goth events tended to involve significantly more than just immediate physical gratification or a one-off escape from everyday life. Rather, subcultural events served to affirm and cement the highly specific and distinctive identities of goths, and to encourage further participation in a variety of ways.

In contrast to the consumption of subcultural music or media at home, goth events facilitated public subcultural participation. While goths undoubtedly enjoyed being 'seen' when out shopping in groups, when participating in the subculture's on-line discussion forums, and indeed at non-subcultural events, specialist goth events were the most important sites at which subcultural capital was earned and claimed, and at which individuals most fully experienced their sense of belonging:

> C4 (*male*): It gives you a central focus, a meeting point, a kind of like you know, where you can affirm your own identity. You go there, and its all shared. Its like going to church really, you know it's a shared belief that you've got – a shared way of thinking.

Such was the importance of events that other elements of the goth scene such as consumables and media tended to be geared toward going out. For example, much of the information in fanzines and web sites was focused on forthcoming or regular events, as was much of the conversation on internet discussion groups. Subcultural shopping was also geared towards public display at events, the excitement of purchasing clothes generated largely from the prospect of being seen wearing them by other goths, whether at regular local events or at large festivals. So crucial was looking the part in subcultural spaces that goths often got together with friends to help one another 'get gothed-up' (see Figure 5.1).

The following respondent explained that such pre-club get-togethers were sometimes highly enjoyable in themselves.

> G1 (*male*): Loads of people went over to [name]'s house and started getting ready and the thing started at nine o'clock and we ended up getting there at about eleven because we were having so much fun getting ready – backcombing hair and getting ready and getting into . . . boots. It was so much fun.

Nevertheless, such rituals were driven, ultimately, by the excitement and anticipation of displaying the finished result to others in the public space of a goth event. In order to realize the potential subcultural capital signified by one's appearance, a significant subcultural audience was required. Specialist styles of consumables, then, may have been goths' most obvious distinguishing feature – but without a suitably specialist forum in which to parade them, their consumption would have lost much of its appeal and significance.

Subcultural events provided a space for collective consumption and appreciation of a shared range of tastes, through listening, dancing and a somewhat competitive sharing of one another's versions of subcultural style and behaviour. So important were the presence, appearance, behaviour and attentions of others to the experience that, effectively, those present can be regarded as consuming one another, a point made by Malbon in relation to clubbing in general terms:

Figure 5.1 Getting gothed-up with friends. (Photograph: P. Hodkinson).

The clubbers consume each other – the clubbing crowd contains both the producers and the consumers of the experience and the clubbers are consuming a crowd of which they are a part (Malbon 1998: 277).

The difference between more mixed clubs and the goth scene was that in the latter case, the clubbers collectively shared and reproduced a very particular set of values and the clear sense of subcultural identity which they symbolized.

As well as reinforcing belonging and individual status within the group, attendance at relatively exclusive goth events played a key role in terms of the creation and maintenance of actual subcultural friendships. After a short initial period of being ostracized, newcomers to the goth scene who adopted some of its tastes and exercised a degree of persistence tended to be over-whelmed by the speed at which they gained acceptance and companions. Respondent K1, referred to earlier in relation to his recruitment to the goth scene, emphasized the importance of people's friendliness to his becoming involved more intensely:

> K1 (*male*): First of all you liked the music, and also you were embraced by a lot of people. People came and talked to you and stuff . . . It was being part of a community. Like I was saying earlier, these people were friendly to you in a club . . . I knew ninety per cent of the people who went to the Phono or Scrumpies. People just introduced you around.

From such a point of social inclusion, many goths gradually accumulated more friendships the more they went out, relative of course to the development of their subcultural capital. The following respondent suggested that the friendships and general acceptance she had gained were the most important aspect of being involved in the goth scene:

> R1 (*female*): I just basically like the goth scene a lot because I've found a lot of friends through it. A lot of people accepted me, which is something I've never had before . . . it gave me a lot of confidence, which is something I'll probably never lose.

Importantly, once friendships were established, maintaining the relationship with such individuals became, in itself, a key attraction of attending further subcultural events. Also, the more subcultural friendships one made, the greater the sense of belonging and status one was likely to experience in subcultural spaces – something which, again, increased their future appeal. The following respondent explained that he had initially been taken by friends to the Phono goth club in Leeds but that, having met other people there, he eventually began to go on his own:

> J3 (*male*): There were a couple of friends in Leeds that were like saying 'come down the Phono sometime', so they dragged me down there . . . and so I got talking to a few people and those other people stopped coming down but a couple of weeks later I thought 'f*** it, I'll go on my own', and I got talking to more people and talking and drinking and I just got to know more and more people and I just go all the time now.

As subcultural events and friendships became more central to the everyday lives of individuals, so did the general importance of their involvement in the goth scene, and their psychological and practical commitment to the subculture. Crucially, at the same time, involvement in social and friendship groups outside of it tended to dwindle somewhat. As the following respondent put it:

> G4 (*male*): People . . . they would have a group of friends and – I know, I did it and I feel really guilty about it – and then you'll meet a load of goths, and you hang around with them and your other friends are then excluded, because they don't fit in socially.

As a result of such a circle of increased involvement, the goth scene came to dominate the friendship patterns of most of its participants. Almost all respondents estimated that the majority of their friends were involved in the subculture, as in this example:

> M3 (*male*): You know, I think there definitely is an identity – I think I can honestly say that ninety per cent of the people I know in Plymouth are goths.

Romantic and sexual relationships with people outside the subculture were even more unusual, once individuals had became involved. Successful adoption of the norms of the goth scene and the consequent gains in subcultural capital tended to make individuals more attractive to other subcultural participants and, in most cases, less attractive to outsiders. In addition, the tendency for goths to attend relatively exclusive subcultural events decreased the chances of meeting, let alone getting together with, an outsider to the subculture. Furthermore, the extent of most goths' subcultural commitment was such that any relationships with non-goths that *did* get underway were liable to suffer from serious practical difficulties:

> T3 (*female*): You usually see a goth with a goth.
> S7 (*female*): because they've met them in a pub or a club.
> T3: and basically if they didn't like the music . . . if there was a goth and a non-goth – because goths are so into their scene it would probably cause problems I think. Imagine dragging a non-goth down to the Mercat – it just wouldn't work, and then they [goth partner] would hate to go to one of their [non-goth partner's] places. And also you're more likely to end up with a goth if you're more attracted to goth-looking people.

While attendance at subcultural events increased the likelihood of romantic involvement with fellow subcultural participants, such relationships – or indeed the prospect of them – provided incentives to further intensify one's practical involvement in the subculture.

The potential spiral we have been describing here, of increased event attendance and ever more exclusive subcultural commitment, contrasts markedly with descriptions of fickle, individualized postmodern consumers who continually move between partial and ephemeral attachments (Bauman 1992b; Maffesoli 1996). While increasing numbers of individuals across society may behave in such ways, the model is largely inappropriate to patterns of involvement in the goth scene or in other subcultures with their own relatively exclusive spaces and relationship circles. This does not mean goths never associated with outsiders, that individuals never drifted away from the goth scene or, indeed, that there were no 'hangers-on'. However, the social rewards which accompanied significant subcultural commitment – in terms of general levels of status as well as of the prospect of romantic relationships and friendships – meant that it often took on a central and relatively long-term place in participants' lives. Conversely, the relative lack of such social rewards for those remaining on the edge of the subculture placed limits on the number of individuals occupying such a position.

Influence and Information

As well as providing the main forum in which goths gained increasing acceptance, veneration, friendships and romance, subcultural events provided individuals with much of the cultural information necessary to attain such goals. While information, knowledge and clues were consistently available from subcultural media, shops and consumables, it was experiences and observations at subcultural events which most informed participants of how they might attain subcultural capital. As the following participant put it:

> B6 (*male*): That is your influence really – your pubs and clubs that you go to – especially if you are going for the first time and that's the sort of music you hear then it's bound to influence the music that you listen to and the way you dress.

Although direct copying was a serious faux pas, other people's appearances at goth events were, for many interviewees, the most important initial source of ideas on what clothes or make-up to buy and how to wear them, as explained by a newcomer to the goth scene from Wakefield:

R1 (*female*): I try as much as possible to observe other goth girlies while they're out and stuff and see what their ideas are, and the blokes as well really, considering half of them wear dresses.

In a subculture largely obscure to radio play or music press coverage, sub-cultural events were equally important as a source of knowledge about and familiarity with goth music. Many respondents tended to discover new music through hearing songs played at goth events, or seeing live bands and then finding out about them:

A6 (*male*): Either I'll see them live – like if they're supporting another band and you go 'wow, they're brilliant' you know 'I'm going to go and find something by them'. Or sometimes somebody will bring a CD down to the Phono and it'll get played for the first time.

The degree of influence events had on the musical knowledge and preferences of their clientele was confirmed by DJs themselves, and also specialist record label proprietors who, because of the lack of radio play for goth music, were particularly reliant upon distributing promotional CDs to clubs in the hope they would be played:

G2 (*male*): DJs are an important part of it. If you've got a track that's being played at Slimelight [London goth club] every night its going to eventually make a difference . . . there is no radio network for gothic music. You've got to use, the next best thing is using the DJs and the DJ club nights.

In addition to the appearance and behaviour of strangers and the music played at events, friends and acquaintances were a key source of influence and information for both new recruits and established goths. The reactions of friends to the appearance of others, for example, would provide clues as to the limits of acceptability within the scene and, conversely, the ways in which one might achieve veneration. In some cases, individuals gave direct suggestions about the ways in which their friends might 'better' themselves. Although, in most cases, the recipient is liable to have been rather more pro-active, the following example illustrates the point, and indeed the potential social rewards involved:

G4 (*male*): We actually did that with someone else – we literally badgered him into it. We dyed his hair black. He didn't want it black, but we dyed it for him. We gave him a catalogue and basically told him what to buy. You know, 'you want to get some tight jeans, some decent boots, and you want to get some shirts and stuff' and he did, and within a week, he had a girlfriend!

Goth events were also important sites for the receipt of practical inform-ation crucial to everyday participation in the scene. Those promoting events, retail operations, fanzines and even societies exploited the concentrated subcultural crowds through a combination of printed flyers and verbal sales-manship. One Birmingham DJ explained the importance of allowing other subcultural producers to advertise at his event:

> B6 (*male*): You have to be aware that other things are going on – you have to support it and you have to make people in your area aware of all these things – I mean you've probably seen we have all the posters up . . . I think it's important to do that.

If a participant failed to notice the relevant flyers or posters within the venue of a goth event, he or she was unlikely to avoid learning about future sub-cultural events, new releases, sources of commodities or fanzines through the channels of word of mouth operating within and around such spaces. In spite of the array of communications media available to them, most respondents explained that 'word of mouth', or 'the grapevine' was their most valuable source of knowledge and information. Two Birmingham respondents, for example, explained that they enhanced their knowledge of goth music and venues through talking to people at subcultural events:

> S7 (*female*): There was just like friends you'd make and you'd ask them about a certain song and they'd go 'yeah, I've got that'.
> T3 (*female*): and you'd ask where else there is to go . . . and it was 'oh, the Toreador, the Mercat'.

In another example the respondent, from Leeds, explained that friends he met at goth events had shown him where to buy goth clothes and music:

> M2 (*male*): I was influenced by other people around me. I made a lot of friends and stuff and they'd like tell you where the shops are and go to the shops with you. You just get into it that way.

Subcultural events and the word of mouth they often played host to, then, were important components in the continual construction of the appearances, knowledges and tastes of their clientele, and in the transfer of practical inform-ation about the subculture. This is particularly significant as an example of relatively independent internal cultural generation, something to be discussed at greater length in the following chapters.

Going out Locally

In terms of facilitating and intensifying the commitment of individuals to the goth scene, and of providing them with ideas and information, events operated both locally and translocally. Usually, local venues accounted for the majority of individuals' social participation in the goth scene, and some goths hardly ever travelled elsewhere for subcultural events, as with the following respondent:

> J3 (*male*): I'm stuck in Leeds. I've got a routine going. I just go to . . . the Phono and I know loads of people there.

Such localized everyday participation meant that goth pubs and clubs were often characterized by a high proportion of regulars. The following respondent contrasts the exclusiveness of the goth night at the Phono with the other events held at the venue:

> C1 (*female*): Friday night [rock night] was sixty per cent regulars, Saturday night [alternative night] maybe fifty per cent regulars, and Sunday night [goth night] you could be guaranteed to know everybody in there.

Large numbers of relatively localized participants were particularly likely within towns or small cities somewhat isolated from other centres of the goth scene. Such areas were especially dependent on local subcultural events in relation to subcultural capital, belonging, friendships, romantic relationships and sources of influence. For example, the relative isolation of Plymouth, in the South West of England, meant that travel to events elsewhere in the country was unusual for the city's goths, as was the appearance in the city of visiting individuals or bands. As a result, the only local goth club assumed a particular significance. As well as providing a safe space in which to claim subcultural capital and affirm identity, this single club played a key role in the facilitation and construction of the subculture in this area. The majority of the city's goths kept up with translocal subcultural trends and, hence, maintained their general subcultural interest and attachment, through the music played by the club's DJ and the information and compilation tapes he sometimes gave to those expressing an interest. The following respondent believed the DJ's efforts, in this respect, had fostered something of a revival of the goth scene in Plymouth:

> S3 (*female*): It's a lot harder to get hold of a lot of music in Plymouth so people don't tend to . . . know of a lot of bands people come across in

London, but I think that's changing because [DJ's name] plays lots
of stuff and lends people CDs and that's getting them into it.

Through bringing Plymouth's goths together, the club also enabled them to
influence each other's appearances, knowledges and CD collections. In particular, it was clear that those who *had* travelled to events elsewhere or who
had engaged with translocal subcultural media were an important source of
influence on those who had not.

In larger, more centrally positioned cities there tended to be a greater variety
of goth pubs and clubs, either locally or in neighbouring cities. However,
certain local venues remained crucial. When Birmingham's main goth pub,
The Barrel Organ, closed down in the early 1990s, for example, a number
of individuals stopped going out and drifted away from the scene as a result,
while others attended general alternative or rock clubs, bringing them into
more regular contact with non-goth styles and individuals and, hence, diluting
their subcultural commitment:

> D6 (*female*): Everybody had heard of the Barrel Organ and a lot of people went
> there before they went on to a club and there were always bands on
> there . . . when that closed it was 'oh God, what do we do now?'
> kind of thing . . . everybody sort of split up. There was like groups
> of people in one place and others went to another.

The reliance of many individuals on local goth events and DJs as sources
of musical influence is also significant in relation to the construction of subtle
local differences in taste. Although commonalities and familiarities generally
outweighed differences between the goth music played in different places,
individual DJs did plug particular favourite songs, bands or styles, something
which one Birmingham DJ believed was liable to influence local clientele:

> B6 (*male*): That's where the pubs and clubs play a bit of a role I think in the way
> that people are, because if the DJ in one area is playing more of that
> sort of music because personally he's more into that . . . that must rub
> off on the people that are in the pubs and clubs especially in a smaller
> area.

In a similar way, it was perfectly possible for general participants to have an
effect on local tastes in clothing, jewellery or make-up as a result of their
individual innovations. As a result of varying levels of popularity and respect,
certain individuals are liable to have had more influence than others, but no
one was entirely excluded from such localized chains of influence.

Translocal Night-Tripping

In addition to attending regular weekly local events, most goths directly experienced the subculture's manifestations outside their area through travelling, at least occasionally and in some cases regularly, to goth club nights, gigs, and festivals elsewhere. Although the sample may have been unrepresentative, since it consisted of those who had already travelled to a goth event, the Whitby Festival Questionnaire provides some evidence here. Only 9 per cent of respondents said they had not travelled outside their locality to attend a goth or goth-related event within the preceding year. Of the remainder, 36 per cent said they had travelled to such events more than ten times during that period (see Appendix, Table 3, p. 201). For a minority, it seemed that goth events in other towns and cities were more important than those within their locality:

WQ3c: Please give details and comments about travelling to events.
108 (*female*): I will travel to anything all over England, mainly because of a lack of such events in Ipswich. This year I have been to London, Bradford, Hull, Leeds, Whitby, Bury and Cambridge, as well as Canada (Toronto).

As indicated in her comments, the extent to which people travelled was sometimes inversely proportionate to the quantity or quality of goth events in their own locality. More importantly, as we have seen from the example of Plymouth, it tended to relate to their proximity to other cities hosting goth events. Thus, in contrast to their counterparts in Plymouth, Birmingham goths frequently made use of their proximity to several significant British cities by travelling to events.

Regular local club nights, depending on the accessibility of the location and the night of the week, tended to attract a minority of travelling goths, but mostly from within their region. The clientele for Birmingham's weekend goth pub and club nights, for example, tended to be drawn from all around the Midlands, as explained by its DJ:

B6 (*male*): I think . . . [a lot] of people who actually club in Birmingham don't actually come from Birmingham definitely. I think they draw in from . . . surrounding counties.

Though such regular events were also prone to being attended by travellers from further afield – if they were visiting goth friends, for example – the numbers were smaller. The exception to this was Slimelight, a subculturally famous all-night club in London, whose clientele every Saturday consisted of a core of regular locals plus numerous goths from across and frequently beyond Britain.

In general, though, more goths travelled greater distances for less-frequent events, such as Afterlife in York and The Wendyhouse in Leeds. As a result of intensive and co-ordinated translocal promotion, these large-scale disco-style events tended to attract a significant minority of travelling participants, largely from within the North and Midlands of England, but more sporadically from further afield, including London at one extreme and Glasgow and Edinburgh at the other. Meanwhile, live gigs, because of the uniqueness of the occasion, motivated even greater numbers of travelling enthusiasts, depending on location, time of the week and of course the subcultural profile of the bands involved (see Figure 5.2).

The uniqueness, spontaneity and perceived authenticity of the live experience (see Cohen 1991:100) as well as the promise of a big translocal attendance sometimes even prompted those normally rooted within their locality to travel, as with the following questionnaire respondent:

WQ3c: Please give details and comments about travelling to events.
71 (*female*): I only travel for concerts of bands I really want to see.

Figure 5.2 Synthetic, playing live in Birmingham 1999. (Photograph: S. L. Wainwright).

Such 'night-tripping', as Hollows and Milestone have aptly called it (1995: 3), sometimes involved public transport but, more frequently, carloads of goths from a particular area would split petrol costs, something reflected in the following comment:

WQ3c: Please give details and comments about travelling to events.
5 (*male*): Clubs and gigs. If someone is going in a car and has space, then I'll be there.

In addition, certain individuals and groups organized minibus or coach trips to particular events. For example, Birmingham University's Goth Society regularly organized a minibus to an annual goth event in Derby, and prom-oters in Manchester and Nottingham had arranged one-off trips to live gigs in Birmingham. Regardless of the mode of transport, though, it was clear from my own participation in many such trips that the process of travelling together was an integral part of the excitement of going out to goth clubs or gigs elsewhere (Hollows and Milestone 1995: 3).

By far the most significant kinds of event in terms of translocal and indeed transnational attendance, were annual or biannual festivals. As well as offering a translocal coming-together of fellow enthusiasts, these events would offer several of the most subculturally well-known bands and DJs over two or more days. As with the Northern Soul events described by Hollows and Milestone (ibid.: 2), they also tended to offer enthusiasts a range of the most obscure subcultural commodities by providing space for subcultural entre-preneurs from across the country to set up stalls and ply their trade. In part-icular, The Whitby Gothic Weekend (see Figure 5.3), a biannual four-day festival in North Yorkshire, always attracted over a thousand people from all over Britain, as well as a significant number of particularly enthusiastic goths from other countries, notably France, Germany and the United States. This particular festival had been attended at least once by most goths I spoke to across Britain, and many explained that it functioned as their annual or biannual holiday – further evidence, if it were needed, of their subcultural commitment. The attractions of travelling to goth events elsewhere, to be described below, were undoubtedly most concentrated at festivals such as this.

In the same way that attendance at goth clubs was involved in a circular relationship with subcultural friendships, and general commitment, travelling to events in other places was tied up with knowing people translocally. The events acted as potential sites of contact with goths from elsewhere and, after the friendships had been established, they provided a further motiv-ation to travel again, not to mention a house in which to stay the night

Figure 5.3 Goths gather outside the Elsinore during the Whitby Gothic Weekend.
(Photograph: S. L. Wainwright).

(Slobin 1993: 68–9). The following respondent, from Leeds, explained that
the friendships he had developed across Britain through previous travel were
a key motivation for the distances he currently covered to attend events:

> T1 (*male*): Personally I'd say that the world doesn't begin and end in one
> town . . . because you get a lot of people, myself included, who have
> their friends scattered all up and down the country, and it's just so
> good to see them again, even if its just for a few hours at a gig or a
> club or crashing over and having Sunday morning bleeueeeerrrrr.

Festivals such as Whitby were particularly enjoyable to goths due to the sheer
number of normally dispersed friends liable to be in one place for a few
days. In the Whitby Festival Questionnaire, 42 per cent of respondents selected
'seeing old friends' among their three most important attractions of the
festival. In addition, 32 per cent selected 'making new friends' in response to
the question, providing evidence of the importance of events to the establishment of new translocal friendships (see Appendix, Table 2, p. 200). Several
respondents specifically mentioned the extra friendly atmosphere at festivals.
The following responses to the open-ended follow-up to this question provide

further evidence of the circular relationship between travelling to events and translocal subcultural friendships.

WQ2b: Please explain in your own words why you have come to Whitby.
81 (*female*): For fun, bands, men, friends . . . to meet new friends, and spend money.
77 (*female*): Because it's tradition – all my friends are here from all over the country.

In addition to the genuine enjoyment of live performances by favourite bands, going to visit friends and making new ones, many travellers enjoyed experiencing a change from their local goth club and its regular clientele. This was the case for the following respondent, from Birmingham, who also emphasized a curiosity about the goth scene in different places. She makes the telling point that, due to the size of the goth scene, the only way of experiencing a choice or variety of clubs or gigs was by travelling elsewhere.

PH: Why did you want to go to Slimelight [London goth club]?
T3 (*female*): Just like to see what's happening there – how it's different to Birmingham – and it's a change as well. It's different because we don't get many places here. Trendy people have lots of clubs to choose from here, but we have like two pubs and one club.

That goths were often more likely to travel hundreds of miles for 'a change' within the translocal boundaries of their subculture than they were to seek variety through non-subcultural clubs in their own locality also demonstrates the extent of their subcultural commitment.

A number of respondents implied that this desire for a 'change' within the goth scene may have involved a hint of vanity as well as mere 'curiosity', as in this example:

PH: What's the motivation for going somewhere else when you've got loads of things going on in Birmingham?
B6 (*male*): Curiosity half the time – a bit of vanity even.

While respondents were reluctant to expand on this, a critical appraisal of my own experiences and observations provide an explanation. As a result of the small number of goths in any particular area, the majority of local participants got to know one another after a time. Once accepted or even venerated as a member of a local scene, the excitement tied up with claiming subcultural capital and gaining new friends was prone to recede slightly, at least until new regulars appeared. At this point, the prospect of being accepted, held in high esteem, or fancied by new people elsewhere would become particularly attractive. Thus, many goths made extra effort with their appearance when attending subcultural events outside their locality! In addition to the motivations of making new friends and spending time with old ones, then, people travelled to goth events in order to enjoy feelings of belonging and status among different crowds of people.

General feelings of subcultural identity and belonging were also strengthened by attending events elsewhere. In particular, the Whitby Gothic Weekend was experienced as something of a pilgrimage of disparate friends and strangers deemed to share common tastes, values, experiences and identity. Numerous respondents enthused about the attractions of a small seaside town full of goths from across the country:

> K1 (*male*): Its just such a good laugh – everyone in this whole town – it's just full of weirdos . . . there's like a mass gathering of people and also because there's going to be some bands there and you know it's going to be a damned good laugh.

Furthermore, many indicated that contact with such a large number of goths from across the country had strengthened their enthusiasm for the subculture and reinforced their sense of identity. This is illustrated particularly well by the following questionnaire comment:

> WQ2b: Please explain in your own words, why have you come to Whitby?
> 61 (*male*): seeing so many goths in one place reminds me of why we do this.

A circular process took place, then, of travelling to subcultural events elsewhere, gaining friends, achieving status and becoming more and more attached to the translocal goth scene. The increasing frequency of travel created concrete links between the goth scene's manifestations in different localities, giving travellers and, of course, regulars at the events to which they had been drawn direct contact with the subculture outside their own locality. As a result of the establishment of translocal friendships through such contact, the links often became long-term and led to more travelling, more friendships, more translocal subcultural capital and at the same time an ever-decreasing involvement with local non-subcultural activities. This direct intercity contact also contributed to the overall translocal consistency of the subculture's values and tastes within Britain. In spite of the local influences referred to, travelling participants were all liable to influence and be influenced by their counterparts in other areas of the country. Similarly, different local DJs, as well as all receiving the same promo CDs, were liable to be influenced by one another through attending each other's clubs from time to time. The national and sometimes international tours of even small goth bands provided further translocal influence. As will become clear in forthcoming chapters, a subcultural network of media and commerce was equally integral to the continual construction of a translocally consistent range of tastes and values. Plymouth's goth DJ pointed out that the increasing contact between local manifestations of the goth scene was making the subculture's range of styles and tastes similar across Britain. He illustrated the point by suggesting there was a similar range of goth 'looks' in each city:

> G4 (*male*): Because people are travelling around a lot more than they used to. People are going to different cities and it [local difference]'s getting diluted again. I don't know if you've experienced this, but going to a place and spotting the likeness of your [local] friends in another city . . . I think there must be some sort of equilibrium that occurs within cities.

This suggestion was largely borne out by my own observation of goth clubs across the country. The level of consistency of the style from place to place was far more marked than any subtle local differences which existed.

Conclusion

This chapter has sought to outline events as the most important practical aspect of the goth scene for individual participants and, probably, for the overall facilitation of their subculture. While the inter-scene contact in non-subcultural events attended by goths was an important recruitment route for the subculture, the going-out habits of most already 'paid-up' goths were dominated by more exclusive pubs and clubs. As the primary site for collective enjoyment of shared tastes, the claiming of status and the establishment of goth friendships and relationships, they tended to be at the centre of a circular process of increasing individual attachment and commitment to the subculture. While often centred around particular local events, for many goths the circular process took place on a translocal level. The fulfilment and friendships gained from travelling to subcultural events outside one's locality would provide a further incentive to do so in the future. That goths were far keener to make the effort to attend subcultural events elsewhere rather than non-goth events locally is a telling indication of their level of practical commitment to the goth scene. Furthermore, once achieved, such specifically translocal capital, belonging and friendships increased the overall proportion of one's time, means of fulfilment and sense of identity accounted for by the translocal subculture.

As well as providing the subcultural forum necessary for the claiming of capital and gaining of friendships, goth events were crucial sources of specialist knowledge, influence and information for individuals key to their participation in the subculture. As such they were significant cogs in the relatively independent facilitation and construction of the goth scene. Although, in some cases, this meant the construction of subtle local differences, the concrete connections created by travelling participants, DJs, bands and promoters contributed to the general translocal consistency of the scene. Of equal or greater importance to the construction of such general translocal consistency, however, were elements of the commerce and media surrounding the goth scene. These crucial aspects of the infrastructure of the subculture will be the subject of the following four chapters.

Note

1. Extracts from discussion group or mailing list posts are attributed to their author. Permission to use the extracts was gained from authors cited in this way. On the basis of the individuals' own wishes, some are credited to real names and others to e-mail pseudonyms.

6

Selling Goth? The Producers of Subculture

In Chapter 2, we established that across a range of theoretical perspectives, there is a tendency for commerce and media to be associated with cultural superficiality or fluidity rather than substantive subcultural groupings as defined in this book. In contrast, the remaining chapters will detail the ways in which commerce and media specifically constructed and facilitated the goth scene – a subculture whose overall levels of distinctiveness, shared identity and commitment are, I hope, beginning to become apparent. Furthermore, we shall see that the involvement of media and commerce need not necessarily imply that autonomy – our final indicator of subculture – is entirely forfeit. Rather than requiring an escape from 'the media or 'the market', as Gary Clarke would have it (1981: 92), relative autonomy suggests that the forms of consumption and communication which facilitate and construct the grouping in question are, to a certain degree, distinct or separate from those connected with outside cultural amalgamations. Therefore, we shall see that, although patterns of buying, selling and media-use were crucial to the goth scene, these were often focused around an internal network of relatively specialist subcultural institutions.

While the following chapters will focus on the extent to which the *practices* of subcultural participants were focused on commercial spaces, objects or media texts oriented toward the goth scene, the immediate emphasis here is on the organizations and individuals responsible for promoting, producing, distributing and selling them. In order to begin to assess the extent to which the goth scene was generated internally, by its own participants, the chapter is divided into discussion of *non-subcultural* producers, located fairly clearly outside the goth scene and motivated essentially by commercial consider-ations, and of *subcultural* producers, motivated wholly or partially by their own involvement in and enthusiasm for the subculture. What will become clear is that the fairly extensive involvement in the goth scene of external producers in the 1980s and early 1990s had declined by the late 1990s, and that many of their roles had been replaced by an internal network of entre-preneurs and volunteers.

Commercial Interest from Outside

As one might expect, non-subcultural producers varied considerably in wealth and influence, ranging from transnational major record companies to local independent shop owners. In the main, non-subcultural producers provided media, consumables and events oriented to a mass or large niche market (Thornton 1995: 122–60), but it is worth noting that they also played their part in certain products which, due to their highly specialist audience orientation or limited availability, could be described as subcultural. The key concern in this chapter, though, is not with the product or its audience, but the position and motivations of those who produced them vis-à-vis the goth scene. It is this which enables an assessment of the level of participation of goths in the generation of their subculture.

While precise origins are hard to trace, it is clear that non-subcultural record labels, distributors and retailers played a significant role in the goth scene right from its beginnings. In spite of the importance of independently organized events such as The Bat Cave in London and the live tours of other bands later to be termed 'goth', it was the simultaneous involvement of the recording industry which enabled the formation of the goth scene on a transnational scale. The commercial success of the likes of Bauhaus, Siouxsie and the Banshees, The Cure and, later, The Sisters of Mercy and The Mission owed itself, in no small part, to the production and distribution of their records by non-subcultural record labels and to the consequent availability of their music in commercial record stores.[1] In a number of cases, the exposure which resulted from initial independent deals soon attracted the interest of larger players. For example, the Sisters of Mercy's label Merciful Release became attached to recording giant WEA from 1984, and The Mission, having released two singles on the relatively unknown independent label Chapter 22, signed a deal with Mercury Records in 1986. Meanwhile, Siouxsie and the Banshees had been signed to Polydor ever since 1978. Such examples of larger-scale commercial interest in specialist sounds are consistent with Keith Negus's observation that, rather than always seeking to 'massify' or standardize, major record labels often seek to maximize niche appeal by cultivating links with generic subcultures:

> Record companies initially position acts sartorially in relation to other artists and genres of music, and signify the adoption of an implicit lifestyle and set of values denoted by these visual codes. (Negus 1992: 66)

The examples of The Mission and The Sisters of Mercy also resonate with Negus's illustration of the tendency for larger labels to exploit already developed niche sounds pioneered by small-scale independents, who effect-ively are left playing the role of talent spotters (1992: 40).

The global marketing and media coverage – of goth bands and the sub-cultural lifestyle with which they were associated – by significant commercial interests, resulted in reasonable shelf space for goth bands in independent and chain record stores across and beyond Britain. High street record stores were, like major labels, becoming more and more focused on supplementing and, indeed, increasing the money made from Top 40 sales to the perceived 'casual buyer' by catering to a diversity of more specialist tastes (see Straw 1997). That having been said, the commercial limits to this inclusiveness were emphasized when the interest, of both independent and major non-subcultural record companies and retailers, in goth bands, declined signif-icantly toward the mid-1990s. While they remained involved in the release of new or repackaged material by initially established goth bands, and in the occasional release of indie or metal music which took on limited elements of goth style, the non-subcultural record industry soon lost interest in seeking or supporting new goth bands.[2] As a result, the availability of recorded music from such bands became almost entirely reliant upon highly specialist record labels and retailers run by enthusiasts for the subculture.

The close relationship between the recording industry and the music media is well documented (see Frith 1983; Negus 1992). In the case of the goth scene, the involvement of record companies intensified and was intensified by the amount of non-subcultural media coverage received by goth bands throughout the 1980s. The majority of 1980s goth bands were featured on BBC Radio One's *John Peel's Sessions*, on niche music television shows such as *The Old Grey Whistle Test* and *The Tube*, and in Britain's music press. While relatively specialist subcultural magazines such as *Zig Zag* played an important part, the labelling practices of journalists working for more broadly oriented publications such as *New Musical Express*, *Melody Maker* and *Sounds* were probably most instrumental in the crystallization of a disorganized hand-ful of sporadic stylistic similarities into an identifiable, coherent cultural movement. That the music press should have played such an important part here re-emphasizes the tendency of such publications to generate interest and sales by focusing not only on music itself but also on its social and cultural significance (Frith 1983: 172). More specifically, it illustrates Sarah Thornton's point that the music press specifically seek to report on, and hence construct, potential new genres or subcultures. As well as serving to add extra interest to the reporting of music, such a move can help generate and maintain loyal committed readerships (Thornton 1995: 153). Certainly, the inclusion of regular coverage of post-punk and, later, goth bands and events during the 1980s had successfully prompted many of the older goths I came across to read *NME* or *Melody Maker* almost every week during the 1980s.

In the same way that major labels fed on the success stories pioneered by independents, larger-scale 'mass' media followed the lead of the music press and became increasingly involved in the dissemination of goth images and music in the latter half of the 1980s. Most notably, in addition to their appearances on late-night radio or television, the best-known goth bands enjoyed occasional appearances on popular music television such as the BBC's *Top of the Pops*, and ITV's *The Chart Show*. Toward the end of the 1980s, there appeared two books by British music journalist Mick Mercer, entitled *Gothic Rock Black Book* (Mercer 1988) and *Gothic Rock* (Mercer 1991). The subcultural popularity of these texts undoubtedly owed itself in large part to an author with considerable personal connections to the goth scene, but non-subcultural publishers and high street retailers accounted for much of their distribution to that audience.

As with the involvement of the recording industry, the goth scene, like many other styles, was only suitably novel to be worthy of mass-media coverage for a short time. Meanwhile, the music press, who were losing readers to new style bibles such as *The Face*, and glossy rock-music magazines aimed at a more mature audience (Shuker 1994: 87), courted and hence constructed various new movements, including an indie scene associated with Manchester (Thornton 1995: 153). The focus of increasingly sparse articles on goth became more and more tongue-in-cheek. One article appeased the majority of its indie readership by stating that:

> You don't want to be one, you don't want to listen to Nick Cave and the Neff and Skeletal Family, you don't want to wear patchouli oil, you don't want to belong to an adolescent tribe who do nothing but hang around . . . looking dour, waiting for the end of the world . . . (Collins 1991: 22–3)

However, it is worth noting that the publication still played its role in the continual construction of the goth scene by helpfully going on to outline many of the subculture's most important elements for those who might in fact want to 'be one'.

During the late 1990s both mass and niche media had become far less significant as producers of the goth scene. Nevertheless, there were occasional reviews or previews of particularly large or notable gigs or festivals.[3] The Whitby Gothic Weekend sometimes attracted journalists seeking to amuse readers of Sunday newspapers and, on one occasion, a teenage girl's magazine.[4] The music press also occasionally reviewed new or repackaged old material by 1980s goth bands and sometimes played up the stylistic references to goth of certain newer indie and metal bands – notably Garbage, Placebo, Republica, Marilyn Manson and Type O Negative.[5] In addition, at a number of points during my research period, non-subcultural media proclaimed the return of, either the popularity of the goth scene itself or its influences on current designer fashion.[6]

While we have detailed, in this section, a number of examples of positive or neutral non-subcultural media coverage of the goth scene, the subculture in Britain had largely escaped the kind of negative moral-panic-style mass-media attention afforded to certain other subcultures (Cohen 1972; Thornton 1995). This was to change, though, in April 1999 when two teenagers opened fire on fellow pupils at Columbine High School in Denver, USA. The British press reciprocated their American colleagues' emphasis on an apparent association of the killers with the goth scene. British tabloid *The Mirror* described the killers' 'gang', known as the 'Trenchcoat Mafia':

> Gang members painted their nails with lurid varnish and wrote poems and stories about death. Smoking pot, quoting songs by shock rocker Marilyn Manson, Vampire games and the Internet also held the group of boys and girls together (O'Sullivan 1999: 7).

The link was also emphasized in British broadsheets. *The Guardian*, for example, asked, 'Did goth culture turn two teenagers into killers?' (Younge and Ellison 1999: 2–3). Such coverage prompted the *NME* to react against the moral panic – devoting its front page to a picture of Marilyn Manson, with the words 'NOT GUILTY. FIFTEEN DEAD IN DENVER. WHY ROCK 'N' ROLL IS NOT TO BLAME' (*New Musical Express*, 1999: front cover). Although a temporary issue in Britain, this was a prime example of the kind of negative moral-panic mass-media coverage which Stan Cohen (1972) and, some decades later, Sarah Thornton (1995) have argued can play a significant role in the construction and popularity of subcultural groupings. While the effects on the subculture will be explored in Chapter 8, my concern here is merely to note the temporary intensive involvement of mass and niche media, as clear commercially motivated external sources of influence and publicity.

We have already established that although they sometimes attended pubs or clubs which involved a mixed clientele, goths tended wherever possible to go to specialist events. Crucially, in either case, non-subcultural producers were liable to be involved. Although they were sometimes sympathetic to it, few of the venue managers, promoters and even DJs involved in 'alternative' events attended by goths during the 1980s or mixed rock events in the 1990s were particular enthusiasts for the goth scene per se. Furthermore, even the much more internally organized and run specialist events which dominated the going-out habits of most goths during the late 1990s remained reliant upon non-subcultural venue managers, P.A. specialists and others. In particular, many events were facilitated by the commercially induced willingness of venue proprietors to orient themselves toward the limited but reliable clientele provided by specialist groups such as goths on otherwise quiet weekdays (see Willis 1990: 67). Furthermore, these subcultural events revolved around pubs, bars and clubs and were linked, therefore, to the large-scale commercial brewing companies which owned most of the venues. Importantly, this involvement of non-subcultural producers in events which were otherwise subcultural, was replicated in other relatively exclusive elements of the subculture. While many specialist goth clothes stores produced at least some of their own stock, they tended to rely upon non-subcultural producers and wholesalers as well. Similarly, goth record labels and retailers often dealt with non-subcultural as well as fellow subcultural dealers and distributors. Even those who produced fanzines and web sites were reliant upon hardware and software provided by the largest-scale commercial interests.

My insistence on pointing out the involvement of non-subcultural individuals or institutions here, there and everywhere may seem to verge on the pedantic. Such involvement is an important reminder, though, that the goth scene and any similar groupings should only ever be described as autonomous in relative terms. The role of non-subcultural individuals and organizations during the early years of the subculture and, to a lesser degree, during the time of my research in the late 1990s emphasizes that the goth scene was not and could not be spontaneous, authentic or self-contained. Such non-subcultural involvement also demonstrates, given the identity, commitment and distinctiveness which characterized the goth scene, that medium- and large-scale commercial interests are not necessarily conducive to the breakdown of cultural substance. Nevertheless, it should also be deemed significant that the relative decline in the involvement of non-subcultural producers in the 1990s prompted goths themselves to take an increasingly important part in the construction and facilitation of their subculture.

Internal Infrastructure

In spite of reliance upon non-subcultural venue owners and managers, most of the events attended by goths during the late 1990s, as well as being targeted at goths, were initiated and organized by enthusiasts. Subcultural promoters, possessing first-hand knowledge of their target clientele, either persuaded venues to employ them to run and promote a night or paid to hire out a space and its staff, and recouped the money for themselves with an admission fee. DJs at goth events were also subcultural enthusiasts themselves, as were many of the bands hired to play. Similarly, there was an ongoing growth in the importance of small-scale producers, distributors and retailers of goods who were personally affiliated to the goth scene. Thus, goths running genre-specific record labels enabled goth bands, unknown outside the scene, to release and sell CDs. Those running specialist retailers of records, often operating trans-locally through mail order, increasingly aided the delivery of such releases to their target audience. Meanwhile, other goths had ventured into the clothing retail trade, producing and/or distributing a range of goods consistent with their own subculture's distinctive tastes. Finally, small-scale narrowly targeted media, produced or organized by goths, had also taken on an important role, whether in the form of fanzines, websites or on-line discussion groups.

Importantly, although they all had certain connections outside the subculture, the producers responsible for these elements of the goth scene collectively formed something of an interconnected subcultural infrastructure character-ized by a spirit of mutual assistance. Most notably, perhaps, subcultural media, from fanzines to on-line discussion groups, functioned to connect together and promote events, retailers, record labels and bands. In turn, events and retailers provided a space for the promotion of websites and discussion groups, and for the sale of fanzines. For their part, record labels and bands continually sent free promotional CDs to goth fanzines, e-zines, retailers and DJs, in order to publicize their material toward a suitable audience. Mean-while, in spite of sometimes being in competition with one another, different goth-event promoters and retailers often distributed or displayed each other's flyers and posters in an effort to raise awareness of all their events and services to their shared translocal market. The proprietor of London record shop Resurrection Records explained that such arrangements could be mutually beneficial:

> A3 (*male*): If the promoters can use us to promote their gigs then obviously that means that they can hopefully get more people there and then they're more likely to actually put things on . . . and it's just like a sort of self-generating thing, and we will then use his gigs to try and promote the shop – putting flyers there, or flyering for new CD releases or whatever.

On other occasions, however, the cooperation had more to do with the well-being of the goth scene as a whole than with the success of their individual activities. Thus, Resurrection Records' involvement in the promotion of Sacro-sanct, a goth festival in London, had not stopped them from selling tickets for the rival Whitby Gothic Weekend, without commission. In return, the promoter of the latter event had included Sacrosanct flyers in her promotional mail-out. Given that many individuals were liable to have chosen between the two festivals, the mutual benefits here are more ambiguous. Another example is provided by goth fanzine *BRV Magazine*'s regular inclusion of a highly sympathetic review section for other goth fanzines – hardly an aggressive marketing move.

In spite of the general prevalence of such a spirit of cooperation there were also instances of considerable rivalry between promoters, retailers, fanzines, bands and record labels. In the case of those with commercial imperatives, it was necessary to compete with others seeking a share in the same limited market. Such competition was often played out on a translocal scale and, particularly in the case of goth record retailers, an international scale. Competition sometimes took on fiercer, more unpleasant tones when motivated by cultural rather than financial factors. Occasional disputes and dislikes arose over a combination of principled differences – in relation to the future direction of the goth scene, for example – and desires for one's own fanzine, event or band to be as successful as possible. In one example, an event promoter and others fell out with a record label over a variety of issues, and a public dispute was played out through goth fanzines and on-line newsgroups for some months. In spite of a general spirit of intense cooperation then, the goth scene's subcultural infrastructure was not entirely united. Crucially, however, such instances of competition and discord further emphasize the common location of such individuals within the same semi-autonomous translocal network.

Although certain individuals and organizations were of particular importance, it was clear that a very large number of participants played their part in this network. It was suggested by one fanzine editor that there were few goths who had never participated in productive or organizational activities of one kind or another:

> G3 (*male*): Its probably one of the most active scenes. Everybody seems to be doing something, either a fanzine, or making clothes . . . I think most goths . . . are active people. They want to try and do something.

While many were or had been, at some point, heavily involved in major activities such as making or retailing clothes, producing fanzines, organizing events or playing music, a much larger number of others contributed via more occasional or small-scale activities. My own experiences promoting a one-off goth event in Birmingham in 1999 provide a useful example. While the venue, the various established DJs involved and I were crucial to its success, attendance was considerably boosted by my receipt of numerous offers of help in printing and distributing flyers, posters and stickers. Small contributions such as giving out flyers, writing the occasional article for a fanzine and taking money on the door at events reflected a general desire to be actively involved in facilitating the development and survival of the goth scene. Such high levels of participation draw attention to the level of 'grass-roots' involvement in the generation of the subculture, as well as re-emphasizing the extent of many goths' commitment to it.

Participation in organizational and productive activities also appeared to be characterized by a somewhat greater gender balance than in much of popular music culture. The absence of females in key positions in much of the music industry has been well documented, for example, in Keith Negus's account of the recording industry (Negus 1992) and Sara Cohen's account of their exclusion from many bands in the Liverpool rock scene (Cohen 1991: 201–23). Indeed, such studies indicate that things may not have improved a great deal from the situation described by Frith and McRobbie in 1978:

> The music business is male-run; popular musicians, writers, creators, technicians, engineers and producers are mostly men. Female creative roles are limited and mediated through male notions of female ability. Women musicians who make it are almost always singers; the women in the business who make it are usually in publicity... In general, popular music's images, values, and sentiments are male products. (Frith and McRobbie 1978: 373)

Those academic accounts of women making more active cultural contributions have often involved relatively gender-specific music scenes such as Riot Grrrl (Leonard 1997, 1998; Triggs 2000), possibly because of the relative scarcity of their involvement in significant productive or organizational cultural activities in more 'mixed' music scenes. As Bayton has put it, 'Looking at popular music as a whole... the main role for women is that of fan' (Bayton 1997: 37).

The situation in the goth scene only partially contradicted this picture. First, it should be acknowledged that, overall, there appeared to be more male than female subcultural producers in the goth scene. Though it clearly was not a representative sample, the fact that just under two-thirds of the subcultural producers I interviewed happened to be male gives a rough illustration of this. There were also horizontal gender inequalities within the goth scene's subcultural infrastructure, based on familiar gender stereotypes. For example, it may not be coincidence that almost half the female producers I interviewed were involved in some way with making or retailing clothes. Conversely, DJs were much more likely to be male than female, as were most non-vocalist roles in goth bands. In addition, those females involved in traditionally male-dominated productive activities were occasionally subjected to stereotypical assumptions based on their gender. The only female member of a team of three goth-event promoters described some isolated experiences of being regarded as of marginal importance compared with her male counterparts:

> J1 (*female*): For example, when at a gig, people sometimes assume that [name] or [name] are in charge rather than me ... Also, when DJing, it's sometimes assumed that I'm just standing in whilst the real DJ has gone to the loo!

Nevertheless, the involvement of females in a variety of activities of significance seemed to be increasingly common and, despite incidents such as that described above, not generally regarded as abnormal by those who consumed their products and services or attended their events. Although their contribution was not on an equal footing with that of men, the number of female producers I came across was considerably higher than I would expect for many other groupings. There were also clear indications that they were more accepted in such roles in the goth scene than in many areas of culture outside it. Indeed interviewee J1 herself was keen to point out that the gendered assumptions she described to me were the exception rather than the rule:

> J1 (*female*): On the other hand, these are isolated incidents and I think that, on the whole, being female doesn't particularly make much difference to the way people perceive me.

This was consistent with a comment from another female goth promoter, from Oxford:

> L3 (*female*): the sexist attitudes in normal society for a woman to succeed don't exist [in the goth scene] and it is perhaps easier for them to get on.

Most notably, the organizer of the Whitby Gothic Weekend – the biggest, most famous British goth event – was female, as were many of the volunteers who helped her. Respondent J1 speculated that the high-profile and successful nature of this female promoter's involvement might have provided a useful role model, making it easier for others to follow suit. She also suggested that a number of high-profile goth vocalists had portrayed a positive encouragement for goth women to take up active roles. Her explanation also involved confirmation of the suggestion made in Chapter 4 of this book (see p. 48) that the goth scene was relatively accepting of femininity more generally:

> J1 (*female*): Women have always played a key role in the scene – Siouxsie Sioux, Danielle Dax – and continue to do so today ... goth would seem less

threatening to women than say the metal or rock scenes, whose culture appear, to me at least, to project an image of testosterone fuelled masculinity.

Therefore, while inequalities and stereotypical assumptions still existed in relation to women's involvement in subcultural productive activities, I would cautiously suggest they were far less pronounced than in most other music scenes. Most importantly of all, however, it was clearly feasible for any goth with sufficient time and energy to contribute in some way to the facilitation and construction of the subculture and, to differing degrees, most had done so.

Volunteers or Entrepreneurs?

G4 (*male*): I think the business side of goth sprung up around the people because they were a niche in the market that wasn't being exploited ... it's meant that the businesses that have come along have been by people that knew what they were doing or what they were fitting into so they might be a bit more sympathetic to people rather than seeing them as fabricated consumers – they'd see them as like the same as they are.

The specific focus of this section on subcultural producers is partly in response to Angela McRobbie's justified call for more research emphasis to be placed on the 'entrepreneurial infrastructure' within youth cultures (McRobbie 1989: 24). Specifically, she attacks a theoretical tendency to conflate commerce with a lack of purity or a fall from grace, and calls for more attention to the importance of small-scale DIY commerce to the emergence and development of youth cultures and, by extension, its potential career significance on an individual level (McRobbie 1989: 36, 1994: 161). She suggests that the tendency in much work on youth cultures to focus on people in their capacity as consumers should be complemented by an in-depth investigation of small-scale profitable practices of cultural production, which often combine work and leisure: 'We ... have to consider cultural practice for a profit, or merely for a livelihood or as a supplement to the dole as now taking over that space in people's lives which we would once have called hobbies or activities' (McRobbie 1999: 26).

Consistent with McRobbie's emphasis, many activities of subcultural producers did involve financial profits, in spite of their personal enthusiasm for the goth scene. Retailers of records, clothes or accessories were the subcultural producers most liable to make sufficient money to make at least a modest living. In particular, the highly specialist CD retail services of

Nightbreed Recordings' mail-order service based in Nottingham and Resurrection Records' shop in London had become successful businesses. Similarly, several goth-oriented clothes retail operations made comfortable, though not excessive, livings for those involved. The proprietor of Morgana, a goth clothes shop based in Wakefield, Yorkshire, summed up the relative success of her business as follows:

> B3 (*female*): We've been here for a long time . . . we have now moved to a bigger shop, and we've opened another shop in Leeds, so we're getting bigger but we're not rich.

Importantly, the goth scene only provided a sufficient market for such businesses if targeted on a translocal scale. Indeed, my continual emphasis on the translocal form taken by the subculture is illustrated very effectively by the insufficient number of goths in any one local area of Britain (with the possible exception of London) for such specifically targeted businesses to survive on their custom alone. For this reason, such operations relied on additional custom from goths outside the locality or from locals outside the goth scene in order to stay afloat. Morgana's success appeared to have resulted from the exploitation of both avenues. The retailer, with outlets in Wakefield and Leeds, targeted its core translocal subcultural clientele through regular advertisements in national goth fanzines, a web page and a mail-order catalogue, and by running stalls at goth festivals. At the same time, local non-goths – from teenagers wanting body-piercings to middle-aged couples wishing to spice up their sex life – accounted for a significant proportion of sales.

> PH: Could you tell me about your clientele?
> B3 (*female*): We get a lot of ordinary people coming in . . . because they want something different for special occasions. We get middle-aged people coming in for some of the fetish things, for the bedroom . . . obviously goths, anybody who knows about the shops. Most goths do actually know the shop. They will come and travel . . . We've had people from Scotland, a lot of people from down South and from Manchester.

Due to the less adaptable nature of their product for local consumers outside the goth scene, specialist music retailers were even more reliant upon a geographically widespread subcultural clientele. Nightbreed Recordings' Nottingham-based mail-order service was promoted nationally and internationally toward a specialist audience, through flyers, advertisements in fanzines, and a regularly updated catalogue, available in website and printed form. In spite of obscurity outside the subculture, the operation enjoyed custom from various countries across the globe as well as throughout Britain. By a rather bizarre coincidence, two New York goths on holiday in Britain visited Nightbreed's office during my interview with the retailer. I took the opportunity to quiz them:

PH: How did you find out about this place?

M10 (*female*): Everybody knows about this place. We buy CDs on mail-order. See they have this magazine called *Dark Side* over there.

M11 (*male*): [to Nightbreed] I've been ordering stuff from you for several years. I still have my letter – I have a credit!

The commercial success of entrepreneurs such as these demonstrates clearly that, even if we were to leave aside the non-subcultural producers described earlier in the chapter, the internal infrastructure of the goth scene could not somehow be regarded as occupying an authentic position outside or in opposition to consumerism. Indeed, from a certain point of view, the importance of DIY entrepreneurs to the goth scene could be seen as entirely consistent with the most neo-liberal of political agendas, most notably perhaps the encouragement of enterprise in the dogma and policies of the right-wing British and American governments in the 1980s and 1990s. Crucially, however, the fact that these operations were able to be successful in commercial terms is conducive, rather than antithetical, to my notion of subculture. That such a small subculture was able to provide a sufficient base of committed regular custom to support its own internal suppliers of goods financially serves to emphasize the group's relative autonomy rather than to undermine it. Through enabling full-time commitment from enthusiastic insiders, the availability and quality of all-important distinctive consumables was increased. As a result, far from being diluted, the distinctive and coherent translocal subcultural form taken by the grouping was strengthened by the entrepreneurial activities of its own participants.

While some were able to make a living from their subcultural key activities, many promoters, bands, record labels and others received a significant top-up to their salary, student loan or other sources of income. The promoter of the Whitby Gothic Weekend was honest enough to accept that the money made from ticket sales and merchandise associated with the event played a small part in her motivations for organizing the weekend:

J8 (*female*): Obviously there is a financial element to it now – although it isn't that big because I still have to work and I still drive a car with 150,000 miles on the clock . . . Put it this way, I make enough to make a slightly better standard of living.

As with those whose activities comprised their main career, such supplementary financial rewards surely enhanced the likelihood of individuals becoming involved in productive activities and, hence, the extent to which the subculture was generated by its own participants.

The importance of profits, though, should not be allowed to obscure the role of cultural motivations for the goth scene's subcultural producers. As well as playing a major role, alongside financial incentives, in inducing the involvement of those whose practices were profitable, cultural factors comprised the sole source of motivation for the efforts of scores of others, who made little or no money from their exploits. The proprietor of Resurrection Records explained that, in spite of the commercial success of some, few subcultural producers were likely to make much money:

> A3 (*male*): There are very few people who are going to get a living out of goth – there's us and Nightbreed . . . I mean none of the promoters are making a living out of it, the bands don't make a living out of it.

Indeed, the testimonies of the majority of organizers, bands, DJs and producers of fanzines and websites indicated that, in many cases, breaking even was not even assured, as illustrated by the following comment from a promoter in Leeds:

> J4 (*male*): It [promoting goth events] wasn't really a major money-making venture even if it was advertised properly . . . there's an awful lot more people that lose money doing promotion than make it – and that's what I found, especially when I put bands on.

As indicated, such individuals were motivated almost entirely by non-financial factors relating to their personal involvement in and enthusiasm for the goth scene. When taken alongside the importance of such cultural motivations, even for those who did make significant profits, this re-emphasizes the role of insider enthusiasm, creativity and initiative in the cultural production of the goth scene and the level of commitment many goths had to their subculture. While commerce and subculture must be regarded as highly compatible with one another, then, the role of cultural motivations and voluntary activities also merit considerable attention. In the following pages, we will examine the precise nature of these non-financial motivations and, specifically, the way they highlight the individual subcultural involvement of such producers.

The Perfect Career

Many of the goth scene's commercial entrepreneurs explained that they became involved in their particular trade due to a desire to combine their occupation with their personal enthusiasm for the subculture. Such a career choice fitted in with a subcultural lifestyle. For example, there was no need to tone down hair, make-up and clothing at work, as in certain other occupations, and it was often easier to take time off in order to attend particular goth events. The owner of Demone, a made-to-order goth clothes store in Leeds, explained that she only put up with the business' excessive workload and modest rewards because it fitted in with her own participation in the goth scene:

> D1 (*female*): I've done this to fit into my lifestyle . . . People think that it's cool but it's a job and its bloody hard work and you don't get that much . . . but I do enjoy it because it fits in with my lifestyle.

In addition to such 'convenience', many commercial and voluntary producers were motivated by the sheer enjoyment of carrying out the particular activities in which they were involved. While the retail side of Nightbreed Recordings was commercially successful, the same was not true, according to the proprietor, for the company's goth record label. This was pursued, he said, as a result of personal passion for producing goth music:

> PH: Is it good business to have a label?
>
> T2 (*male*): No! [laughs] The thing you've got to understand is that we're motivated because we're musicians, and musicians of a specific genre . . . the whole scene relies totally on love for the genre . . . the wheels grind on interest and love for the scene and the music.

I received a similarly amused response, when I asked the vocalist from American band Faith and the Muse about financial rewards. In spite of an international high profile within the goth scene and the release of numerous CDs, she cited the band's desire to produce and play music on their own terms as their central motivation:

> PH: Does Faith and the Muse make a living for its members?
>
> M7 (*female*): Faith and the Muse is a very expensive hobby for us!
>
> PH: Do you think it ever will?
>
> M7: No, I really don't. To make a living would mean to extend our music in a way to grab a larger fan base, to water it down actually . . . Allow me to open a small window for you . . . to tour we need transportation, petrol, hotels, food, equipment, rentals . . . To tour means to bring along live musicians . . . We can't afford to pay them . . . thus, they, like everyone, do it for the experience, the adventure, the love of music.

Subcultural Perks

As well as convenience and enjoyment, the activities of subcultural producers often resulted in significant perks related to their subcultural involvement, such as free entry to goth events or free CDs. Those who helped out promoters by distributing flyers or taking money at the door at goth events were usually content to play their part in return for free entry and in some cases a complimentary drink from the promoter. On a larger scale, key individuals whose activities made them well-known throughout the goth scene were often able to be guest-listed for events across Britain. This benefit was emphasized by the producers of high-profile British fanzine *BRV Magazine*:

> S4 (*male*): If we want to go to a goth or alternative gig we just phone up. We either know the band or the promoter and we get on the guest list and get free beer half the time!

Producers of fanzines, alongside goth DJs, also received subcultural perks of a more material kind. Those who made themselves known to record companies and bands regularly received free advance promotional goth CDs. Meanwhile, producers of subcultural clothing were able to use their skills to produce their own garments, and retailers could keep for themselves occasional items purchased at bulk wholesale prices. One proprietor gleefully explained to me that she ordered a lot of things in her own size! Of course, that such subcultural goods and privileges constituted desirable personal rewards again underscores the personal interest in goth music and fashion of those who received them. Such personal interest also came into play for some fanzines producers, in relation to their ability to meet and interview bands for whom they, every bit as much as their readers, were enthusiastic fans. The producer of Glasgow-based fanzine *Naked Truth* explained:

> G3 (*male*): We were really excited about talking to bands that we were into. I don't know, it sounds sad now but you've heard a band on CD or tape, and they'd phone you up, and you were like 'ohhh!!', you'd get a buzz out of it.

Subcultural Capital

Alongside factors such as appearance, knowledge and ownership of the right consumables, being seen to undertake subcultural organizational or productive activities constituted strong evidence of subcultural commitment and tended to raise the general profile of those involved. As such, it was a key source of subcultural capital. This was most obviously the case for those involved in bands, who, as well as being centre of attention at their own live performances, were liable to have their names on flyers, their pictures in fanzines, and their CDs played in goth clubs. To differing degrees they took on something of a celebrity status within the goth scene. The vocalist from the band Manuskript admitted that this was a key appeal:

> M5 (*male*): Not everyone gets to go out and be a rock star on a very minor scale even for 40 minutes every month.

Although few received the level of fandom enjoyed by high-profile goth bands, subcultural capital also motivated the activities of many other subcultural producers. At the top end of the scale, the promoter of Whitby Gothic Weekend cited her subcultural high profile as a key reward of her considerable efforts. She particularly indicated the value of this status when it was translated into translocal friendships within the subculture:

> J8 (*female*): The other aspect of it that I get is like my celebrity status [laughter] . . . it is a good thing because I can go out on my own on a night anywhere in any town and I will always see someone that I know.

Others involved in DJing, fanzine writing, website construction on various scales, or even sitting on the door at the smallest of goth events were liable to experience some kind of increase in standing, whether in the context of a particular local crowd or across the country. As a result of the importance of authenticity, creativity and commitment in the goth scene's subcultural ideology, many were somewhat reluctant to emphasize personal status as a motivation for their activities. The producer of *Naked Truth* fanzine was not one of them, however:

> G3 (*male*): It's quite a good thing to do. It's like minor fame! Especially at things like the Whitby weekend.

The following exchange between two goths who maintained their own websites demonstrates the value of interviewing people together. They extract from one another a reluctant admission of the importance of personal status as a reward for their activities:

> P1 (*male*): It [website] was . . . trying to do something which I thought people would use.
>
> B1 (*female*): So you could go 'look what I've done!' . . .
>
> PH: So why do you have a website then?
>
> B1: Oh I don't know.
>
> P1: Go on admit it!! . . . It's just an ego trip basically.

B1:   I think they all are really . . . It's just a big 'look at me' pointer isn't it?

P1:   It's like your fifteen minutes of fame isn't it . . . on mine, the goth map's useful but . . . the rest of it is 'this is me, here I am, you can mail me!'

Importantly, while rewards like subcultural status and the gaining of friends may be regarded as self-serving, they also relate very clearly to the cultural affiliation of those involved to the goth scene. Status and friendships within the confines of such a subculture would constitute little reward for those whose social lives revolved outside it.

Contributing to 'the scene'

The most common answer I received to my questioning as to key people's motives and rewards was that they wanted to contribute something to the survival, development and, sometimes, improvement of the goth scene. Producers of various kinds emphasized a desire to play a part in the subculture's advancement, as in the following quotes from the designer of a goth information website and the promoter of a goth event in York:

D3 (*male*):   I thought it would be useful to compile a list of clubs so people who were travelling around could work out where to go in certain cities . . . It just occurred to me that it could make a big difference.

J2 (*female*):   I like seeing people enjoy themselves – there's no other night really in the area and I really wanted to put York back on the map.

For some, the intention was not just to facilitate the goth scene, but to change it. The promoter of Whitby Gothic Weekend explained that she wanted to use the festival, and her own position of influence, to change the general atmosphere of the subculture:

J8 (*female*):   I run it for the scene because I'm kind of on a moral crusade to make goth a happier place to live sort of thing . . . I mean the slogan on my compliments slips is 'The Gothic Weekend – putting a smirk on the face of goth'.

In his account of the growth of sociality and neo-tribalism, Maffesoli (1996: 17, 96) has argued that while they have no particular external objectives, the emerging affinity groups he describes involve a strong moral imperative for their own survival and regeneration: 'the "tribes" we are considering may have a goal, may have finality; but this is not essential; what is important is the energy expanded on constituting the group as such' (ibid.: 96). This kind of desire to contribute to the development and survival of 'the group as such', alongside more individual rewards such as subcultural capital, perks, and sheer enjoyment of particular creative activities, is clearly demonstrated here, on an individual level, in the motivations of the goth scene's subcultural producers. As Maffesoli suggests, there is no external rationale for the importance attached to the constitution and reconstitution of the goth scene. The priority relates to the ideology of voluntary commitment described in Chapter 3 or this book, but was also rooted in a very genuine personal desire of participants not to lose a lifestyle and identity which was of considerable personal importance to them.

So strongly held was the ideology of voluntary commitment to the subculture's well-being that many goths in interviews, general conversation and internet discussion indicated that they found the idea of making significant financial or other personal rewards from organizational or creative activities somewhat distasteful. In fact, though, the desire to contribute to the well-being of the goth scene often went hand in hand with a number of more individual rewards. In particular, the goth scene's criteria of status ensured, rather ironically, that being seen to undertake apparently selfless activities in the interests of the subculture was liable to induce particularly high levels of personal admiration and status. While the most cynical of commentators may suggest that this observation invalidates all claims to altruistic motives, my own conclusion is that the activities of subcultural producers were usually attributable both to a genuine desire to contribute something *and* to a mixture of more individual rewards. The following Birmingham promoter's contribution to an e-mail list discussion came across as a particularly honest assessment:

Re: It Used to be about the music man
Let's be honest, we do it for the same reason every else does, partly because we care about the goth scene a lot and want it to keep going, but mainly because we like the idea of being promoters, we get to talk to bands and pretend we're really 'cool'.
(De Bie 2000)

More significant than asking which of the non-financial motivations outlined was most important, though, is emphasizing that all of them allude to the committed involvement of the individuals concerned, within the goth scene. They draw further attention, therefore, to the significant extent to which the subculture was generated by its own participants.

Conclusion

This chapter should leave the reader in little doubt that commercial motivations and rewards are entirely compatible with the levels of substance of the goth scene. At the same time, however, it is crucial to emphasize that the relative importance of small-scale subcultural entrepreneurs, compared with niche and mass non-subcultural businesses, is an important indicator of the autonomy and, hence, substance of a particular grouping. Furthermore, the importance of cultural rather than financial motivations, both to such entrepreneurs and to the far greater number of voluntary subcultural producers, is worthy of emphasis. This is not because commercial motivations or rewards are somehow antithetical to the concept of subculture, but because non-financial motivations serve to illustrate the unambiguous position of such producers as committed participants of the subculture.

Notes

1. Non-subcultural record labels involved with early goth music included independents and majors. Some examples of independents included Beggars Banquet, who released material by Bauhaus and The Cult among others; Jungle Records, who released material with Specimen; 4AD, who released material with various bands, including The Birthday Party and Dead Can Dance. Examples of major labels included Polydor, involved most notably with Siouxsie and the Banshees and WEA, who contracted the Sisters of Mercy and their previously independent label Merciful Release in 1984.

2. Examples of 'cross-over' bands marketed partially at goths included Garbage (Mushroom Records) and Placebo (Elevator Music). Compilations involving 1980s goth bands include Sisters of Mercy – *Slight Case of Over Bombing* (Warner UK 1993) – and Siouxsie and the Banshees – *Twice Upon a Time* (Polydor 1992) – and a genre-specific goth compilation called *Nocturnal* (Procreate 1998).

3. Examples of non-subcultural media previews or reviews of goth events encountered during my research included Salter, *Big Issue in the North*, 1998; Myres, *Melody Maker*, 1997; Thompson, *New Musical Express*, 1999.

4. Examples of coverage in mass media include Gilbert, *Independent on Sunday*, 1996; Matherson and Simpson, *Minx*, 1997.

5. Examples of articles reviewing or featuring the release of new or repackaged material by well-known 1980s goth bands include Malins, *Q Magazine*, 1998; Udo, *New Musical Express*, 1996; Seagal, *New Musical Express*, 1998. Examples of references to the goth influences in metal or indie music include Dalton, *New Musical Express*, 1998; Oldham, *New Musical Express*, 1996; Tsarfin, *Terrorizer*, 1999; Tovey, *Terrorizer*, 1999.

6. For an example of proclamations of the return of the goth scene itself, see Myres, *Melody Maker*, 1998. Examples of coverage of goth's influences on designer-fashion trends include Paterson, *Scotland on Sunday*, 1997; Davidson, *The Herald Magazine*, 1999; Alford, *Observer Life*, 1993.

7

Buying Goth: Subcultural Shopping

The selection, purchase and consumption of particular kinds of subcultural goods, most notably recorded music, clothing and accessories, was a key element in participants' experience of the goth scene. When asked to indicate the most important aspects of their participation, 53 per cent of Whitby Festival Questionnaire respondents selected fashion/appearance and 49 per cent, recorded music as one of their three choices (see Appendix, Table 4, p. 201). Answers to the open-ended follow-up question involved constant reference to clothes, music and sometimes other consumption-related aspects of the scene:

WQ5b: In your own words please explain what is the goth scene all about?
11 (*female*): The clothes, the style – the general interest in things that are dark and macabre.
44 (*female*): It's about dressing up in your best stuff . . . and listening to great music.
64 (*male*):   We enjoy the books, films, music and clubs.

The following interviewees provide extra weight to the point, specifically indicating that accumulating personal collections of particular kinds of recorded music was important to the process of intensifying their initial involvement in the goth scene:

T3 (*female*): Well there were songs that we'd heard and we wanted to know who they were by . . . yeah 'who's this? we must get this song' . . .
S7 (*female*): Yeah, you'd hear the odd track, and then I used to buy the album and the album was brilliant.
T3:   And then you'd buy the next album.

Purchasing particular styles of clothes and make-up were equally significant to the development of their individual identities within the goth scene:

S7: We [first] went to Edwards with a trace of eye-liner, a trace of lipstick.

T3: and now people don't recognize us . . . There was a stage when we were like 'ripped fishnets – yuk', and then a few weeks later [*mimes ripping of tights*], and that was like three pairs of ripped fishnets . . .

S7: and then it was like, 'PVC tops, no!', and now I've got a couple.

To a significant extent, it was through ownership and use of consumer goods that goths claimed their subcultural capital, differentiating themselves subtly from one another and more overtly from groupings and individuals outside the subculture. Collections of commodities provided the material manifestation of the subculture's distinctive range of tastes. The process through which individuals developed their subcultural 'look' and enhanced their knowledge and appreciation of music revolved around selecting, purchasing, combining and using particular kinds of object, as did the consistency and distinctiveness of the goth style as a whole. Furthermore, as well as being crucial as a means to an end, the act of shopping was often an important subcultural activity in itself (see McRobbie 1989: 24; Shields 1992a: 5).

Moving on from the emphasis on production in the last chapter, here we illustrate the importance of consumption to the goth scene, emphasizing the significance to the shopping routes of goths of first a variety of non-subcultural retailers, not especially oriented to them, and second a translocal network of specialist subcultural sources of goods. At the same time, we will focus on the differential levels of creativity and critique involved in the selection and use of consumables by goths. The purpose of this is not to identify or celebrate a unified degree of creativity or active consumption among goths, but rather to emphasize that their subcultural consumption tended to be characterized by varying levels of discernment and innovation. More specifically, it involved the selective, creative appropriation of goods from non-specialist sources alongside the rather less active purchase and use of more pre-packaged, subcultural items. For different reasons, both will be regarded as consistent with this book's conceptualization of the goth scene as a substantive subculture.

Sifting Through (for 'the odd gem')

Whilst emphasizing the importance of consumer goods to subcultural styles, Dick Hebdige (1977, 1979) positions the creative use of these, prior to the moment of commercial incorporation at least, as resistant to hegemonic capitalism. More specifically, subcultural styles involved a 'semiotic guerrilla warfare', whereby external everyday consumer goods were appropriated into a subcultural context and took on new, subversive meanings (ibid. 1979: 105). This book has already questioned notions of stylistic subversion, and this chapter will not be seeking to argue that the consumption habits of goths were somehow resistant to hegemony, whether symbolically or otherwise. However, if we leave aside this question of stylistic subversion, Hebdige's discussion of the appropriation of mass commercial objects into a subcultural context is not in itself inappropriate, either in the past or in the present (Muggleton 2000: 146). The creativity exhibited when objects are used in ways not envisaged by producers and marketers, alongside the general levels of effort, thought and knowledge involved in their selection and use, are legitimate grounds for investigation, whether or not the latter represent any realistic threat to dominant ideology as a whole.

There is little doubt that some of the consumption practices of goths indicated both creativity and appropriation. They frequently made use of goods purchased from market stalls, high street chain stores and retailers of second-hand goods, all of which being outside the internal networks of their subculture. When asked about their shopping habits as part of the Whitby Festival Questionnaire, 21 per cent of respondents selected 'local chain stores' as an important source of clothing, and 27 per cent as a key source of music. Meanwhile, 68 per cent selected local independent stores as key sources of clothing and 63 per cent chose the same option for music (see Appendix, Tables 5 and 6, p. 202). Ethnographic experience indicates that a reasonable proportion of such local independent stores are liable *not* to have been specifically targeted at the goth scene. As with events, non-subcultural sources of consumables tended to be particularly important for those participants who lived in areas where more specialist stores were unavailable. Such selection and use of goods from external retailers often involved considerable discernment and innovation on the part of subcultural consumers, fitting nicely with a somewhat depoliticized notion of subcultural appropriation.

Goths utilized a particularly wide variety of retailers in order to search for clothes which fitted with or added to their own current version of the subculture's style. At the least critical level, general 'alternative' clothes shops offered, under one roof, a range of reasonably pre-selected items of clothing associated with the metal, punk, crusty and sometimes underground dance scenes as well as with goth. The appropriative skills of goths, though, were much more apparent in their careful selection and use of items from the highly diverse range of clothes and accessories on offer from rag markets, charity shops and high street stores. They partook in a creative assembly of subcultural style, through selecting, sometimes altering and combining a variety of objects from external sources, into their own individual version of the goth style. The following interviewee, from Birmingham, explained that his subcultural look was assembled in this way, and that few of his goth clothes were marketed as such:

J12 (*male*):   A lot of the stuff I wear is like recycled. It's normal sort of clothes. Like jeans which I've had for ages, and shirts which I've just sort of like changed the style about and added bits on and stuff.

PH: Right, rather than buying *this* specific goth item?

J12:   Yeah, I've only bought a fishnet top thing – that's the only piece of goth clothes that I've actually bought.

While in the case of this last respondent the majority of his clothing and accessories were purchased from markets and charity shops, others made frequent use of high street chain stores for the same purpose. The following questionnaire respondent indicates the occasional rewards for those prepared to sift carefully through the diverse range of clothing available in such stores:

WQ6c: How easy or difficult is it for you to find goth music and clothes to buy?

11 (*female*): Sometimes you can find the odd gem in ordinary shops such as M&S.

Clothes shopping, then, was often a matter of identifying the small number of potentially suitable items from a majority that were unsuitable, and then placing them into an overall look which entailed an individual interpretation of the goth style. The way in which items of clothing were worn and the integrity of the overall look into which each item was placed were of far greater importance than the whereabouts of its purchase (Muggleton 2000: 146). In further illustration of this point, some also made selective use of the specialist shops or mail-order services of other styles or subcultures. Most notably, many sought out certain kinds of rubber or PVC clothing from retailers of fetish or general sex accessories. Such items also constituted a useful example of appropriation since, when placed into the context of the overall goth style and worn in goth spaces, they were often stripped of most of their sexual connotations and appreciated largely for their aesthetic, stylistic value. Indeed, although they did not necessarily reflect the views of most or all other goths, the respondents quoted next, who had discovered clothes they liked at sex stalls at a fashion show, seemed to dislike having to purchase clothes from retailers associated with the sex industry:

S7 (*female*):   There was another stall there that was PVC.

T3 (*female*):   A lot of it was page-three-girl type stuff.

S7:   I don't know if they get the impression that you're dodgy – that you have to be dodgy to wear it.

T3:   That annoys me – sometimes you have to go to these places and get the stuff that you want.

S7:   Yeah, there's that sex shop down Dale End isn't there and they do really nice stuff in there – but it's a sex shop.

Compact discs and records are less adaptable than items of clothing, making the notion of appropriation more ambiguous in its relevance to goths' consumption of music. Nevertheless, non-subcultural retailers formed an important part of their shopping routes, and knowledge, selectivity and creativity were demonstrated in a variety of ways. The negotiation of second-hand-record shops, market stalls and record fairs tended to require considerable expertise, for example. Such institutions provided both newcomers and established participants with the ability to improve the credibility of their collections by spending considerable time searching out or stumbling upon items from the back catalogues of bands associated with the subculture. In particular they tended to be the most useful source of rare goth or goth-related records of the past which were unavailable from other non-subcultural shops. They also offered potential bargains to those prepared to search long enough. While records were often organized under generic titles, it was increasingly rare for 'goth' to be one of these. Searching out goth or goth-related records, then, often required effort, patience and knowledge. While often this involved awareness of the names of bands and releases, the following respondent explained that he had also learned to select records on the basis of an assessment of the style and content of covers:

M2 (*male*): You know sometimes you are thumbing through a load of twelve-inches, and you just come across one and think 'oh that's got to be a goth band' and so you buy it, just from the look of it. I've bought records on that basis and not been disappointed. You can just tell can't you? Or sometimes I got records of bands that I'd vaguely heard of but knew nothing about the band, but thought 'oh, I'm going to try that'.

The fact that the majority of music purchased by goths was already associated with their subculture rather negates the use of a Hebdigian notion of appropriation to describe this process. However, selection of the desirable items certainly involved skill and knowledge, alongside elements of greater innovation and individuality.

Notably, while usually dominated by bands associated with subculture and consistent with its style, the record collections of goths were usually given a particular sense of individuality by the non-subcultural music they included. Most selected and purchased examples of music they deemed somehow compatible with the goth style, even when its marketing involved no overt subcultural associations. Others consistently sought selected items from other genres for which they had developed a personal liking – most frequently in the form of indie, metal, punk or new romantic music. Some goths even engaged in the consciously ironic purchase of popular commercial titles deemed to contradict the stylistic conventions of their subculture. Notable examples of the latter included Shampoo and Aqua. As explained in Chapter 3, such individual transgressions as these, so long as overall collections and tastes in clothes and music retained sufficient consistency with the subculture's shared tastes, were potentially beneficial to one's standing, and certainly demonstrated a degree of individual selection and creativity.

While, in the examples described above, we have demonstrated independence, knowledge or creativity on the part of consumers, it should be noted that goths also engaged in the purchase and consumption of items from non-subcultural sources in rather less active ways. Although the overall availability of goth music in high-street or general independent record stores had declined considerably since the early 1990s, the CDs of well-known 1980s goth bands were still sometimes purchased in such non-subcultural spaces by goths. Although the selection of music from such a mixed non-subcultural context indicates considerable knowledge, we should recognize that many of these products had very well-known associations with the goth scene due to deliberate niche marketing. In particular, many goths in my study had purchased retrospective compilations, either of particular 1980s bands or of goth music generally, which were explicitly marketed at them, and available from most general record stores. In addition, some bought CDs featuring newer bands such as Garbage, Placebo and even Marilyn Manson which were partially targeted, via their image and media publicity, at goths, alongside indie or metal fans more generally.

The significance of such externally available but subculturally targeted CDs and merchandise should not be underestimated. The external availability of the music of certain goth bands meant that, like non-subcultural events, they constituted initial points of contact for potential new participants. The following interviewee explained that hearing a Sisters of Mercy album played in a record shop in the late 1980s, and subsequently purchasing the CD, had been an important step in his becoming involved in the goth scene:

S2 (*male*): I suppose when I first got into it properly, it's the old clichéd answer – The Sisters of Mercy . . . I was wandering past a record shop . . . and they were playing it . . . and I thought 'I vaguely recognize this'. I'd obviously heard it on the radio or whatever and so I went up to them and said 'what's this?' and they told me . . . and I had a spare tenner in my pocket and ended up buying it. And then after that, I started kind of fishing about for other stuff that was similar.

In addition, many who were already affiliated to the scene emphasized the importance of externally available and very clearly targeted goth compilation CDs, for the ongoing development of their music collections.

J3 (*male*): Compilations are a good way of finding out about stuff really I guess . . . there's like Gothic Rock, Gothic Rock 2, Hex Files, the new Nocturnal thing . . .

Such CDs offered a useful taster of a number of bands labelled and marketed as goth, whose other releases could then be followed up individually using more specialist subcultural sources:

S2 (*male*): I've got a habit of once I've got one track by a group I generally back-track through their whole back catalogue and buy everything they've released.

The popularity of such externally available compilation CDs was illustrated by the following goth DJ, who suggested that songs included on a late 1980s compilation were, as a direct result of this, guaranteed to go down particularly well at goth events:

G4 (*male*): Do you remember how you used to be able to play any track off the first Gothic Rock album and lots of people would dance to it, but you'd play something similar and people wouldn't because they didn't know it – so lots of people must have had that album.

The use of objects from non-subcultural sources of various kinds was clearly very important, then, to the make-up of individuals' recorded music collections and their versions of the goth 'look'. More so, perhaps, than any other individual aspect of the subculture, the practices of shopping and consumption underline significant links between the goth scene and the commercial world outside it. The selective consumption of non-subcultural sources of goods, though, is not inconsistent with the goth scene's conceptualization as a subculture. First, the term subculture – as used in this book – indicates a *relatively* independent grouping within a diverse society. It therefore does not require opposition to or isolation from any unified 'dominant culture', or indeed to or from the capitalist system which penetrates all elements of Western societies. Secondly, the fact that a significant degree of this consumption from external sources involved the selection, whether 'innovative' or not, of items relatively consistent with an already established subcultural set of tastes re-emphasizes the commitment of participants to the distinctive style of the goth scene. Finally, the role of active appropriation, independent creativity and occasional transgressions in this assemblage of style emphasizes the important role for participants themselves in the ongoing development of their shared style.

Pre-Selected Goth Style

For Hebdige, subcultures remained authentic and significant only so long as they were based on the critical appropriation and subversion of everyday goods. It was only during a process of commercial incorporation and dilution of the subcultural style, *after* it had existed in its spontaneous form for a time, that explicitly marketed subcultural objects emerged:

> Once removed from their private contexts by the small entrepreneurs and big fashion interests who produce them on a mass scale, they become codified, made comprehensible, rendered at once public property and profitable merchandise. (Hebdige 1979: 132)

This suggestion is problematic in two respects. First, it dismisses in rather an elitist fashion the significance and substance of subcultural groupings after the point at which their style has been exposed 'on a mass scale' (G. Clarke 1981: 82). One of the key contentions of this book is that the substance of subcultures, in the form of shared identity, distinctiveness, commitment and relative autonomy, is both significant in itself and entirely compatible with exposure to commerce and media. Secondly, Hebdige underestimates the importance throughout the life of subcultures, including their early moments, of objects which are overtly packaged, marketed and sold as subcultural commodities. As Clarke, McRobbie and others have pointed out, the marketing of ready-made punk style, not least by the likes of McClaren and Westwood, was a key part of the very development of the subculture (see G. Clarke 1981: 92; McRobbie 1989: 24, 25 and 1994: 161).

Clarke rightly argues that there is little point in lauding supposed initial innovators and disregarding those who took on subcultural styles after they were marketed as such, when the time period between the two is at best negligible (G. Clarke 1981: 92). Developing the point further still, there is a need to challenge the very suggestion of distinct periods characterized exclusively by *either* appropriation of external objects *or* the purchase of marketed subcultural objects. We have already demonstrated clearly that some two decades after the initial involvement of non-subcultural commercial interests, the goth scene involved *both* the genuine appropriation of formerly non-subcultural goods *and* the rather less active purchase of more subculturally targeted objects. Crucially, however, the externally available goth-oriented CDs and records we have described thus far constituted merely the tip of the iceberg of pre-packaged goth style. Highly specialist retailers, which deliberately stocked items oriented mostly or wholly toward the subculture, were becoming ever more important.

The loyal, enthusiastic market provided by the goth scene enabled a number of subcultural retailers to profit from providing such an already selected and filtered range of clothes, music, accessories and even household decorations, many of which were not available externally. In the Whitby Festival Questionnaire, some 39 per cent of respondents indicated that one of either mail order, shops outside their locality or gigs and festivals was their single most important source of music, and 34 per cent cited one of these as their main way of obtaining clothes (see Appendix. Tables 5 and 6, p. 202). Participation, observation and interviews emphasized that such non-local and event-based sources were liable in most cases to have a specialist orientation toward the goth scene. The need to seek non-local and/or specialist sources of consumables was also indicated by open-ended responses to the questionnaire:

WQ6c: How easy/difficult is it for you to find goth music and clothes to buy?

82 (*male*):   Reasonably easy by mail-order, much harder from shops . . .

52 (*female*): Easy at festivals, easy when travelling to London.

Importantly, while it certainly indicates a significant degree of self-generation for the goth scene, such internal consumption, far from being anti-commercial, was also enabled by the diverse free-market economy within which the subculture operated. Furthermore, compared with the selection of items from non-subcultural sources described in the previous section, it implies somewhat lower levels of innovation or creativity on the part of subcultural consumers. Rather than appropriating and adapting miscellaneous objects or even searching for the small number of ready-made goth items available in non-subcultural stores, the customers of specialist retailers chose from items which had already been selected as compatible with the goth scene by the retailer. Therefore, it would seem that in this case, Hebdige's suggestion that 'it is basically the way in which commodities are *used* in subculture which marks the subculture off from more orthodox cultural formations' (1979: 103) underestimates the importance of the pre-selection and marketing of distinct subcultural items by specialist entrepreneurs. It may be the case, as Muggleton has argued, that the purchase and use of pre-packaged subcultural style retains a degree of individual adaptation and subversion, but levels of creativity surely are less marked than in the case of the appropriation from the diverse array of goods from the high street or the market (see Muggleton 2000: 144).

Nevertheless, the importance of consumption from specialist retailers, in terms of facilitating participation and continually constructing the goth scene's range of style, is significant in illustrating the subculture's relative autonomy. Subcultural producers and suppliers of goth clothes and, particularly, music provided a range of the most obscure and distinctive subcultural consumables, many of which weren't available externally. Therefore, even the most creative users of rag markets, charity shops and the high street tended to combine the items they appropriated with more standard subcultural goods obtained from specialist retailers.

While general record stores, markets or record fairs were valuable sources of older goth music, obtaining more up-to-date subcultural music often required highly specialist record labels, distributors and retailers. Some respondents explained that occasionally they had been able to order particular obscure goth CDs through helpful local indie record shops and, indeed, to purchase demo or commercially released CDs directly from bands themselves. However, even this required prior knowledge of the bands and releases concerned. In contrast, specialist goth-record shops provided their clientele with a space to browse, listen and discuss preferred bands and CDs with subculturally knowledgeable assistants. The owner of London goth-record store Resurrection Records explained that he often recommended releases to customers on the basis of their previous purchases.

> A3 (*male*): I think a lot of people come in without a clue what they want. Particularly when you think that there is a thousand different gothic titles in there on CD – a lot of the new stuff that's coming out gets reviewed but a lot of it doesn't . . .
>
> PH: But you can still shift them by knowing about them and letting everyone else know about them?
>
> A3: Yeah, and knowing what people like. As the shop's got bigger that's become more difficult . . . but there still is a lot of that going on.

This confirmed what I had already heard from a Birmingham respondent who frequently visited the London shop:

> W1 (*male*): There's a goth record shop in London called Resurrection Records and I found out about a lot of the new music through them because I've gone quite frequently . . . they'll say 'you might like this, have a listen', and you say yes or no.

While they did not offer a physical space or the same kind of face-to-face interaction with staff, mail-order services were centred around informative printed or internet-based catalogues, containing similarly specialist alphabetically listed titles, each with a helpful description for the consumer. The following interviewee found the latter particularly useful in this respect:

> C2 (*male*): I've started getting a lot more things mail order, because [in mail order catalogues] you've got the name of the band and then you've got a

little sentence underneath saying 'sounds a bit like' somebody else you might have heard of.

Subcultural CD retailers then, delivered to goths a range of already filtered goth music, enabling browsing, learning and purchasing on impulse. They both facilitated pre-planned purchases and induced discovery of new bands and releases. The constant availability of a range of new goth music facilitated by such retailers, and the labels they dealt with, was crucial to the constant regeneration of interest and enthusiasm among new and old participants in the subculture.

Such specialist CD retailers, though, certainly did not exist in every locality. London was the only city with anything like sufficient number of local goth consumers to support them alone. This meant that, having made the most of what limited goth music was stocked in local chain and independent music stores, goths without their own local specialist store tended either to travel to specialist shops elsewhere, or to use mail-order services. Resurrection Records' proprietor explained that his shop was often visited by non-locals, many of whom he had come to recognize due to the frequency of their appearances:

A3 (*male*): We've got quite a lot of locally based customers who come in once a week or once every two weeks ... but we've got a hell of a lot of irregular customers ... who'll come every six months, once a year.

PH: Do you recognize them?

A3: Oh yeah, normally, and its not just people from England either ... there's a sort of little band of Germans – about twenty of them – that come over about six times a year.

A number of users of Resurrection Records and their mail-order rival Nightbreed also emphasized the importance of the subcultural orientation of these businesses, which were consequently far more important to them than local chain stores or general independent record shops:

PH: Where do you get new music from these days?

S1 (*male*): from basically Nightbreed – that's the main place. It's only very rarely that I get anything from a record shop now. I gave up years ago. It's all mail order.

Nevertheless, it should be noted that an equally important subcultural source of recorded music for many goths and particularly for newcomers was home taping. Paul Willis's observation of the reliance of many young people on the receipt of tapes filled with music from friends with greater knowledge or bigger record collections than them was certainly applicable to the goth scene (Willis 1990: 63). While ownership of originals tended to entail greater subcultural capital, those individuals who did not often use specialist goth retailers were able to obtain goth music through friends who did. Equally, there was a tendency for individuals to use tapes their friends had recorded for them as a tester, to decide whether they wanted to purchase particular CDs themselves. In this respect, as Willis points out, the supplier of the tape takes the role of a 'trusted and accepted consumer guide' (ibid.). Given that the tapes received by goths were often compiled by other goths, home taping and, indeed, the related practice of lending out records and CDs can be considered a largely internal form of music distribution. However, it also played a crucial role in the process of the recruitment of individuals into the goth scene and the cementing of initial contact with the subculture. The following questionnaire respondents suggest that it was compilation tapes or lent records which sparked their initial interest in the goth scene:

WQ7b: Please give details about what or who got you into the goth scene.
48 (*male*): Got lent some records.
61 (*male*): A friend gave me a compilation and I loved it.

Similarly, the following interviewee suggested that being lent a considerable number of obscure goth records by a friend he met at college helped him transfer from listening to a small number of externally exposed goth bands to becoming self-consciously passionate about goth music:

J7 (*male*): He came into college and brought a bag full of records . . . and there was stuff that I'd never heard of before . . . I just went home and that night musically things really changed . . . I realized . . . that other bands did exist and that the stuff I was listening to was so tame in comparison to what was available. I think that was where . . . I really started to believe in what I was listening to. It got me emotionally; it was like 'yeah, this is the sort of stuff you want to listen to'. I think it was then – when I got the Birthday Party stuff and the Bauhaus stuff . . . that I'd got this stuff that I called goth.

In a similar fashion to the operation of subcultural word of mouth in general terms, then, the informal transfer of recorded music between friends was of crucial importance to the construction and facilitation of the goth scene. Like subcultural retailers and commercial compilation CDs, subcultural friends tended to offer a pre-selected range of subculturally acceptable material.

Goth, or potentially goth-compatible clothes and accessories were slightly more likely to be available in various local stores than music was. The greater adaptability of clothes meant garments or accessories from non-subcultural sources were far more suitable for appropriation or adaptation than CDs or records. Nevertheless, most goths increased their choice and obtained particularly obscure subcultural items through mail order or through travelling to particular subcultural shops elsewhere. Such translocal subcultural shopping was most important for those with fewest facilities close by. As the following interviewee from Plymouth put it:

PH: So how about clothes then?
S1 (*male*):   Mail order again really – there's never been any really goth shops down here.

As a result of such travelling and especially of mail order, many respondents from small or remote towns and cities *did* feel satisfied with the overall availability of goth music. The following respondent was from a coastal town in North Wales:

D4 (*male*):   I buy goth music every month. This is mail order from Nightbreed or Resurrection Records . . . choice isn't really limited by living in Llandudno as long as you don't mind putting your faith in mail order.

Many, though, found mail order of less value for clothing than for music, as a result of practical difficulties, such as the inability to try things on for size and the costs of postage. As a result, travelling to visit specialist shops elsewhere was often preferred. The proprietor of Morgana, a well-known goth clothes store with branches in Wakefield and Leeds, explained that they were frequently visited from across the country (see Figure 7.1). She also explained that the company's mail-order service had proved a valuable translocal means of promotion, in that many customers who had initially ordered clothes by post had subsequently travelled to the shop in order to browse through the stock first-hand.

B3 (*female*): [mail order] has worked really well. It worked not only in terms of turnover, but also worked in terms of getting people down here and getting our name about. You know a lot of people that order something and then they'll travel to see us . . . we've had people up from London, the Midlands, Newcastle, Scotland, Wales – literally from all over the place.

Stores such as Morgana also raised their custom by running stalls at certain translocal goth events. Along with travelling to the shops themselves, such events were also a popular and useful source of a variety of obscure goth clothing. While she used mail order for music, the following respondent

Figure 7.1 Inside Morgana's specialist clothes store in Wakefield. (Photograph: P. Hodkinson).

regarded travelling to shops and events outside her home town of Bedford as crucial to developing her collection of goth clothes:

> S6 (*female*): I personally find mail order useless . . . except for music, for which it is indispensable. London is within easy reach for clothes . . . occasionally I get to other towns, most recently Leicester and Oxford . . . London sprees happen about once a month, otherwise I wait for gigs, Whitby, etc.

Like respondent S6, lots of goths relied to some extent on the subcultural retail stalls at goth events. These ranged from bands selling demo tapes and T-shirts at low-profile gigs to entire markets including subcultural retailers from across Britain, at big translocal festivals. In particular, the Bizarre Bazaar during the daytime at the Whitby Gothic Weekend regularly enticed most of the goth retailers I came across to hire a pitch. The Bazaar had become a key part of the festival for many participants due to the range of obscure subcultural items available in one place (see Figure 7.2). When asked to choose

Figure 7.2 Faithful Dawn/Dark Beat Records stall at the Whitby Gothic Weekend Bizarre Bazaar. (Photograph: S. L. Wainwright).

their three favourite aspects of the festival in the Whitby Festival Question-naire, 21 per cent included 'buying new clothes, music, accessories' as one of their choices (see Appendix, Table 2, p. 200). On the same questionnaire, in response to questions asking how they obtained goth clothes and music, 53 per cent selected 'gigs and festivals' among their three choices (see Appendix, Tables 5 and 6, p. 202).

Constructing Translocal Consistency

Specialist retailers continually provided goths with a relatively easy and reli-able source of additions to their subcultural appearance or music collection. As well as helping to generate and maintain the enthusiasm of participants, the pre-selection of items by a relatively small number of businesses reinforced the consistency and distinctiveness of a style which would surely have dissip-ated rather more had it been reliant entirely upon individual appropriations. As will be discussed in the following pages, goth retailers, through the way they and their customers operated translocally, played a particularly important part, alongside media, events and word of mouth, in the consistency of the goth style from place to place. However, they also contributed to subtle local differences.

It has already been suggested that subtle variations in clothes and music occurred as a result of the particular play-lists of local DJs or indeed the tastes of other influential individuals. Equally important in this respect were the particular items stocked by local retailers. In Plymouth, for example, a number of goths wore rubber and PVC clothes that they had been inspired to purchase as a result of the opening of a new fetish-wear shop in the city. As a result of the general lack of local goth-specific retailers, and the distance of Plymouth from major shopping cities, this retailer became one of the main sources of clothing for goths in the city. A number of respondents suggested that for this reason the Plymouth goth scene was particularly fetish-oriented:

> G4 (*male*): If you consider fetish wear – you know, very extreme – that's more common in Plymouth, because of Westward Bound [fetish shop] . . . Because there's no goth shops at all down here, if you want to buy bizarre clothes you have to go there and so people . . . went 'cool clothes to buy' and so they wore it and so naturally other people come along and think 'what do goths wear? Aha they go to Westward Bound'.

Such local differences should be placed into perspective, however. The distribution throughout Britain of general styles and, often, exact same items of clothing and music, whether through direct mail order, or via local retailers, played a significant part in the continuing consistency of the subculture from city to city and its distinctiveness, as a whole, from other styles. In relation to the above example, PVC and rubber clothing may have been of particular prominence among goths in Plymouth, but it had been sold by goth retailers, and worn by enthusiasts across Britain for some years prior to my research there. It is liable to have been the initial development of interest in this particular style, through translocal subcultural networks, that first prompted goths in Plymouth to regard a fetish shop as compatible with their scene. More generally, my observations revealed few significant differences between the record and clothes collections of goths in the three cities of Plymouth, Leeds and Birmingham on which the majority of my research was focused. In spite of perceptions of local differences by certain respondents, my overall impression, as already indicated, was that each city had a similar range of goth fashion and music tastes, broadly consistent with the themes described in Chapter 3.

While non-subcultural selections and adaptations made by individual participants were important to the development of the style, its translocal consistency was reliant upon the network of individuals involved in the production and retail of subcultural consumables, most of whom – as we have seen – were involved in the goth scene themselves. Bands – by the kind of music they recorded, the images they presented, and the merchandise they sold – could influence the general tastes of their translocal audiences and, indeed, those of other goth bands. Record labels, too, due to being labelled by themselves or others as goth, played a role in defining and constructing the boundaries of the genre through the particular bands they chose to work with, and the stylistic directions in which they sometimes encouraged or discouraged them to go. Because of the specialist nature of their music policy, some labels were regarded as guarantors of genre and quality and because of this, some goths religiously collected their releases:

C2 (*male*): These days, if it's on Apocalyptic Vision . . . then I usually like it.

The consumables stocked or recommended by goth-specific retailers, though, played perhaps an even bigger role in constructing the boundaries of inclusion and exclusion of the goth scene. If a band or album was included on the shelves of a well-respected subcultural record shop, or in the catalogues of a specialist mail-order retailer, its acceptability among goths throughout Britain and indeed further afield was liable to be significantly strengthened. As a useful example, a mail-order service known as Cheeky Monkey (1999), run by the well-known and influential organizer of the Whitby Gothic

Weekend, included under the title 'alternative, goth and credible' a number of 1980s chart recordings as well as goth music. As well as reflecting the existing nostalgic penchant of some older goths for such music, this move, in the context of a catalogue regarded by goths to reflect their tastes, is likely to have helped construct such music as generally consistent across Britain with being a goth. In similar ways, all goth retailers acted as subcultural gatekeepers. Furthermore, it was clear from a number of the interviews I did with retailers across the country, that they had considerable influence upon one another. If one goth-clothes store discovered a new supplier or clothing line which became popular, it was only ever a matter of time before similar items could be found in other goth stores across the country. Needless to say, this chain of influence within the network of subcultural retailers further cemented the translocal consistency of the overall goth style.

Shopping as Subcultural Participation

As well as being important to the ability of goths to develop their collections of subcultural goods, and to the construction of a translocally consistent and distinctive style, subcultural shopping was an important source of information about other consumables, sources of consumption, or subcultural events. Thus, if one purchased a goth CD on mail order, it usually arrived accompanied by flyers advertising other goth CDs, or forthcoming subcultural events. Furthermore, once on the mailing list of this company or any similar one, the consumer would be subject to occasional mail-outs containing such flyers. Similarly, goth retailers, as well as some general alternative record and clothes shops, tended to simultaneously play the role of information points, through displaying a multitude of posters and flyers advertising goth events, demo tapes, fanzines and even other retailers. As the owner of Resurrection Records put it:

> A3 (*male*): I think that in London it's helped to get a focal point for the scene, not just for people to come and buy things, but there's posters all over the walls telling people about gigs. There are times when I feel like an information post.

This notion of shops as a 'focal point' for certain groups of individuals is consistent with the findings of Sara Cohen (1991: 54) and Ruth Finnegan (1989: 275), both of whom emphasize the importance of record and/or music shops as centres of information and gossip for local music scenes. As Finnegan puts it: 'They [shops] were both formally and informally involved in the musical life of the area . . . they and their staff were part of local music networks . . .' (Finnegan, 1989: 277). The difference in the case of subcultural goth retailers was that rather than being oriented toward a diverse localized music scene, they tended to operate within and facilitate a specialist translocal subculture. Although the subcultural information on their walls tended to have a local or regional emphasis, most also promoted goth events, products and bands based elsewhere in Britain and further afield.

Shops played the role of focal points for the goth scene, not only through the information displayed on their walls, but also in providing a day-time social space for subcultural participants and, hence, an important setting for channels of word of mouth. One interviewee explained that the Morgana clothes shop in Wakefield was central to her learning about and then becoming involved in the goth scene. As well as offering a choice of pre-selected goth clothing, accessories, and fanzines, the shop became an important space for observing, learning and socializing. I noticed for myself a tendency for regular customers to drop into the shop for a chat, something which had enabled this individual to both take part in and learn more about the goth scene. It was all the more important in this respect because she was under sixteen and only rarely able to go out at night.

> R1 (*female*): I used to go into Morgana every Saturday because basically I had nothing else to do and I was just there observing people, what they were wearing, what they were doing, what they were talking about. And of course at that point I was too young to go out.
>
> PH: Yeah, because I guess most people . . . would see people in clubs and things . . . but I suppose the shop has lots of people in there all the time talking and stuff.
>
> R1: Because it's such a small-scene shop . . . they [proprietors] know most of the people that come in and so therefore I listened to the conversations and later on I joined the conversations . . . and people who came regularly got to know me and introduced me to more people and then I made friends with them.

Albeit in a rather more limited form, then, such shops offered the kinds of facilities available at events, in terms of a specialist social space and the provision of subcultural information.

More generally it was clear that, as well as operating as a means to an end, in terms of developing a personal appearance and offering subcultural connections, shopping was often a fulfilling subcultural activity in its own right. While almost always regarded by respondents as secondary to goth events, going shopping and hanging around in certain town- or city-centre locations in the daytime was sometimes – consistent with the general observations of

Rob Shields relating to shopping malls – an important group social occasion (Shields 1992a: 5). Often participants would meet up with one another by chance, while on other occasions group shopping trips were organized in advance. Most notably, in the same way that goths travelled in groups to events elsewhere, they sometimes organized trips to different cities with the express purpose of negotiating the subcultural routes through their shopping centres.

Though to a lesser overall extent than at goth events, identities were affirmed and subcultural friendships were expanded and cemented in the course of shopping trips. Considerable subcultural capital and, hence, social rewards were on offer because of the likelihood of encountering other goths, even if shopping alone. Individually and collectively differentiating between and selecting from a range of subcultural and potentially subcultural goods in the spaces in which they were sold were means by which shared tastes and individual differences were played out, as well as comprising a perfect way to demonstrate the depth and appropriateness of one's knowledge and tastes. Although they did not make the kind of effort they would have done for an event, many goths spent time dressing up in order to go shopping, something which maintained or enhanced their level of acceptance from their companions and enabled them to experience maximum group camaraderie. It also made them and their friends particularly visible to other subcultural participants among the crowds of shoppers. At the same time, the effort made with appearances served as a defiant means of collective differentiation from perceived outsiders to the subculture, who, given the constant movement between different subcultural and non-subcultural spaces, would be encountered far more frequently than in the course of a subcultural night out. Any receipt of abuse, though certainly not enjoyed, would ultimately serve as a rite of passage for newcomers, and a reinvigoration of defiant subcultural commitment and collective identity for established participants.

Conclusion

That the selling, buying and use of certain objects were critical to the goth scene's continual construction and facilitation is clear, I feel. Obtaining and displaying the right commodities was, more than anything, the key to subcultural capital, and hence to identity. An understanding of the sources of such consumables and the ways in which they were consumed is, therefore, central to any discussion of the facilitation and construction of such a subculture. In general terms, while the consumption so crucial to the goth scene cannot be regarded as entirely innovative or active, it embodied such qualities in part. It involved a mixture of the creative appropriation of objects from non-subcultural commercial sources and the somewhat less imaginative use of pre-packaged subcultural goods, which were often obtained from within the goth scene's own translocal networks. While neither indicates absolute authenticity, both are consistent with this book's notion of subculture. The consistent ways in which goths selected and used non-subcultural objects emphasized their commitment to a relatively distinctive set of stylistic subcultural themes. On the other hand, the increasing importance of clothes, accessories and music produced, promoted or retailed within essentially subcultural networks serves to emphasize the relative self-generation and, hence, autonomy of the subculture. Finally, going shopping was significant in providing goths with up-to-date information about other aspects of the goth scene, and often constituted a minor subcultural social occasion in its own right.

8

Communicating Goth: *'Traditional' Media*

Much subcultural theory has positioned media, like commerce, as part of the cultural 'mainstream' and hence external to subcultures. In some cases, theorists celebrated the initial spontaneity and authenticity of subcultures, which were deemed, essentially, to be outside and in opposition to media until their subsequent incorporation back into the realms of mass culture (Hebdige 1979). Meanwhile those who described the inadvertent strengthening of subcultures through the labelling effects of moral panics still located media in a negative relation to subcultures from outside (Young 1971; Cohen 1972). The notion of an essentially oppositional relationship between media and subcultures is also retained by those who cite societal saturation with the former as evidence for the redundancy of the latter as a concept (Redhead 1993: 5; Muggleton 1997). The possibility that media operating essentially *within* subcultures might play a positive role in the construction and facilitation of their substantive form is often rather marginalized by theorizing which, for the most part equates 'the media' with either a superficial mass culture or a fluid postmodern diversity.

The value of Sarah Thornton's work (1995) on the media construction of club cultures, in the removal of such an assumption and hence the assertion that subculture can retain relevance in a media-saturated society, is therefore considerable. Crucially, her insistence on the importance of media to the development of club cultures rests on a distinction between different forms of media. While detailing an important labelling and publicizing role for *mass*-media moral panics, she demonstrates that more specialist media simultaneously played positive roles in the construction of club culture. On the one hand, *niche* media, in the form of music and style magazines, are argued to have constructed a coherent subculture out of what was 'little more than an imported type of music with drug associations' (Thornton 1995: 158). On the other, even more small-scale specialist *micro* media, notably flyers and fanzines, are deemed to have been significant in distributing practical information about music and events. Through identifying these distinct roles,

Thornton is able to demonstrate that together, mass-, niche- and micro-media are crucial to the very existence of subcultures:

> Youth subcultures are not organic, unmediated social formations, nor are they autonomous grassroots cultures which only meet the media upon recuperative 'selling out' or 'moral panic'. On the contrary, the media do not just represent but participate in the assembly, demarcation and development of music cultures. (ibid.:160)

Though Thornton does not emphasize it herself, the importance of media is particularly apparent in relation to the translocal form taken by many sub-cultures. The spanning of geographical distance by such substantive groupings implies a particular dependence upon communications technologies – a point which surely applies as much to the supposedly spontaneous movements of the 1960s and 1970s as to those at the turn of the millennium.

Useful though her distinctions are, we will adapt Thornton's media typol-ogy, somewhat, consistent with the subcultural/non-subcultural taxonomy used throughout this book in relation to key elements of the goth scene. As before, the purpose is to differentiate between those elements and institutions of the goth scene which were relatively exclusive and autonomous (subcultural), and those oriented to a larger, more diverse market (non-subcultural). Importantly, the notion of subcultural media here implies those which operate largely within a single subculture, something which contrasts with Thornton's choice of the term 'subcultural consumer magazines' (ibid.: 155) to describe niche media which actually tend simultaneously to court a variety of different music scenes. Our concept of subcultural media is also rather more specific than the general notion of 'alternative media' which has been utilized by some theorists to describe a particular variety of non-corporate forms of communication (Atton 2002). Such distinctions are important, since the goth scene in Britain had become particularly reliant upon media forms which, as well as being small-scale, do-it-yourself and targeted, were essentially internal to a particular subcultural community. Specifically, the sharp decline in non-subcultural media coverage of goth music at the beginning of the 1990s was accompanied by an increasingly important role for printed subcultural media, discussed later in this chapter, and equally specialist forms of internet com-munication, discussed in Chapter 9. The growing importance of such internal media, produced and consumed by goths, further emphasizes the levels of relative independence and self-generation we have identified in relation to shopping and, even more so, to going out. First, though, we shall examine the roles played by past and present non-subcultural media coverage of the goth scene.

Consuming Non-Subcultural Media

It should be clear from the discussion in Chapter 6 that mass and niche media played a key role in the initial construction of the goth scene during the early to mid-1980s. In particular the niche-music press constructed and then re-emphasized the boundaries of the scene again and again through regular coverage of goth bands and their fans. Niche or mass-media coverage of the goth scene also played a role, throughout the 1980s, in the recruitment of new participants to the music, the style and the conscious sense of identity and distinctiveness which now accompanied them. For the following respondent, a *No. 1 Magazine* article around the middle of that decade, which he had photocopied and kept, was crucial to his initial discovery of the goth scene.[1]

PH:	What is the first thing you can remember about goth or anything like that?
S1 *(male)*:	Well actually that [indicates photocopied article] was one of my first references.

As well as publicizing the goth scene to potential recruits, the article he showed me contained numerous illustrations and provided lists of bands, types of clothes, hair styles and jewellery which were associated with the goth scene. As such it both constructed the boundaries of the subculture and facilitated recruitment. Many other respondents who discovered the goth scene in the 1980s suggested that mass-media coverage, in the same way as non-subcultural events, shops and friends, acted as an initial hook which triggered off the conscious search for less well exposed aspects of the goth scene. The following interviewees, for example, indicated the importance of television and radio coverage of goth bands during the 1980s:

L2 *(female)*:	Ooh, what was it called? What was that really cool music programme called? They had the Cure in concert on it. What was it called?
D2 *(female)*:	*The [Old Grey] Whistle Test?*
L2:	Yeah that was it – they had lots of stuff on.
D2:	There was also *The Tube* as well . . . they had live bands on.
D2:	I used to like the music anyway. I didn't actually know that it was goth. I used to listen to John Peel, in the evenings and I used to tape off the better stuff, that's how I first got to hear like The Chameleons and Alien Sex Fiend, and The Sisters of Mercy.

The point was also emphasized by the following responses to the Whitby questionnaire:

WQ7b: Please give details about what or who got you into the goth scene.

14 (*male*):   Seeing Sisters of Mercy on TOTP [*Top Of The Pops*] and Mission on radio.

16 (*female*): Heard a song by the Cure on television – bought the album and albums by related bands, then discovered the clothes.

In spite of the sharp decline in coverage from the early 1990s onward, occasional instances of niche and mass-media coverage, alongside occasional exposure of the goth style to society outside it in non-subcultural retailers or nightclubs, continued to constitute a potential link into the subculture for some would-be participants. While most respondents emphasized events and friends as the primary factor behind their recruitment, it certainly seems plausible that the occasional pictures, articles and information in general alternative and rock music magazines may have complemented the impact of interpersonal factors.

As well as being a recruitment tool, however, niche and mass-media appearances by goth bands seemed something to be collectively enjoyed and celebrated by those already enrolled. Contrary to Thornton's assertion that positive mass-media coverage is the 'subcultural kiss of death' (1995: 135), it seems, in small quantities, to have been something which generated further enthusiasm and strengthened the sense of identity of many goths. In spite of the fears they had of their subculture becoming over-popular, there was a certain pride in occasional displays to the general populace of the music and fashion so close to their hearts. Many interviewees were as keen to show off videos they had compiled of television appearances by their favourite bands in the 1980s as they were to dig out their old copies of music magazines.

Music-press coverage during the period of my research tended, as a result of its rarity, to provoke enthusiastic discussions among goths as to its degree of accuracy and its possible effects on their scene. Numerous threads of discussion on goth internet discussion groups focused on media coverage of the subculture. For example, an article in *Melody Maker* (Myres 1998) on the supposed return of the goth scene provoked the following post to a goth internet discussion group, prompting the expression of a variety of positive and negative opinions on the article and the chances of a revival for the subculture.

Subject: Melody Maker Goth feature
Melody Maker have devoted a whole page on Goth for the first time this decade. Very predictable but not a complete waste of space and does happily announce that "Goth is Back" with good plugs for Slimelight, Full Tilt and the Deviant Society. Either way, it's something to build on . . .
(Wilson 1998)

For some respondents, niche music-press coverage, as well as being a source of enthusiasm and debate, provided useful practical information about CD releases and gigs. The limited coverage of the goth scene in metal magazines such as *Kerrang!*, *Metal Hammer* and *Terrorizer* toward the late 1990s had attracted some goths to take advantage of the ease of finding and purchasing them, compared with more specialist fanzines, and to use them as a means of keeping up with what was happening:

> S7 *(female)*: There is the odd thing [article] like about the Sisters of Mercy or whatever . . . and you find out about concerts in the goth scene.

While most of its material was focused on bands which most goths considered to be metal, *Terrorizer* frequently emphasized goth influences in such music. In one issue, for example, it referred to the music of Moonspell and Type O Negative as 'Goth Metal' and 'Gothadelic' respectively (Tsarfin 1999; Tovey 1999). Apparently aware of the possible interest of goths themselves, the magazine had also begun to include a very small but regular section focused on recent CD releases associated with the more exclusive subcultural world of the goth scene. Knowledge of the tendency for some goths to read such magazines, alongside a hope that their products would appeal to other readers, also led some goth entrepreneurs to purchase advertising space in them, as in the case of a mail-order goth clothing business:

> A4 *(female)*: My boyfriend at the time always got *Terrorizer* magazine – which happens to be a hard-core metal magazine and . . . all the blokes in it wore gothic clothing, so we put a big ad in it – and it had a massive, massive response . . . that first advert was in a Marilyn Manson special, which helped.

Meanwhile, from the point of view of readers, another respondent explained that, for him, a variety of niche-music magazines had been a useful source of free posters with which to decorate his bedroom walls as well as an influence on his music purchases:

> G4 *(male)*: I did have like lots of posters from magazines and that on my walls . . . They [magazines] did influence me musically in that after reading them for a while you get to recognize reviewers' names and that. If they've reviewed an album you like anyway and they thought it was good, and then you see their name reviewing something else and they thought it was good then that's like a friend's recommendation.

Importantly, the role of non-subcultural media in terms of providing information and influence, provoking enthusiasm and facilitating recruitment also implies that such publications and broadcasts constructed what was included and excluded within the boundaries of the goth scene. Nowhere was this more notable than those articles which addressed the possible re-emergence of the goth scene as a whole. For example, an isolated *Melody Maker* article insisted that:

> Goth is back. Look over your shoulder: the shadows are stretching, darkness is encroaching and with it comes a mutated form of the human race. They dress differently, they talk differently and they group together in secret, hidden haunts. (Myres 1998: 23)

Alongside the inevitable photographs of goths, the text of such articles often selectively referred to, and hence reinforced and constructed, the consistent defining characteristics of the subculture. This can also be illustrated by an extract from an article entitled 'The New Black', which reported on a 'goth comeback' in the 'Lifestyle' section of *The Big Issue*:

> Look closer at the people out on the streets when the sun's gone down and you'll see how many have started painting the world black – nails, lips, eyes, and bedroom walls. Then layering themselves in black leather and lace and backcombing their hair . . . Pale faced kids with . . . acne poking through a layer of talcum powder. (Owen and Mitchell 1997: 31)

As part of the discussion of non-subcultural commercial producers in Chapter 6, I described a recent moral panic about the goth scene, in the British press, which had been triggered by the apparent connections to the subculture of those responsible for the Columbine High School shootings. We have already seen that, according to some traditional subcultural theorists, negative moral-panic-style mass-media presentations of subcultural groupings can inadvertently become self-fulfilling prophesies (Young 1971; S. Cohen 1972). While attacking their somewhat one-dimensional notion of 'the media', Thornton reproduces elements of moral-panic theories in her explanation of the media construction of club cultures. She argues that negative mass-media coverage of the Acid House phenomenon in the 1980s served to 'baptize' participation in club culture, to confirm its status as a genuine form of transgression and, hence, to strengthen the resolve of those involved and the attractiveness of the subculture to others (Thornton 1995: 129). On the basis of this, there are three main ways, perhaps, in which the goth scene might have been affected by its sudden public notoriety in relation to the school shootings. First, the notion of a self-fulfilling prophecy would suggest that the values of the subculture might have changed in accordance with its media portrayal as, among other things, racist and violent. Secondly, the strength of identity of existing members could have been enhanced due to a collective feeling of victimization. Thirdly, recruitment levels could have risen as a result of the general publicity and notoriety.

In relation to the values of the goth scene, there was little if any discernible movement, in Britain at least, toward the values or actions with which it was associated in the media during the year which followed the shootings. The long-term rootedness of the subculture's values, the extremity of the incident in question and, sometimes, the ability to dismiss it as a reflection of a perceived 'American culture', meant that participants in Britain distanced their subculture as far as possible from the shootings and the alleged values of its perpetrators. This can be illustrated by the widespread condemnation of the two killers and, indeed, of media scapegoating, on a British goth internet newsgroup, whose members expressed horror at the media's association of their subculture with the incident.

Subject: Re: US killings Rant rant rant . . .
After all Goth is a medium for free expression; killing people, no matter what the justification, is the ultimate form of counter argument to this ideal. Does any goth, anywhere, really derive pleasure for the knowledge that some school children were gunned down?
It is a shame, albeit very convenient for the powers-that-be, that American culture is unable (or unwilling) to question the free availability of fire-arms and seeks to blame any form of outsider for this atrocity. Am I the only one who can find some allegory in the racism that seems to have been connected with these murders and the need to blame anyone who looks or sounds different.
(Tudway 1999)

While there was no sense whatever in which the media association of the goth scene with violence and intolerance became a self-fulfilling prophecy, the incident did appear to reinforce the sense of collective identity of goths. It was apparent that their sense of being misrepresented and scapegoated by the mass media served to unite them and engender reinvigorated camaraderie. As well as discussing the accuracy and implications of the media coverage, many goths took it upon themselves to write to newspapers in defence of the subcultural lifestyle they so cherished. Consistent with elements of Thornton's observations, then, there was a sense in which, although its participants were horrified, the goth scene gained from the attention and misunderstanding. The collective dislike of a prejudiced 'mainstream society' – the perceived source of the injustice – was intensified and, with it, the defiant sense of identity they shared.

Also, the moral panic, through the sheer weight of publicity it and the niche-media reaction to it gave the goth scene, is likely to have contributed to recruitment. As well as making the subculture visible to an unrecruited audience, the disapproving moral tone may have attracted teens in search of an apparently rebellious identity. What is less clear, of course, is whether the original negative mass-media coverage, or the subsequent defensive articles in the niche-music press were most significant in this respect. As Thornton and McRobbie have pointed out, the critique of tabloid moral panics has sold numerous copies of 'alternative' niche music and style magazines (Thornton and McRobbie 1995: 190). On the whole, although this sudden mass- and niche-media coverage could hardly have failed to affect the goth scene, its impact, in Britain at least, was less noticeable than many (including myself) had expected. This was partly because, unlike with the continuous flow of religiously inflected moral-panic-style coverage in parts of the American media both before and after the shootings, British newspapers appeared to lose interest in the demonization of the goth scene after a few weeks.

The purpose of this section has been to emphasize the variety of particular ways in which non-subcultural media contributed to the goth scene as a cultural entity both prior to and, to a lesser extent, during my four years of research. In spite of their importance, the overall decline in niche- and mass-media coverage of the goth scene from the beginning of the 1990s served, ultimately, to increase the subculture's level of obscurity from society outside it, and its reliance upon specialist or subcultural media produced by and for subcultural insiders. As explained earlier, the media forms included in this category roughly correspond to Sarah Thornton's notion of 'micro-media', the definition of which is worth citing:

> Flyers, fanzines, flyposters, listings, telephone information lines, pirate radio, e-mailing lists and internet archive sites . . . An array of media, from the most rudimentary of print forms to the latest in digital interactive technologies, are the low circulating, narrowly targeted micro-media . . . (Thornton 1995: 137)

Increasingly, subcultural communication was taking place through the internet, something focused on at length in Chapter 9. However, the decline in mass- and niche-media coverage of the goth scene also had enabled fanzines, flyers, posters and mail-outs, all of which had existed from the very beginnings of the goth scene, to acquire a greater significance in the translocal facilitation and construction of the subculture. The discussion of subcultural print media, here, will be split into two parts, the first of which covers fanzines, and the second, flyers and posters. Essentially, we will examine the extent to which each media form should be considered subcultural, and investigate the role each played in relation to the survival and development of the goth scene as a translocal subculture.

Goth Fanzines

Marion Leonard, writing about the small-scale media networks of Riot Grrrl, usefully defines fanzines, or 'zines', as 'self-published, independent texts devoted to various topics including hobbies, music, film and politics [which are] usually non-profit making and produced on a small scale by an individual or small group of people . . .' (1998: 103). Preceded by early science fiction fan magazines and then overshadowed, in some respects, by the larger-scale 'underground press' associated with 1960s counter-culture, the growth of fanzines culminated in their well-documented part in the punk phenomenon (Sabin and Triggs 2000: 7, Atton 2002: 56). After that point, as well as continuing to be commonly associated with popular music, science fiction and politics, fanzines emerged as a key grass-roots means of communication among football fans. Chris Atton has rightly pointed out that the orientation, form and readership of fanzines is diverse and that consequently, the medium should not be regarded as subcultural by definition (2002: 57). At the same time, however, it is clear that a number of fanzines *do* take the form of subcultural media as defined in this book – that is – written by, about and for enthusiasts of the same substantive lifestyle grouping.

Thornton (1995: 139–40) rather plays down the significance of fanzines relating to club culture, arguing that most emerged after, and were overshadowed by, the extensive coverage of acid house in mass and niche media. This conclusion is consistent with the comparatively marginal role played by the numerous goth fanzines of the 1980s. With possible exceptions, including a publication called *Artificial Life* toward the beginning of the decade, such self-produced media were rather eclipsed by the far higher-profile niche-music press coverage of the subculture. The focus of this section, though, will be on the more crucial subcultural role played by mid- to late 1990s goth fanzines in the absence of extensive non-subcultural media coverage. As will become clear, such publications varied considerably in terms of regularity, longevity, content, circulation, numbers involved in production, and quality of printing. However, they shared a number of features which related to their status as subcultural media.

In spite of charging a cover price and, in some cases, generating revenue from advertising, significant financial profit from fanzine production was, consistent with the general findings of Atton, a poor prospect (2002: 59). Consistent with many other elements of the subculture, then, goth fanzines were edited and written by enthusiasm-motivated goths. Indeed they were an extremely participatory form of print media. The increasing ease of access to word-processing and photocopying technologies meant that almost anyone prepared to exert the considerable effort required could edit, print and distribute his or her own fanzine (Leonard 1998: 105). Thus, there were a multitude of small-scale, A5-size, black-and-white goth fanzines which often took a relatively personal tone. One example I came across was *Cyber Optic*, which consisted of approximately thirty A5-size pages of news, reviews and interviews relating largely to its author's own musical and stylistic preferences. However, as the costs of higher-quality printing were also declining, A4-size glossy fanzines had emerged, including *Kaleidoscope*, *Naked Truth*, *Meltdown*, *The Black Box*, *BRV Magazine* and its off-shoot *TombRaver*. Some of these had begun to draw a distinction between themselves and their more amateur-looking A5 counterparts by referring to themselves as magazines. They are

Figure 8.1 Selected goth fanzines: *Kaleidoscope* issue 9, *BRV Magazine* issue 22, *Tomb Raver* issue 25, *Meltdown* issue 7, *Gothic Times* issues 2,4,5, *Dawn Rising* issues 11,12,13 (Photograph: S. L. Wainwright). Fanzines reproduced with the kind permission of Faithful Dawn (Dawn Rising) and the editors of *Kaleidoscope*, *BRV Magazine, Tomb Raver, Gothic Times* and *Meltdown* [www.meltdownmagazine.com, PO Box 543, Beaconsfield, HP9 1WL].

referred to in this chapter, though, as fanzines because they were independent, voluntary, specialist and motivated by enthusiasm as well as having low circulations.[2]

Even the most high-profile goth fanzines, though, were highly participatory, in the sense that, although edited and produced by a very small number of individuals, a diversity of contributors were responsible for their content, particularly in the case of letters, poems, pictures, reviews or advertisements sent in by readers. The producers of the well-known fanzine, *BRV Magazine*, explained that articles were often sent to them without any prompting and that, in addition, they sometimes actively called for voluntary contributors:

J9 (*female*): We've got six regular reviewers at the minute and they all like different stuff . . .

PH: How did you get in contact with them?

S4 (*male*): They were subscribers anyway. They started sending stuff off their own bat. You know, they'd review stuff that they'd bought themselves.

J9: and then we put an advert in an issue saying 'wanted – music reviews, in exchange for free issues and free promo stuff ' telling them to send an example of their writing in.

Importantly, such fanzine contributors were usually geographically dispersed, both emphasizing and reinforcing the internal translocal connections within the goth scene. Though the fanzine was edited and printed in a single location, *BRV Magazine*'s regular reviewers, for example, lived in various locations across Britain and, in one case, in Hungary. Similarly, *The Black Box*, a professional-looking glossy fanzine based in Madrid, had regular reviewers of gigs and CDs based in Germany and Scotland. The latter contributor, who was brought up in Spain and moved to Scotland to attend university, explained that his involvement was initiated by himself when he was a reader of the fanzine:

M6 (*male*): I thought the people in Spain would be interested in knowing something about the gothic scene in Scotland, or in the UK in general, so I sent them [the fanzine] a letter saying 'if you are interested I can write about bands, interview bands, whatever you want' and they were very pleased.

The internal means of distribution of goth fanzines – and, hence, their audience – was also key to their description as subcultural media. Whether posted directly to subscribers, peddled at goth gigs and festivals (see Figure 8.2) or retailed in sympathetic clothes or record shops, they were rarely visible outside subcultural networks.

Figure 8.2 *Meltdown*, peddled at the Whitby Gothic Weekend. (Photograph: S. L. Wainwright) Publication reproduced with the kind permission of the editor of *Meltdown*.

With the exception of a one-off advertisement in non-subcultural metal magazine, *Kerrang!* and availability within a very small number of general 'alternative' record or clothes shops, *BRV Magazine* was confined exclusively to the goth scene. Its producers had rejected the idea of distribution via a chain-store newsagent due to the extent of their reliance on a small regular goth readership:

S4 (*male*): It just wouldn't work. Even if the [goth] scene did get bigger and a bit more popular again it's only going to be very short-term, and the costs of actually setting up a full-on distribution with a magazine and stuff for something that's only ever going to last about a year or two before the scene sinks back into the underground again . . . it's just not financially viable.

The implication of such lack of external availability was that to discover and purchase goth fanzines, one had already to be involved in subcultural networks. Outsiders were unlikely to know about, never mind attend, the subcultural retailer or festival at which they were displayed and sold, and even less likely to find out the relevant address to set up a postal subscription. Leonard makes a similar point in relation to the Riot Grrrl fanzine network:

> Acquiring the addresses of zines involves tapping into the informal friendship networks active within riot grrrl. Whilst some grrls produce contact lists, other addresses are printed in review sections of zines or enclosed with the publication in the form of small 'flyers' . . .
> (Leonard 1998: 106)

Unlike non-subcultural media, then, fanzines played little if any part in the recruitment of individuals to the goth scene. Far from being conducive to movement or 'flow' between groupings, as emphasized in notions of neo-tribalism and other postmodern-oriented theorizing, they emphasize the substantive, bounded form taken by the goth scene.

Furthermore, like the subculture itself, they operated translocally. While the readers of some smaller publications were concentrated in the same region as the fanzine's producers, larger fanzines reached widely dispersed subcultural readerships. The producers of *BRV Magazine* estimated that its sales spanned most of Britain and that, on top of this, approximately 15 per cent were exported to Europe, the United States, Australasia and South America, either by direct subscription or via small-scale subcultural record distributors. Similarly, the producers of Glasgow fanzine *Naked Truth* suggested that their base country of Scotland accounted only for a tenth of sales, and that a quarter of the remainder went beyond British shores.

> G3 (*male*): Next week we'll sell about a hundred at Whitby [i.e. to geographically dispersed festival goers], and then the subscribers ones will go out all over the world, and then we'll probably sell about two in Glasgow the week after!

The geographical dispersal of fanzines can also be illustrated from the point of view of readers. The following individual, for example, explained that as well as reading various fanzines from across Britain, she ordered some from the United States:

PH: Which fanzines do you get then?

S3 (*female*): I get Bats [*BRV*] and *Legends*, I did get one called *Blurred Victorian Child* . . . I do tend to get things like *Propaganda* as well, and a lot of the other American zines because it's nice to know what's going on over there as well.

Fanzines' status as specialist subcultural media, and their role in facilitating the substantive form taken by the goth scene, can further be illustrated by their content. In spite of differing from one to another in their precise focus, they rarely went beyond the blurry outer boundaries of the subculture's range of stylistic themes. *Cyber Optic*, mentioned above, took a self-consciously light-hearted approach and emphasized techno, industrial or 'cyber-goth' styles in which its producer was most involved. Other publications, such as *Crimson*, were dedicated to the interests many goths had in vampires. Meanwhile, some fanzines were targeted at the fans of particular goth bands. *Dawn Rising*, for example, was a free newsletter dedicated to and produced by the band Faithful Dawn as a means of promotion. Larger zines such as *BRV Magazine*, *The Black Box*, *Naked Truth* and *Kaleidoscope* were usually more inclusive in terms of content – covering a wide range of styles associated with the subculture.

The particular ways in which the subcultural content of fanzines served to facilitate and construct the goth scene as a subculture is a key concern in their discussion here. Most importantly, perhaps, they provided centralized specialist notice boards for the pooling of practical information relating to subcultural consumables, forthcoming gigs, festivals and CD releases. Although such information was often available on separate flyers produced by the organizers of such events or services, fanzines acted as subcultural filters, pulling together and co-ordinating a multitude of relevant information. Larger fanzines also sometimes included free compilation CDs, which enabled fans to sample for themselves the sounds of various bands, rather than relying on the views of a reviewer.

Importantly, such information, in line with fanzines' widespread circulation, tended to involve geographically dispersed subcultural events and products. The 'Gig Dates' section of issue twenty-four of *BRV Magazine* (1998), for example, included details of forthcoming events in London, Nottingham, Torquay, York, Birmingham, Bristol, Southampton, Sheffield, Newcastle Upon Tyne, Edinburgh, Derby, Blackpool, Morecambe, Leeds and Whitby in the UK, as well as goth festivals in Leipzig and Hanover in Germany. Meanwhile, the issue's CD reviews section involved globally dispersed artists and record companies from New Zealand, the United States, Belgium, Italy, France, Germany, Australia, Spain and Austria, as well as Britain. Through the provision of such translocal information, fanzines created concrete links between goth bands, businesses, promoters and of course general participants across Britain and further afield.

When asked how they found out about music and events, most respondents mentioned flyers, the internet and word of mouth as most important. However, fanzines were often mentioned as a partial factor:

> R1 (*female*):   Now I tend to read a lot more of the fanzines that people are producing. I basically go on recommendation really. If a fanzine recommends something then I'll bear it in mind and if I hear more people saying they like it as well then I'll buy a CD.

That fanzines played a significant informative role in these respects was clearly beneficial not only to consumers but also to those providing the music, commodities or events who were able, through such internally targeted media, to reach their highly specialist, geographically dispersed market. The vocalist of goth band Manuskript linked coverage in the goth scene's internal network of fanzines with his band's early development, particularly in terms of their being asked to play outside their immediate locality. He compared his band with other student bands who, due to the lack of equivalent subcultural media infrastructure, remained local and largely unsuccessful:

> M5 (*male*):   There were people writing fanzines, and we could get gigs at other places, and it took off in a very small way– getting your name about in a few fanzines and doing gigs in other places. For a band that's only really been going for a year and can't really play properly, the chance to go off and do some gigs in towns far away is quite exciting . . . while all the other student bands were just knocking about at university and not doing anything . . .

In something of a circular fashion then, goth enthusiasts were able to use the information in fanzines to get the most out of the translocal goth events and products available, which increased the chances of success for those responsible for producing or providing such services. This in turn contributed to more and possibly better music, events or clothes becoming available and greater numbers of individuals becoming involved in their production and distribution.

Fanzines also helped construct the values of the goth scene. They had the ability, to some degree, to reinforce or alter the tastes held by their readers and to define the boundaries of the subculture they came to represent. This was partly because, due to their insider status and specialist content, they tended to have considerable subcultural credibility (Thornton 1995: 137). As the following respondent from Plymouth put it:

S1 (*male*):   Fanzines are not watered down, they're pure goth. You know you are going to get a decent read and that it's going to be about things that you want to read about.

Although fanzine readers, like any other media audience, inevitably brought their own experiences, tastes and viewpoints to their interactions with the publications, the general credibility of such media meant their content was liable to exert some influence over at least a proportion of their readership.

Most notably, they played the role of gatekeepers. Whether they were praised or lambasted, the fact that particular events, bands, images, books or films were deemed zineworthy was potentially influential in itself. Furthermore, some fanzine readers were in positions of influence themselves, and liable to pass on their agendas. One DJ said specifically that during a year in which he was unconnected to the internet, fanzines became his main way of keeping up to date with new goth music. Given the importance of DJ playlists in shaping the tastes of participants (see Chapter 6), fanzines can be regarded in this case as having a potential indirect effect on the tastes of non-readers as well as those of readers themselves. I probed the producers of *BRV Magazine* about the ways in which they decided what kinds of music to include in their reviews section. Their reply usefully reveals some of the ways in which judgements were made and boundaries drawn:

S4 (*male*):   The thing I've told record companies is, 'if it's melodic, if it's musical and it's got vocals that you can see that they are remotely vocals then we'll do it, but anything that's just noise with people grunting over the top just goes in the bin' . . . There is a lot more mainstream stuff that is getting a lot darker . . . we had Tour of Satana in the last issue . . . she does look quite gothy . . . and then we've got Stream – they've got a goth background . . .

They accepted that such decisions about inclusion and exclusion, in such a subculturally well-respected fanzine, were liable to be influential:

J9 (*female*):   It has a big role because it's a central point for all the reviews, gig dates, current interviews, where people discover who they like and who they don't. You have to be careful what you put in because to a certain extent you can influence the gothic community as a whole . . . you're in a position where you have a bit of power I guess.

While the potential agenda-setting influence of large fanzines such as *BRV Magazine* was of most significance here, smaller, more taste-specific publications also played a role. The producer of *Cyber Optic*, for example, revealed that he had hoped to introduce more humour into the goth scene by including it in his fanzine:

M9 (*male*):   When I started up properly I rounded up some other zines and discovered most goth rags were sadly lacking in humour and frankly most of them were rather dull. I suppose I wanted to show people that being a goth didn't mean you had to amputate your sense of humour.

He also hoped that *Cyber Optic's* particular focus on bands claiming to merge traditional goth styles with elements of dance music would influence readers. While such influences were increasingly accepted by some within the goth scene, it seems likely that the coverage would indeed have functioned to further legitimize this aspect of the subculture.

As well as influencing subcultural agendas and boundaries, fanzines played a role in maintaining and generating enthusiasm and interest for the goth scene. Reading them allowed individuals to feel involved and up to date with their subculture from place to place. Such knowledge was a potential source of considerable subcultural capital for those in possession of it. The following respondent, though, suggested that in addition to any importance in terms of status, fanzines enabled her, as a fan, to indulge her genuine curiosity about the bands she liked:

PH: So what is the appeal of fanzines then?
R1 (*female*): You know the gigs that are coming up and everything . . . and also, this sounds very teeny [ie. teeny bopper], but you get interviews with the bands and everything – and it lets you find out more about the people who are doing it professionally and stuff – it's just interesting.

Finally, the best-known fanzines functioned to reinforce the translocal sense of shared identity within the goth scene. Their exclusiveness to the subculture and their construction of a common agenda meant that, abstractly, they connected their geographically dispersed goth readers with one another through their common consumption of the publication. Consistent with Benedict Anderson's well-rehearsed argument that early print media functioned to construct 'imagined' national identities in the past, it is clear that, on a smaller-scale, the accessibility of more and more advance forms of such technology enabled goth participants, in the absence of external media interest, to produce fanzines which helped construct and reinforce the translocal sense of community which characterized their subculture (Anderson 1991). As Atton has put it, in relation to the medium in general terms, 'fanzines can . . . activate or establish a community' (Atton 2002: 54). In this respect and the others described, fanzines contributed internally to the ongoing generation of the goth scene as a committed, distinctive and relatively autonomous cultural entity. However, it would be mistaken to overestimate their centrality to the construction of the goth scene. Although most read them occasionally, and their content was often passed on indirectly through DJs, bands, promoters and word of mouth, only a minority of my interviewees were avid, regular fanzine readers. In general terms, as more and more individuals gained internet access, fanzines were beginning to be eclipsed by the more instant interactive forms of communication offered by such technology. Furthermore, as a direct source of practical information, fanzines were probably of less overall significance than posters and flyers.

Goth Flyers and Posters

While fanzines constituted independent subcultural commodities in their own right, the sole function of flyers and posters was the direct promotion of events, record releases or businesses. Even during the period when the goth scene received extensive non-subcultural media coverage, flyers remained a crucial means of letting a specialist clientele know about local gigs or regular nightclub events too small-scale to make it into the pages of the music press. Since the decline in niche-media coverage of goth, the importance of flyers and posters extended to almost all goth events and, indeed, to some of its subcultural retail operations and record labels. While still crucial to the local advertising of events, we shall see that flyers in particular had also become translocal media. Arguably they were the most effective source of practical subcultural information in the goth scene, whether viewed or received in pubs, in shops or through the post.

Goth flyers and posters constituted subcultural media due to their highly specialist audience targeting. Most overtly, they functioned to select a largely subcultural audience through the pictures, symbols and information about music which they included (see Thornton 1995: 112). Most flyers for goth events, products or services emphasized the term 'goth' and often other genres or subgenres which goths were known to like or whose fans were known to be sympathetic to goth, such as 'industrial', 'darkwave' and sometimes 'alternative'. It was generally understood that, in spite of the mention of such additional genres, the stipulation 'goth' anywhere on a flyer tended to indicate, more than anything else, the orientation of the night. After all, few people but goths themselves would emphasize such a marginal genre. In addition, flyers or posters for nightclub events targeted their clientele by naming live goth bands, listing examples of the recorded music played, and occasionally naming individual DJs.

Figure 8.3 Selected goth flyers. With thanks to their producers. (Photograph: S. L. Wainwright).

While the content of flyers and posters played an important role in inform-ing the audience of the musical or stylistic orientation of an event, the most important factor in their targeting was the selective ways in which they were displayed and distributed. Thus, in the local area of the event concerned, flyers would be given out and posters displayed in pubs and clubs whose clientele consisted largely of goths. Sometimes potential punters were targeted even more explicitly, by distributing flyers selectively to individuals, on the basis of their appearance. Posters and flyers were also placed in particular local subcultural record or clothes shops and non-subcultural stores known to be popular among goths. Although the content of the flyers usually ensured that few non-goths would turn up, their presence in non-subcultural niche record shops was an instance of exposure of information about goth events outside the internal networks of the subculture. For the most part, though, events were advertised exclusively to local goth enthusiasts, through attempting to catch their eyes during their day- and night-time routes through the city (Thornton 1995: 141). This strategic positioning of flyers is illustrated in the account the following promoter gave of the ways he advertised a regular nightclub in Birmingham:

K3 (*male*):   We just spent about two months fly-posting every other [goth] night everywhere in Brum [Birmingham] . . .

PH: Where did you put [the flyers], what sort of places?

K3:   . . . years and years ago all the goths used to hang about outside the Virgin Megastore – that used to be like the in place on a Saturday afternoon . . . everybody used to congregate there – so we put loads of flyers there.

Although lots of flyer and poster advertising was weighted towards goths who lived in or close to the town or city concerned, they were increasingly distributed further afield. In the case of events deemed likely to attract travelling clientele, they were sometimes sent to sympathetic subcultural producers based in other cities who would distribute and display them at their own particular event or business or, if particularly enthusiastic, throughout the goth routes in their areas. This often tended to be confined within a few regions within reach of the event. One of the promoters of The Wendy House, a monthly goth club night held in Leeds, indicated he had generated such a regional network of flyer contacts:

K1 (*male*):   For the Wendy House more and more people will travel up, because we advertise it everywhere. I've got flyer contacts in York, flyer and poster contacts in – you know its all this goth network thing around the North . . . you just send loads of flyers to people and just expect them to give them out!

PH: It sounds like its mostly a regional thing, rather than being national or international?

K1:   Yes, we've tried to get people from London and stuff like that but it's going to mainly be people from roughly our region.

As well as being placed in regular events and shops in other areas, flyers and posters were distributed by promoters at goth festivals. Such events provided access to a large specialist group of people who had travelled from elsewhere and, hence, might be willing to do so again. The value of such a large, captive, translocal audience explained the barrage of flyers for events, products and businesses all over Britain which one was liable to encounter at goth festivals. Flyers were also distributed translocally by post, using lists of addresses volunteered by interested individuals at events or via e-mail. Often, those promoters or bands without their own mailing list were able to get their flyer included in the envelopes sent out by those who did have one, in return for a reciprocal favour of some kind. For example, it was common for fanzines mailed to subscribers to be accompanied by numerous flyers. As one fanzine reader from Plymouth explained to me:

S1 (*male*): You generally find that fanzines . . . you open them up and half a million
leaflets fall out . . . I get so many leaflets for bands that are playing in
London.

Even more so, perhaps, than targeted local means of flyer distribution, such
mailing lists functioned to facilitate the participation of an already initiated
subcultural audience rather than to induce the recruitment of newcomers.

The low costs and potential for precise subcultural targeting of posters
and, especially, flyers made them important means of distribution of subcultural information. The ability of the target audience to pocket flyers and
refer to their information later, as opposed to remembering or copying down
details, also contributed to their effectiveness. As a means of direct promotion,
then, they were a crucial practical facilitator both for the participation of
individuals and for the promoters or proprietors of events and services whose
exploits were more likely to be successful. Alongside fanzines, then, this medium
also formed a key part of the contribution of subcultural participants themselves to the general survival of their subculture.

Conclusion

Emphasis on the importance of various kinds of non-subcultural media
coverage to the initial development and subsequent recruitment to the goth
scene during the 1980s serves to avoid the trap of regarding it, or indeed any
other subculture, as somehow spontaneous, authentic and independent. There
is no necessary inconsistency between the important roles played by such
external media coverage and the defining criteria of subculture emphasized
throughout this book. The second section of this chapter, though, has begun
to establish a separate point, that the goth scene was increasingly reliant upon
its own autonomous forms of subcultural communications. Fanzines, flyers
and posters produced by goths for goths played a crucial role in the facilitation
of event attendance, the promotion of subcultural commerce, the generation
of enthusiasm and the forging of concrete translocal links within the
subculture. As well as further demonstrating the degree of participation by
goths in the survival and development of their own subculture, this emphasizes
the invisibility of elements of the goth scene from outside society. In contrast
to suggestions that media saturation might result in the destruction of substance and community, the case of the goth scene begins to demonstrate that
certain forms of media can play a critical role in the development and survival
of the most committed, distinctive and autonomous forms of collective
identity. We shall see in Chapter 9 that, contrary to some expectations, this
point held every bit as true for the internet as it did for off-line media.

Notes

1. According to the respondent, this article appeared in *No. 1 Magazine* in 1986.

2. For example, the editors of one of the highest-profile British goth fanzines, *BRV Magazine*, estimated a circulation of approximately 2000, while *Naked Truth*'s editor said his well-known fanzine's figure was closer to 400.

9

Communicating Goth: On-line Media

We are struck, as we use the internet, by the sense
that there are others out there like us. (Jones 1997: 17)

Having established the significance of the goth scene's network of printed media, the focus now turns to the role played by on-line communications in the facilitation of the subculture, as more and more of its participants gained access to the internet and became what were known to some insiders as net.goths. If the appropriateness of my description of fanzines, flyers and posters as relatively autonomous subcultural media was reasonably uncontroversial, my insistence that the internet might also have enhanced the autonomy and substance of the goth scene may, at first, appear more open to question. After all, as well as being linked with the most large-scale and powerful of commercial interests, the internet is accessed every day by millions of diversely oriented individuals around the globe. In his famous work *The Virtual Community*, Howard Rhinegold emphasizes the potential of the internet to bring the most diverse of individuals into 'a world in which every citizen can broadcast to every other citizen' (Rhinegold 1994: 14). Referring to Usenet's network of on-line discussion forums in the singular as 'arguably the world's largest conversation' (ibid.: 130) he argues the case for conceptualizing the net as a mass medium: 'It is a mass medium because any information put onto the Net has a potential worldwide reach of millions' (ibid.: 130).

Meanwhile, for those of postmodernist persuasions, the diverse yet fluid nature of the internet accelerates the breakdown of boundaries between established social categories and, hence, the fragmentation of individual identities and stable communities (Poster 1995; Turkle 1995). Sherry Turkle describes a 'culture of simulation' characterized by the ability to 'invent ourselves' by moving freely between an infinite number of potential identities and, indeed, playing out several at any one moment in time (1995: 9–26). In relation to this book's notion of subculture, such a perspective implies that groupings such as the goth scene would have their distinctiveness, commitment, identity and autonomy thoroughly dissolved by the ability of individuals to move from one virtual affiliation to another on a mouse-click. Consistent with this, Marion Leonard suggests that on the internet, 'the ease of accessing any site disrupts the concept of underground community' (Leonard 1998: 111). In line with more general postmodernist interpretations of contemporary culture, then, the implication is of the melting if not the evaporation of cultural and subcultural boundaries by a mass medium which offers a taste of everything to everyone.

In practice, however, the use of the World Wide Web and on-line discussion groups by goths couldn't have contrasted more with such a picture. Far from distracting them into other interests or dissolving the boundaries of their subculture, the internet usually functioned, in the same way as goth events, to concentrate their involvement in the goth scene and to reinforce the boundaries of the grouping. The key general point here is that regardless of the number of individuals on-line, the internet does not, in practice, function as a singular mass medium but rather as a facilitating network which connects together a diverse plurality of different media forms. Some of these are widely used and well known, as in the case of web sites associated with already established media or commercial organizations, while the vast majority are smaller-scale specialist sites and discussion facilities, many of which associated with particular interest communities or subcultures. Crucially, the technical ability to engage with each specialist culture represented on the web does not mean that anyone is likely to do so. Furthermore, the means by which websites and discussion groups are accessed can have the effect of clustering them together by subject matter and of encouraging users to pursue existing interests rather than to discover new ones. It is through elaboration of this key point that we may begin to understand how websites and discussion groups related to goth were more a part of the overall subcultural infrastructure of the goth scene than they were a part of any all-encompassing, fluid internet culture.

Goth Web

World Wide Web searches I conducted on the word 'goth' always resulted in pages and pages of relevant sites, the vast majority of which seemed directly related to the goth music and fashion scene in which we are interested. These goth sites ranged from personal homepages, to promotional devices for particular goth bands or businesses, to general subcultural information sites. In spite of the huge potential audience and the apparent ease with which they could have been accessed by anyone, the practical reality was that the users of goth websites tended to be involved in the goth scene. This is because more than any other medium the World Wide Web requires users to choose in advance what to view. As a result, the chances of stumbling accidentally upon specialist sites without any prior interest are rather slim. Thus, while keyword searches were an efficient way of guiding existing goth participants and initially interested potential newcomers to a wealth of material on the subculture, they were hardly likely to result in non-participants accessing goth sites by chance. Similarly, hypertext links enhanced goths' ability to navigate precisely between subcultural websites, but not their chances of contact with non-subcultural content or individuals. Put simply, the vast majority of links to goth sites were located on other goth sites, something which meant that, collectively, they formed a specialist and relatively auton-omous sub-network. Furthermore, there were certain particularly well known sites, such as *Darkwave*, which acted as nodal points directing users to a variety of useful subcultural resources in the sub-network (*Darkwave*, accessed 2000).

This goth web was connected more closely to other elements of the subculture – both on- and off-line – than it was to non-subcultural parts of the web. Further exclusive 'links' to goth sites, then, were provided in the form of addresses included on printed subcultural flyers, fanzines and CD inlays and transferred from one goth to another in conversation, whether face to face, over the telephone or via personal e-mail. In addition, URLs included as part of e-mails to the goth discussion groups comprised a part-icularly important means by which websites were accessed because they usually appeared in the form of active hyperlinks. A number of interviewees said that links in the body of discussion group e-mails were an important way in which they discovered new websites:

> B2 (*male*): I find that a lot of the links that I follow do tend to be links that have been advertised on UPG [*uk.people.gothic* newsgroup].

All these modes of access, of course, required a clear prior involvement in the goth scene, both in terms of coming into contact with the information and having the motivation to use it. Although hard to prove empirically, then, the weight of logic suggests strongly that most users of goth websites were already interested in their themes.

Similarly, the ability to decide for themselves what content to view tended to mean that the leisure-time web use of goths themselves, consistent with their commitment to the subculture in other ways, tended to be particularly concentrated on goth sites. Many goths in the late 1990s would surely have identified with the following respondent's explanation of her keenness, when she first gained access to the internet, to investigate its goth-related contents:

> M8 (*female*): When I first went to [university] they said 'oh yes, the internet is a wonderful new research resource you can use, go and find all these sites about anthropology', and I was like 'sod that!' and typed in 'goth' and wahey!

To differing degrees, all respondents also used non-goth sites in their leisure time, from on-line newspapers or comics, to railway timetables, to on-line gaming. However, all who were asked about it said that such additional uses were less frequent than those related to the goth scene.

> M8 (*female*): the goth stuff tends to be something which you do every day, and the other stuff tends to be every now and again.

As well as functioning as yet another illustration of the practical commitment of goths to their subculture, the specialist web-use of individual goths, alongside the relative obscurity of goth pages to most outsiders, clearly emphasizes that such sites were consistent with the relative autonomy of the grouping rather than antithetical to it.

The conceptualization of goth websites as subcultural media is further reinforced by the involvement of most of their producers in the goth scene, whether the sites were personal home pages or promotional devices for subcultural events or products. The availability of free web space was conducive to considerable grass-roots participation by goths in the construction of their subculture. The ability to create as well as consume subcultural media without paper, scissors, photocopying, envelopes or a cover price led a high proportion of net.goths to create their own sites. As a rough illustration, in January 1999, out of 366 goths who left details on one respondent's website map of British goths on the internet, 156 had indicated they had their own web pages (*Net.Goth Map*, accessed 1999). Inevitably, only a relatively small number would become well known among goths, but there remained the potential for anyone to reach a significant translocal audience. Posting links to a new site on a goth newsgroup or mailing list, for example, was an effective means of encouraging potentially interested visitors. Having advertised my own hastily cobbled together website on a goth e-mailing list, I not only found that its number of visitors trebled in the following days, but that some months later, other goths on the list had placed links to my site on their own. Therefore, as well as being largely used by a specialist audience, goth websites also gave individual participants the potential to involve themselves in the construction of their subculture.

Goth Discussion Groups

The most significant aspect of the internet for most goths and, therefore, the construction of the goth scene as a whole, was not in fact the World Wide Web, but discussion facilities such as Usenet newsgroups and e-mail lists.

> P1 (*male*): It's mainly mail and newsgroups . . . for us, I only use the web if I want to go and find something.

Preceded by various academic and government conferencing systems in the 1980s, both newsgroups and e-mail lists consist of an ever-developing pool of posts on various issues (threads) to which any subscriber can add his or her own contribution. In other words, they are far more interactive than most websites, allowing ongoing all-to-all communication. The first goth newsgroup, *alt.gothic*, was formed as an international, though in practice largely American-centred forum, in the early 1990s. A few years later, as the number of subscribers and posts increased, British goths formed a smaller, national group known as *uk.people.gothic*. More recently, a number of e-mail lists emerged, based on the goth scene in particular areas of Britain and Ireland. Examples included *Contaminatii* and *Tainted* (both for England's West Midlands), *Mancgoff* (Manchester), *North Goths* (North of England), *Scotgoth* (Scotland), *Iegoth* (Ireland), and *Tarts* and *Sluts* (both for London).

Subscribed to by goths, and highly participatory, these newsgroups and mailing lists, even more so than goth websites, were subcultural media. Notions of Usenet as a singular mass-mediated conversation among millions (Rhinegold 1994: 117) or a meta-community (ibid.: 121) simply weren't borne out by this example. Rather, the distinct and separate nature of goth discussion groups fits in to Hill and Hughes's point that facilities such as Usenet function to reinforce existing beliefs and affiliations rather than fundamentally to change attitudes and that, as a result, they 'tend to draw people into isolated groups, conversing among themselves' (Hill and Hughes 1998: 73). Those who accessed goth newsgroups or mailing lists, then, were liable to do so as a result of a prior interest. It was possible for outsiders to find out about them, through Usenet's listing of groups for example. However, the likelihood of an individual without an initial interest subscribing to a mailing list with 'goth' in its title was surely only slightly higher than that of the same person deciding to spend the evening in a goth pub as a result of having coincidentally walked past it. Conversely, the following respondent, who was a member of the subculture, said that as soon as he found out about Usenet, the first thing he did was to search for and join a goth group:

> J11 (*male*): A friend told me about newsgroups. I looked to see if there was a goth one, and there was – it went downhill from there!

It seemed even more common, though, for respondents to learn directly about particular goth discussion groups through off-line word of mouth with other goths.

> V1 (*female*): My experience [of discovering *uk.people.gothic*] is that I got told about it from someone else who got told about it from someone else who got told about it from someone else.

In the unlikely event that a non-goth *did* subscribe to a goth discussion forum, however, the chances of their persevering for long were also relatively faint, due to the specialist and exclusive nature of discussion, and the tendency for mistrust and hostility towards outsiders. The ways in which internet communities tend, in the words of Hill and Hughes (1998: 69), to 'vigorously and successfully defend their electronic boundaries' has been a key concern of the growing body of literature on discussion-group-based, computer-mediated communities (see Jones 1995, 1997, 1999, 2000; Smith and Kollock 1999). Nessim Watson, for example, describes ways in which the norms and relations of an on-line group of Phish fans were informally regulated via responses from established members. In particular, Watson emphasizes the role of flaming – the practice of sending aggressive messages, either to an individual's e-mail address or to the whole group – as a means of controlling the behaviour of newcomers and excluding outsiders (Watson 1997). Consistent with this, the posting of inappropriate or ill-informed messages by those not sufficiently socialized into goth discussion-group norms was liable to result in being flamed. While sometimes goths found themselves on the end of such treatment, it was particularly effective in excluding perceived outsiders:

> M8 (*female*): Anyone who's not really interested in goth and just starts posting loads of crap usually gets told to sod off.

A less direct but equally effective means by which the content of discussion groups was regulated occurred when particular messages or individuals were completely ignored by other members of the group. The following respondent explained that when he was a newcomer to *uk.people.gothic*, he found it hard, initially, to get anyone to respond to his messages because he had not learned what sort of topics and modes of behaviour people were interested in:

B2 (*male*): I made the big mistake of not finding out about UPG [*uk.people.gothic*] before posting to it and I made a least three posts before reading the FAQ and everyone completely ignored me for a week.

If the passer-by, in my previous analogy, did decide to enter the goth pub out of curiosity, it seems likely that the music and decor of the building, alongside the clothing, body language and stares of other clientele, will have created a specialist and exclusive atmosphere and made the individual feel uncomfortable. Consistent with this, in the virtual space of a goth discussion group, having one's comments ignored, receiving directly hostile replies and generally feeling unable to participate in the specialist conversations was potentially just as effective. It is, of course, possible to *lurk* on discussion groups, without disclosing one's presence to the rest of the group. However, while many goths did spend time learning the conventions of such groups before they began to take part properly, it is not at all clear why an uncommitted outsider would have wished to spend his or her time doing so.

As well as being even more internal and exclusive than goth websites, discussion groups were more interactive. As Rhinegold (1994: 130) rightly observes, 'every member of the audience is also potentially a publisher'. There is no need, therefore, to advertise one's contributions to ensure they are read, as in the case of a website, because subscribers will automatically receive the message. Any goth with net-access, then, was able to express opinions, request information, or promote events, services or websites to a specialist subcultural audience. Of course, just as certain websites became well known, some discussion group members developed a particularly high profile. The maintainer of a prominent goth-scene information website suggested that this had raised his profile on goth discussion groups:

D3 (*male*): because I provide information . . . it has the side effect that people tend to pay a lot more attention to my opinions in posts.

However, the fact that certain individuals commanded more attention than others did not stop anybody, through his or her on-line social skills or merely the subject matter of his or her posts, from having on occasion significant influence or, indeed, developing a more permanent reputation over time.

Enhancing Subcultural Participation

Goth websites, then, and, even more so, newsgroups and e-mailing lists, contributed to and illustrated the autonomy and self-generation of the goth scene through their relative exclusiveness and their high levels of participation. Crucially, rather than leading to the replacement of an off-line lifestyle with an on-line one, resources and forums on the internet functioned to facilitate the subculture as a whole through providing specialist knowledge, constructing values, offering practical information and generating friendships. In particular, due to being more up-to-date, more interactive and easier to access than fanzines, goth on-line resources became more and more significant in comparison to their printed counterparts, during the course of my research.

First, various kinds of socially valuable subcultural knowledge could be gleaned from the internet. In-depth details about particular bands, for example, could be obtained from either official or unofficial sites dedicated to them in part or in full. For example, as well as offering practical information on gigs and releases, Faithful Dawn's official website offered a history of the band, several photographs and a section detailing the current music tastes of the two band members (*Faithful Dawn* site, accessed 1999). More independent e-zines, such as *Gothicland*, meanwhile, offered a range of articles on goth bands, clubs, fashion and various other aspects of the goth scene (*Gothicland*, accessed 2000). A number of Frequently Asked Questions sites were designed to provide basic knowledge to potential newcomers to the goth scene. The *alt.gothic FAQ*, for example, offered a definition and history of the goth scene, giving examples of past and current bands, acceptable styles of clothing, pictures, and links to other useful sites (*alt.gothic FAQ*, accessed 2000). Newsgroups and e-mailing lists also offered subcultural knowledge, opinions and values. Through reading and taking part, one might learn about new developments in goth tastes or behaviour, or gain the latest knowledge about goth bands. The following post to *uk.people.gothic*, for example, enabled readers to be 'in the know' by informing them of the recent split of a goth band. Though the news was quickly passed on to subscribers of other goth groups, many without net access were unaware of it for some time.

Subject: The end of Nekromantik (sob weep etc)
Go and look at the web site if you didn't already know, all the explanations are there apparently. Really shit to lose one of the few 'goth' bands that actually looked to be going anywhere.
(Sneekybat 1999)

In addition to satisfying genuine interests, up-to-date knowledge was important to the development of individual subcultural capital, whether in relation to the impressiveness of music collections and personal appearance or merely through the ability to hold one's own in conversation with other goths.

However, the material and opinions included on websites and discussion threads also played a role in the overall construction of subcultural shared tastes and values. On frequently asked questions sites, even the most thorough, open definitions overtly constructed the translocal boundaries of the goth scene and are liable to have been particularly influential for those newcomers toward whom they were often targeted. In the following short extract from the *uk.people.gothic FAQ*, particular hairstyles and items of clothing and jewellery are specifically established as suitable for late 1990s goths:

> Goth fashion changed subtly [in the 1990s], with crimped hair, high ponytails and combat trousers from the Grebo/Crusty scene, long straight hair, velvet and lace from Victorian Horror, leather and rubber wear from the fetish scene, hair bunches, zip tops and hooded tops from techno. There is also a slow take-up of tattooing and piercing . . . By far the most popular goth fashion item remains skintight black jeans.
> (*uk.people.gothic FAQ*, accessed 2000)

Just to be clear, the point is not to assess the accuracy of such accounts, but merely to emphasize that by what they chose to include and exclude, they played an important gatekeeping role in reinforcing and developing the value system of the subculture.

The interactions on discussion forums are also liable to have affected perceptions of the scene's boundaries of inclusion and exclusion. Discussions about bands and items of clothing were common. The positive mention of artefacts in question by even one or two subscribers was sometimes sufficient to establish their acceptability within the subculture, even if they were not appreciated by all. In a particularly good example, the growing acceptability of male goths wearing certain kinds of skirts was reflected, and thus reinforced in a discussion on the *Contaminatii mailing list*. Below is an extract from one of the contributions:

> Re: Skirts on Blokes
> I quite like blokes in skirts – not the 'HEY LOOK AT ME – I HAVE A PVC MINI SKIRT ON' style but more subtle longer skirts can look quite good.
> Thought [name] looked quite swish in his long skirt at Whitby. Not very keen on blokes in very short, tight mini-skirts . . .
> (Hemming 1999)

If it was important for communicating knowledge and constructing subcultural tastes and values, the internet played an even more crucial role in providing everyday practical information to goths. Via discussion-group threads or relevant web pages, up-to-date details could be obtained about forthcoming events, CD releases, retailers or fanzines. Respondents emphasized that on-line information tended to be more accurate and up-to-date than was the case for even the most reputable of fanzines. Although some websites did become out-of-date, others had developed particular reputations for containing the very latest subcultural information. One site, *Helix*, had become particularly well known and trusted for providing regularly updated information about goth and 'goth-friendly' clubs and events across Britain (*Helix*, accessed 1997–2000). The author of the site explained that, as a result, much of the information had started to be posted in by promoters and bands themselves, something which further enhanced the site's accuracy:

> D3 (*male*): When it first started all the information I got was people saying 'I've found a flyer that says this'...these days I'd say that at least half...comes either from the bands themselves...and from the promoters.

Nevertheless, it was discussion groups that were the most important on-line source of information for British goths. For this reason *Helix*'s maintainer complemented his website by posting regular events updates to the newsgroup *uk.people.gothic* and to subscribers of his own e-mailing list. Event promoters, bands, record labels and retailers also made announcements about events or services on discussion forums. In the example below, a message to *uk.people. gothic* provides information about the opening of a new branch of a well-known goth clothes shop in London. The information is passed on by a prominent goth promoter:

> Subject: A new Black Rose emporium in Camden
> Apologies if this has already been mentioned, but...
> The Black Rose, London's prime outlet for clothing of the goffick variety, will shortly open a new branch in Camden. The new Rose (ha!) will be located in the Stables Market, i.e. at the top end of the market area, beyond the railway bridge. (Johnson 1999)

It was also common for participants specifically to request information on discussion groups, something which invariably resulted in a positive reply. One request on the *Contaminatii* group, for information about the forthcoming Whitby Gothic Weekend, resulted in several replies, including one which included the entire line-up for the event. The maintainer of *Helix* explained that subscribers to newsgroups and mailing lists were unlikely to avoid receiving such information due to the regularity of their participation in the groups. In illustration of the point he used the example of his regular posting of information about the Whitby Gothic Weekend:

D3 (*male*): Every single net.goth in the UK knows that Whitby happens and they know exactly what date the tickets go on sale and every single week they have it drummed into them by Helix.

Information posted to newsgroups became even more effective, from the point of view of promoters, if it managed to spark off discussion among subscribers. For example, the aforementioned request on *Contaminatii* for information about the Whitby Gothic Weekend prompted another subscriber to ask which list members were likely to be going to the event. Below is one of the responses:

Subject: Re: Whitby
Let's see . . . Me, [name], [name], [name], [name] . . .
the 20+ other Cov people who [name] has sold tickets to, and [name] from Leicester, [name] from Bristol . . . And a few I've forgotten. Last year's ticket shortage seems to have scared people into deciding early . . .
(White 1999)

A collection of individuals enthusing in such a way about their intentions to attend an event was liable to attract far more additional people to it than a non-interactive, impersonal advertisement from its promoter. The interactive nature of such forums enabled something of an on-line equivalent of 'word of mouth' to take place. Its advantage over its traditional face-to-face equivalent, though, was the size of the audience for each contribution. Its effectiveness in terms of encouraging attendance at events was pointed out by one subscriber to a goth mailing list as part of a discussion about the large number of messages the list was getting:

Subject: Re: Toreador on Saturday
I *like* reading lots of posts about things that are going to happen. It gets me excited, and makes me look forward to things more. It also serves to make me jealous when I don't go to events, and therefore gets me off my backside more.
(Harvey 1999)

Another important reason why many relied upon discussion forums as their source of information about events and clubs was that, as well as finding out what was going on where, there was a chance of arranging to meet up with fellow subscribers at the venues concerned. Gaining new contacts and friends with whom, ultimately, to socialize off-line was another important aspect of interactive on-line communications within the goth scene:

> J11 (*male*): I have met many people on the net. First by e-mailing them and then arranging to meet at gigs etc.

In particular, some found online introductions easier than approaching people in goth clubs:

> P1 (*male*): I mean . . . she's made a lot more friends . . .
> B1 (*female*): Yeah, people who I never would have spoken to . . . because in real life I'm too shy. It's a good icebreaker – you get chatting to them without you having to be face to face. You can find out about them.

While, for some users, interactive goth discussion groups constituted forums for the full playing out of subcultural friendships, for many others, interacting on-line was regarded predominantly as a facilitator of off-line socializing:

> B2 (*male*): I don't count posting to *UPG* as socializing! Posting to *UPG* and *Contaminatii* is in order to organize and meet to socialize. Socializing to me is about face-to-face stuff.

The new goth friendships enabled by on-line interactive communications not only increased the attraction of continuing to take part in goth discussion groups, but also provided further incentive for participants to attend 'real-life' goth events. The following interviewee explained how this worked for him and his friends:

> P1 (*male*): We'd have a lot less nights knowing where people are [without the internet] because people post and say 'well I'm going out' and you think 'well I haven't seen so and so for a long time so I'll go out'.

The fact that the specialist information, collective enthusing, and on-line friendships facilitated by the internet encouraged attendance at goth events was the most significant contribution of the medium to the goth scene in general. Given the capacity of events themselves to encourage further participation, it is clear that the internet formed a key link in enhancing participants' practical commitment to the subculture. More generally this very effectively illustrates Wellman and Gulia's point that, rather than spelling the end of face-to-face interaction and community, on-line technologies can function to complement and enhance off-line social activities and affiliations (Wellman and Gulia 1999: 170). Far from being a separate social or cultural entity, the internet consists of a range of resources used to enhance, facilitate and complement distinct lives and affiliations off the screen (Kendall 1999: 60).

Worldwide Goth?

It has been emphasized at various points during this book that, thanks to a mixture of subcultural travel, commerce and communication the goth scene provided a clear illustration of Ulf Hannerz's point that small cultural group-ings need not be narrowly confined in space (Hannerz 1996). As one might expect, the internet played an important part in the translocal connections within the subculture, enabling the instant transfer, across any geographical distance, of highly specialist information, knowledge, views and conversation. In a similar way to fanzines, sites on the World Wide Web offered details of releases and tours of goth bands based in countries across the world. Mean-while, official band sites and CD retailers offered the opportunity for globally dispersed fans to purchase CDs and merchandise directly by credit card. There was also a fully international list of goth clubs organized under the names of towns, cities, countries and continents (*International Goth Club Listing*, accessed 2000). Clicking on the name of a club connected the user to further information, sometimes in the form of the relevant promoter's own site.

Such facilities clearly enhanced the ability of goths with internet access to find out what was happening in the goth scene in those areas of the world in which it had manifested itself. In particular, those participants able physically to cross national boundaries used websites to find congregations of goths in otherwise unfamiliar countries. The British information on *Helix* was fre-quently accessed by non-British goths intending to visit the country, something illustrated to its author when, to his delight, he came across a Danish goth in London with a print-out of his site:

> D3 (male): The best thing of all was when I was running around in London shopping and some chap from Denmark came up to me and he said 'excuse me I'm trying to find this place' and he had a bit of paper and it was a print-out from my web site, and I was well impressed. He'd printed it out in Denmark and brought it with him to England.

Non-British goths visiting the country also used *uk.people.gothic*, to find out practical information about goth events. The questionnaire respondent below, from the United States, had relied upon the forum to find out about the Whitby Gothic Weekend:

> WQ1b: How did you get information about the Oct '97 Whitby weekend?
> 46 (*male*): Endless babble on UPG transfers over to America . . .

As well as constituting a resource for those already intending to visit different countries, the discussion about high-profile events on newsgroups sometimes prompted transnational travel among those receiving it. Large-scale events were sometimes attended by goths from outside Britain, specifically in order to meet up with transnational friends made through discussion groups and personal e-mail. An e-mail interviewee from the United States illustrates the point:

> C3 (*male*): Virtually all 'goth contact' I have is with people outside of my [local] community... In fact, I came to the Whitby Gothic Weekend as a vacation to meet many people with whom I'd been corresponding [on-line] for years.

It seems reasonable then, to conclude that many such individuals would have had less incentive to travel internationally were it not for the internet.

As well as facilitating international travel, the connections created by websites and discussion forums are liable to have contributed toward greater transnational consistency of the values and tastes of the subculture. For example, the definitions of the goth scene provided on high-profile goth sites, such as the *uk.people.gothic* and *alt.gothic* FAQs, tended to be relatively consistent with one another. Equally important, though, was the potential transnational influence created by a multitude of smaller sites, as well as international conversations on discussion groups and, of course, the trans-national travel they encouraged.

In spite of the potential for any participant with an internet connection to access all manner of subcultural material, resources and individuals from around the world, in practice the goth scene did not approximate a globalized 'village' or community. While the technological potential for everyday inter-national communication was utilized by some individuals, the majority of British goths seemed to focus their internet use rather more precisely. First, language differences ensured that much foreign correspondence engaged in by British goths was liable to be concentrated on English-speaking countries. More importantly, because the net was used largely as a facilitator for particip-ation in goth scene off the net, users tended to seek information which was of most practical use in this respect. Consequently they sought to find out about events they were able to attend, and to interact with individuals with whom face-to-face contact was a realistic possibility. While they seemed to recognize the potential of international information and conversation for those able to travel abroad regularly, most respondents did not have the time or money to do so, and hence focused their internet use on the British goth scene.

> B2 (*male*): It's one hundred per cent UK events and UK people really... I've visited Swiss and German web sites and I speak a bit of German... but really I'm only interested in the UK scene.

PH:	Why is that?
B2:	Foreign language and I haven't got the money to go there.
V1 *(female)*:	But I mean of course it would be very useful if we wanted to go on holiday to Madrid, and we wanted to go to a goth club in Madrid . . . but since we haven't got the money to do that there's no point.

Using the web as a means to participate in the 'real-life' goth scene, then, meant that British respondents tended to use websites such as *Helix* and *Darkwave*, and discussion groups such as *uk.people.gothic* in preference to their international equivalents. The material was liable to be more relevant and, in the case of discussion groups, there was a smaller number of messages to sift through and a greater likelihood of getting to know fellow subscribers. Due to its smaller subscription base, *uk.people.gothic* was more cohesive than *alt.gothic*, and enabled each individual poster to gain the attention of others:

P1 *(male)*:	In *alt.gothic* you're going to get a couple of thousand messages a day, *uk.people.gothic* you're going to get less people, so people will read more. It's a smaller group, you get more coverage, more people will actually read your messages and they'll have more time to answer it.

If its role as a connector between nations was somewhat limited, the internet played a key role in enabling dense translocal communications within the subculture across Britain. This came across clearly when I asked the following interviewee what, for her, was the most important effect of the internet on the goth scene:

M8 *(female)*:	I think it's created much more inter-city socialization and the ability – its easier to go to places and meet people and go to events and things and you know, not feel so intimidated by – because you're likely to know people and stuff.

Most notably, then, on-line communications contributed to the cycle of translocal friendships and intercity travel described in Chapter 5, and in turn, the consistency of goth values and tastes across Britain. The feasibility of travel within the country meant that the information, the on-line enthusing, and ease of arranging somewhere to stay the night encouraged participants to travel out of their localities to attend goth events. In particular, a desire to meet up with translocal subcultural contacts made on the internet provided an extra motivation.

Whilst groupings such as *uk.people.gothic* or websites delineated as national were of most obvious importance in enhancing translocal travel, individual local e-mail lists also played their part, through enabling groups of local enthusiasts to arrange collective day or night trips with maximum ease. In the example below, the author is enquiring, on a British West Midlands list, about a possible trip to a club in Leeds:

> Subject: Wendyhouse
> it's rumoured that brumites [Birmingham people] are going. Who are you and what is in the boot? will [name] fit in?
> (Hobberstad 1999)

Local lists were equally useful for those intending to travel *to* events in the area they covered. In the following message to the *Contaminatii*, the author requests a place to stay the night for some goths travelling from Manchester to attend a forthcoming goth gig in Birmingham:

> Subject: Dream Disciples
> Seeing as a bunch of the mancgoffs seem to have acquired a strong liking for road-trips, we will be descending on Brum for the Dream Disciples gig . . .
> Now, the traditional request, anyone got any falling over space that we could impose upon? If I can persuade people, we'll be down on the Friday for clubs and stuff before heading north on Sunday.
> (Amison 1998)

It was equally common for goths visiting certain towns or cities within Britain to request and receive information about the goth scene in their destination area, whether on *uk.people.gothic* or the relevant local mailing list.

On-line translocal contact and the travel it facilitated and encouraged, then, made a clear contribution to the concrete connections between goths from different areas of Britain and, as a result, to the translocal consistency of the subculture. What may come across as rather less expected, however, is that the internet was also used by goths as a means of enhancing their localized, day-to-day subcultural participation. It has recently been argued that, while it can certainly be used to 'connect with people and cultures in faraway places' the internet also enables users to 'find out about one's neighbour and events in one's own municipality' (Sanderson and Fortin 2001: 191). Although focused on highly specialized material and individuals rather than local communities in any general sense, goth e-mailing lists designated as local or regional were otherwise consistent with this point. Even to the most ardent of translocal night trippers, they provided a useful way to communicate regularly with local goth friends, to find out about low-profile events nearby, and to arrange to meet up with one another. For many, such lists had become as important as *uk.people.gothic*, a particular attraction being the frequency with which one was liable to meet other subscribers face to face:

PH: So is the local list more useful to you then?
B1 (*female*): Yeah
P1 (*male*): Its because there are more people that you know on it . . . you can talk to them on- and off-line, it's a good thing.

The greater relevance of a high proportion of posts to local mailing lists, due to the ease of meeting fellow subscribers at the local events discussed, gave them a unique value.

At the same time, though, such local lists did not stop people from involving themselves in regular translocal communications. The following respondents explained that the two served different purposes and that, as a consequence, they used both:

B2 (*male*): I subscribe to *UPG* to find out what's going on in the country and *Contaminatii* to find out what's going on in the West Midlands.
V1 (*female*): I'm the opposite, I mostly read *UPG* because it's a lot wider spec.

Furthermore, certain individuals subscribed to several different local mailing lists, some of which were supposed to be focused on areas hundreds of miles from where they lived. Often this was because they had visited such areas and made goth friends there. As a result of such multiple subscriptions, it was common for information and discussion on one group to spill over onto others, and indeed for the subscriber-base of each 'local' list to extend well beyond its intended area. This meant that in spite of their use in terms of facilitating everyday provincial participation, local and regional lists were very much part of a national subcultural network.

A Temporary Sub-Subculture?

As explained, goths tended to use the internet as a means to enhance their general participation in the goth scene. It was increasingly significant to their level of commitment to and attachment to the subculture off-line. Nevertheless, the shared experience of taking part in the goth scene on the internet had led, to start with at least, to the positioning of those involved as something of a sub-group within the subculture as a whole. Most overtly, their self-description as net.goths demonstrated a consciousness of affiliation, not only to the translocal goth scene, but to a particular on-line sub-group. The term net.goth was even specifically defined on newsgroup FAQs. Although most participants themselves might have used wider definitions, the version associated with *uk.people.gothic* read as follows: '"net.goth" is now applied to anyone who frequently posts to uk.people.gothic, aus.culture.gothic or alt.gothic, and a strong sense of community has grown up around this Internet culture' (*uk.people.gothic FAQ*, accessed 2000). This 'sense of community' was particularly obvious during the late 1990s when, at large-scale translocal events such as the Whitby Gothic Weekend, subscribers to *uk.people.gothic* wore net.goth badges displaying their e-mail pseudonym to identify themselves to subscribers who had not, as yet, seen one another in the flesh.

The sense of identity was also manifest in practice, in that interactions on the net were complemented by a tendency to socialize with fellow net.goths in off-line situations.

> P1 (*male*):   How many people can we say that we know now that aren't on the net, barring [name] and [name]?
>
> B1 (*female*): But that's barring all the ones I was going to mention!

It was clear that using the goth scene's online facilities, whether in terms of individual friendships or general discussion groups, gave net.goths a shared set of experiences – something which sometimes resulted in cliquish behaviour at events and clubs:

> M1 (*male*):   Net-goths are a clique, no matter how much they deny the fact. Naturally there are people who span both worlds, and I'm not saying that the rest are associating only with other net.goths consciously. But it's a natural thing to get together in real life with people who you've had a conversation with via the net. It's common ground.

Although they incorporated a similar range of appearance and music-related tastes and values to those of the subculture as a whole, goth discussion groups also involved certain on-line norms and values distinct from those of the subculture as a whole. As I was to find out when I first came into contact with them in 1997, although it remained extremely important, acceptance or veneration in the goth scene in general terms was not sufficient, in itself, to fit in with net.goth discussion groups. It was also necessary to gradually learn specific on-line codes of behaviour. Factors such as the extent of one's ability effectively and appropriately to express oneself on-line, and the perceived subcultural quality of one's personal website, became additional sources of subcultural capital, or the lack of it. Occasionally then, individuals who, due to their appearance, might have been regarded as low in subcultural capital were able, through the perceived subcultural quality of their on-line behaviour or achievements, to become veritable celebrities among net.goths.

> D3 (*male*): I believe there is such a thing as a net-celebrity – someone who . . . because of their behaviour on-line . . . they are more important than the average person on the net.

However, internet access throughout Western societies has increased at an astounding rate during the late 1990s and beyond. As more and more goths gained access to the internet, whether from home, work or university, the distinctiveness, both perceived and actual, of net.goths as a subgroup started to become less and less marked toward and beyond the year 2000. Rather than being something which made one distinctive, use of the internet was becoming a normal aspect of participation in the goth scene. As a result, the notion of being a net.goth became less significant and instead, an ever-increasing proportion of goths had their participation enhanced and intensified as a result of the resources, information, ideas and friendships on offer. The role of the internet in the general construction and facilitation of the goth scene, then, seemed liable only to increase in importance.

Conclusion

In relation to the goth scene, on-line media functioned as subcultural, in that they were produced and used mostly by goths, or interested potential goths, and obscure to most outsiders. As well as contrasting with general suggestions that media induce the disintegration of substantive cultural groupings, this raises important questions about suggestions that the internet operates as a singular mass medium or a separate 'virtual' world. The way in which goth on-line media operated made them more comparable to small-scale communication forms such as fanzines, flyers and word of mouth than to television, tabloids or even the music press. Nevertheless, their interactive potential and capacity for the rapid and ongoing translocal transfer of data meant that, as the proportion of goths using them multiplied, they became more effective and important than their off-line equivalents in the construction and facilitation of the goth scene.

In general terms, the role of the internet in relation to the goth scene provides further evidence of the consistency of the grouping with all the indicators of subculture outlined in Chapter 2. That goths so often chose to concentrate their leisure-time internet use on specialist subcultural material provides us with yet another illustration of both their practical commitment and their strength of identity. Furthermore, the knowledge, information, friendships and enthusiasm provided by these goth websites and discussion groups played a direct role in enhancing the intensity of participation and sense of belonging of their users. Although its transnational effects may have been limited, the internet, more than any other medium, increased both electronic and face-to-face contact between goths from different localities and, in doing so, enhanced individuals' sense of their subculture as translocal. Such connections also served to reinforce the consistency of the subculture's distinctive range of tastes and values from place to place, particularly within, but also outside of Britain.

The role of such exclusive subcultural media in enhancing the three defining characteristics of identity, commitment and consistent distinctiveness also serves to emphasize its consistency with the fourth. The importance, to the translocal facilitation and construction of the goth scene, of media produced and used predominantly by goths, illustrates the relative autonomy of the subculture. Far from disrupting the notion of underground community, a translocal network of specialist, interactive forms of communication, operating as an increasingly important part of a general subcultural infras-tructure, underlines the contemporary relevance of such a metaphor.

10

Concluding Thoughts

In spite of the obviousness of the goth scene's distinctiveness and group identity, I was impressed, at the start of the research on which this book is based, by theories which rejected the notion of subculture, in order to emphasize the rather more partial and temporary nature of contemporary affiliations. Four years on, I remain sure that lifestyles and groupings characterized by considerable fluidity and multiplicity are increasingly prevalent throughout consumption-oriented Western societies. Notions such as neo-tribalism, as developed by Maffesoli (1996), Bauman (1992a, 1992b) and, later, Bennett (1999), may prove useful in understanding such trends where they apply. However, as my subjective interest in the goth scene was transformed into an in-depth research project, it became ever more clear that, although this grouping embodied elements of diversity and ephemerality, it was far more notable for traits which indicated greater levels of cultural substance.

This level of substance has been illustrated by a range of research data throughout this book, in relation to the four key indicators outlined at the end of Chapter 2. First, we have seen that the goth scene was characterized by a set of values and tastes which, although diverse and changeable, were sufficiently distinctive and consistent, from time to time and place to place, to enable participants easily to differentiate insiders from outsiders. Second, the majority of participants, during the time of their involvement, shared a translocal sense of affiliation and collective distinction, which tended to be prominent in their overall sense of identity. Third, while it did not account for all their practical activities, the grouping tended to dominate the leisure time, consumption habits, social lives and internet use of its members for a significant period of time. Fourth, without being in any way isolated, the 1990s British goth scene operated *relatively* autonomously. In spite of the continued role of certain external goods, services and businesses, we have seen that the key interdependent practical elements of the goth scene – events, consumables and media – were often produced by and oriented toward goths. Forming something of an interconnected subcultural infrastructure, such specialist products, services and spaces often served to limit the frequency with which goths came into contact with lifestyles and groupings outside their subculture. In more general terms, they played a highly significant role in facilitating the aforementioned distinctive values, shared identity and practical commitment, thus emphasizing the *relative* self-generation of the goth scene.

Through offering a redefinition of the concept of subculture based on the indicators of relative distinctiveness, identity, commitment and autonomy, this book attempts to provide a means for conceptualizing the goth scene and other elective groupings characterized more by their substance than by their fluidity. In so doing, it avoids the over-generalization of superficiality, mean-inglessness and the breakdown of substantive groupings which, in different ways, characterizes theories of mass culture, of postmodernism and, sometimes, of fluid collectivities. At the same time, it avoids a tendency to regard localized face-to-face cultural practices, identities and communities as the only possible example of small-scale, substantive cultural groupings in an otherwise media-saturated world. Rather than proposing a new subcultural theory as an equally sweeping alternative way of conceptualizing society, though, the intention has been to clarify and, hence, place limits upon the use of the term, without being over-prescriptive. The suggestion is that alternative terminology, notably the notion of neo-tribalism, might also be clarified and limited, in order to describe and understand those contemporary lifestyles and affiliations, which, in contrast to subcultures, *are* fundamentally ephemeral and partial.

While retaining the term it provided us with, this book also avoids key problems with traditional subcultural theory, particularly its Birmingham School incarnations. In particular, this book's conception of subculture does not rest upon spontaneous expression of shared structural contradictions and need not involve any other form of symbolic or direct 'resistance'. While it is certainly conceivable that they may apply in certain cases, external political goals or effects were less important, in the example of the goth scene, than the desire to feel distinctive and to belong to a community. Furthermore, rather than being entirely reliant upon 'authentic' processes of mutual gravitation or spontaneous reaction, the goth scene was and always had been thoroughly reliant upon media and commerce in a variety of forms. Consistent with elements of the work of McRobbie (1989, 1994, 1999) and Thornton (1995), it is a key finding of this research that the involvement of profit motives and communications media can be highly conducive to the cultural substance deemed here to characterize subcultures. Meanwhile, partly thanks to the involvement of specialist media and commerce, it is clear that substantive forms of affiliation such as the goth scene can take an interconnected and consistent translocal form.

While I have often stressed the levels of cultural substance which embodied the goth scene, the book should not be taken as a celebration of the subculture or the form it took. In spite of my obvious emotional attachments as an insider, the intention has been to avoid moral judgements relating to the possible virtues or drawbacks, to participants and to society as a whole, of subcultures as compared to more fleeting forms of affiliation. Aside from my emotional attachments as an insider, there *were* particular characteristics of the goth scene which I became particularly impressed by; most notably, the extreme creativity of some goths as consumers, the levels of insider participation in the facilitation and construction of the subculture, the relatively high levels of gender equality and the partial transgression of boundaries of gender and sexuality. Equally, however, I often found myself somewhat frustrated with the boundary-drawing which was engaged in by many goths and the resulting tendency for a degree of narrow-mindedness towards fashion, music, individuals and cultural groupings deemed incompatible with the subculture. In some respects, perhaps, such pros and cons reflect more general debates over the social desirability of substantive communities, whether in relation to ethnic, sexual, national, local, political or leisure-based forms of affiliation. In all these types of community, the higher the level of overall substance, the greater will be the prospect of meaningful identity and fulfilment, active cultural or political participation, independence from external control and transgression of norms. Equally, however, it would seem that as substance increases, so does the rootedness of each community's alternative set of norms and the strength of the boundaries and exclusions they give rise to.

Though they may warrant more specific attention in future research or theory, though, such judgements about moral advantages and disadvantages are perhaps of lesser overall consequence, in the context of this particular piece of work, than the lessons I hope that it might provide toward an understanding of the ways in which particular elements of contemporary consumer societies can work. Whether celebrated or decried, for example, the case of the goth scene clearly shows that various forms of commerce and off- and on-line media can be conducive to substantive translocal cultural groupings. Similarly, the detailed account of the processes through which, in a society characterized by increasing instability, most goths came to reject multitudes of fleeting affiliations in favour of a single intensive subcultural lifestyle, provides an important contribution to social understanding, regardless of whether such a choice of lifestyle is deemed virtuous. As a final example, whether or not their efforts are deemed morally worthwhile, descriptions of the considerable control exercised by goths over the facilitation and construction of their subculture make an important contribution to crucial debates over the general potential for grass-roots agency and active participation in contemporary society.

Moving briefly onto some methodological reflections, the decision to conduct in-depth, multi-method ethnographic research of one grouping rather than more superficial accounts of several should enable confidence in the findings of this book relating to the British goth scene. If nothing else the project has convinced me that it is better to achieve a thorough, detailed and cross-verified understanding of one grouping than to rely on a far less well-grounded account of several. While it would be odd if all goths thoroughly agreed with my every observation and argument, I would hope that the largely positive implications of my position as critical insider within the project might add further weight to them. Nevertheless, there are inevitable limitations to the scope of my conclusions. As well as being based on a particular grouping, the findings described in this book are largely focused upon a particular country and a particular period of time. Whether the levels of cultural substance I unearthed in the case of the late 1990s British goth scene would be replicated in a study based on the United States or mainland Europe remains open to question, as does the extent to which the translocal British goth scene will survive and retain its subcultural form in years to come.

Such limitations in terms of breadth, however, are more than compensated for, in my view, by the depth and quality of knowledge provided by the long-term focused ethnographic approach. Although its acknowledgement is important, the specificity of my case study does not somehow render the levels of affiliation, commitment, consistent distinctiveness and autonomy which characterized the late 1990s British goth scene entirely peculiar to it. The mixture of malleability and clarity offered by this book's reworking of subculture and, indeed, its development of a conception of translocal, should hopefully make them useful for future researchers, whether as suitable descriptors for the groupings they focus on, or merely as yardsticks for comparison and contrast.

In respect of future work, I would stress in particular that acknowledging the need to examine individual negotiation and movement between different affiliations should not lead to an abandonment of research which is focused on the workings of particular groupings. I would especially encourage further research, not only on other examples of subculture, as defined here, but also on translocal and media-facilitated forms of community in general terms. Further development of the growing body of literature on virtual communities would clearly be an important part of this, although such research needs to do more to place the analysis of on-screen interactions in the context of off-line practices, identities and facilitating institutions. Consistent with this book's reworking of subculture, I regard it as important both to outline and account for the levels of substance or fluidity of different communities and, particularly, to investigate the extent of their relationship with both on- and off-line forms of media and commerce. Though other valuable criteria may emerge, my hope is that a focus on levels of consistent distinctiveness, shared identity, commitment and autonomy may provide a useful starting point here.

Appendix: Quantitative Questionnaire Results

These tables show those results from quantitative sections of the October 1997 Whitby Festival Questionnaire which are referred to directly in the text of the book.

Table 1. Social Profile of Respondents

	%
1.1 Age	
16–20	19
21–25	40
26–30	35
30+	6
(valid cases 109, data rounded to nearest valid per cent)	
1.2 Gender	
Male	51
Female	49
(valid cases 109, data rounded to nearest valid per cent)	
1.3 Occupation (based on Std. Occupational Classification – categories merged)	
Managers/Administrators	11
Professional/Associate Professionals	24
Clerical/Secretarial	3
Personal & Protective Services	3
Sales	4
Plant/Machine Operators:	3
Unemployed:	12
Students (undergraduate and postgraduate)	39
(valid cases 99, data rounded to nearest valid per cent)	
1.4 Ethnicity	
White	97
Other/mixed	3
(valid cases 107, data rounded to nearest valid per cent)	

Table 1. Social Profile of Respondents *(continued)*

	%
1.5 Do you live with a partner or spouse?	
Yes	33
No	67
(valid cases 109, data rounded to nearest valid per cent)	
1.6 Do you have any children for whom you are responsible	
Yes	9
No	91
(valid cases 109, data rounded to nearest valid per cent)	

Table 2. Attractions of Whitby Gothic Weekend

WQ2a – What, for you, are the most important attractions of the Whitby Gothic Weekend?

Respondents invited to rank their top three choices from a list of fourteen (including 'other'). Table shows percentage of respondents selecting each option as their first choice and then percentage selecting each option somewhere among their three choices. Table shows most popular options.

Attraction	Proportion selecting option as 1st choice %	Proportion selecting as either 1st, 2nd or 3rd choice %
Social atmosphere	43	68
Safe environment	2	10
Seeing particular favourite bands	5	20
Live goth music	14	38
Making new friends	9	32
Romance/sex	3	10
Seeing old friends	13	42
Dressing up	3	25
Buying clothes, music, accessories	4	21
Large goth discos	2	17

(valid cases 109, data rounded to nearest valid per cent)

Table 3. Travelling to Events

WQ3a – **In the past year, how many goth or goth-related events have you attended which involved travelling more than 30 miles from home?**

No. of events	Proportion selecting option %
None	9
1 to 3	31
4 to 10	24
More than 10	36

(valid cases 109, data rounded to nearest valid per cent)

Table 4. Most Important aspects of goth scene

WQ5a – **Which of the following are most important to your participation in the goth scene?**

Respondents invited to rank their top three choices from a list of eight (including 'other'). Table shows percentage of respondents selecting each option as their first choice and then percentage selecting each option somewhere among their three choices.

Attraction	Proportion selecting as 1st choice %	Proportion selecting selecting as either 1st, 2nd or 3rd choice %
Socializing	43	71
Nightclubs/pubs	11	66
Fashion/appearance	10	53
Recorded music	19	49
Live music	15	38
Books	1	10
Films	0	3
Other	2	4

(valid cases 105, data rounded to nearest valid per cent)

Table 5. Sources of Goth Music

WQ6a – Where do you buy goth music from?

Respondents invited to rank their top three choices from a list of seven (including 'other'). Table shows percentage of respondents selecting each option as their first choice and then percentage selecting each option somewhere among their three choices.

Source	Proportion selecting as 1st choice %	Proportion selecting as either 1st, 2nd or 3rd choice %
Local Independent Shops	42	63
Local Chain Shops	5	27
Shops Outside Locality	13	33
Gigs/Festivals	9	53
Mail Order	17	45
Don't Buy	11	11
Other	5	5

(valid cases 103, data rounded to nearest valid per cent)

Table 6. Sources of Goth Clothing and Accessories

WQ6b – Where do you buy goth clothes and accessories from?

Respondents invited to rank their top three choices from a list of eight (including 'other'). Table shows percentage of respondents selecting each option as their first choice and then percentage selecting each option somewhere among their three choices.

Source	Proportion selecting as 1st choice %	Proportion selecting as either 1st, 2nd or 3rd choice %
Local Independent Shops/ Market Stalls	47	68
Local Chain Shops	3	21
Non-Local Shops	21	41
Gigs/Festivals	10	53
Mail Order	3	26
Home Made	5	6
Don't Buy	10	10
Other	2	3

(valid cases 102, data rounded to nearest valid per cent)

Bibliography

Books and Academic References

Adorno, T. (1941), 'On Popular Music', in S. Frith and A. Goodwin (eds) (1990), *On Record: Rock, Pop and the Written Word*, London: Routledge.

Adorno, T. (1944), 'The Schema of Mass Culture', in J. Bernstein (ed.) (1991), *The Culture Industry: Selected Essays on Mass Culture*, London: Routledge.

Adorno, T. and Horkheimer, M. (1944), 'The Culture Industry: Enlightenment as Mass Deception', in J. Curran, M. Gurevitch and J. Woollacott (eds) (1977), *Mass Communication and Society*, London: Edward Arnold/Open University Press.

Anderson, B. (1991), *Imagined Communities*, London: Verso.

Ang, I. (1985), *Watching Dallas*, London: Methuen.

Atton, C. (2002), *Alternative Media*, London: Sage.

Baudrillard, J. (1983), *Simulations*, New York: Semiotext.

Baudrillard, J. (1988) 'Simulacra and Simulations', in M. Poster (ed.), *Baudrillard: Selected Writings*, Cambridge: Polity.

Bauman, Z. (1992a), *Intimations of Postmodernity*, London: Routledge.

Bauman, Z. (1992b), 'Survival as a Social Construct', *Theory, Culture and Society*, 9(1): 1–36.

Bauman, Z. (2001), *Community: Seeking Safety in an Insecure World*, Cambridge: Polity.

Baym, N. (1995), 'The Emergence of Community in Computer Mediated Communication', in S. Jones (ed.), *Cybersociety: Computer Mediated Communication and Community*, London: Sage.

Baym, N. (1997), 'Interpreting Soap Operas and Creating Community: Inside an Electronic Fan Culture', in S. Kiesler (ed.), *Culture of the Internet*, New Jersey: Lawrence Erlbaum Associates.

Bayton, M. (1997), 'Women and the Electric Guitar', in S. Whiteley (ed.), *Sexing the Groove: Popular Music and Gender*, London: Routledge.

Becker, H. (1963), *Outsiders: Studies in the Sociology of Deviance*, New York: Free Press.

Bennett, A. (1999), 'Subcultures or Neo-Tribes? Rethinking the Relationship Between Youth, Style and Musical Taste', *Sociology* 33(3): 599–617.

Bennett, A. (2000), *Popular Music and Youth Culture: Music, Identity and Place*, Basingstoke, Macmillan.

Blumer, H. (1969), *Symbolic Interactionism: Perspective and Method*, Englewood Cliffs, Prentice Hall.

Bourdieu, P. (1984), *Distinction: A Social Critique of the Judgement of Taste*, London: Routledge.

Butler, J. (1990), *Gender Trouble: Feminism and the Subversion of Identity*, London: Routledge.

Butler, J. (1991), 'Imitation and Gender Subordination', in D. Fuss (ed.) (1991), *Inside/Out*, London: Routledge.

Butler, J. (1993), *Bodies That Matter: On the Discursive Limits of 'Sex'*, New York: Routledge.

Came, H. (1996), 'Towards a Free and Loose Bisexual Future', in S. Rose and C. Stevens (eds), *Bisexual Horizons, Politics, Histories, Lives*, London: Lawrence & Wishart.

Chambers, I. (1985), *Urban Rhythms: Pop Music and Popular Culture*, London: Macmillan.

Chambers, I. (1988), *Popular Culture: The Metropolitan Experience*, London: Routledge.

Chaney, D. (1996), *Lifestyles*, London: Routledge.

Clarke, G. (1981), 'Defending Ski-Jumpers: A Critique of Theories of Youth Subcultures', in S. Frith and A. Goodwin (eds) (1990), *On Record: Rock, Pop and the Written Word*, London: Routledge.

Clarke, J., Hall, S., Jefferson, T. and Roberts, B. (1977), 'Subcultures, Cultures and Class: A Theoretical Overview', in S. Hall and T. Jefferson (eds), *Resistance Through Rituals: Youth Cultures in Post-War Britain*, London: Hutchinson.

Cohen, Albert (1955), *Delinquent Boys: The Culture of the Gang*, London: Collier-Macmillan.

Cohen, Anthony (1985), *The Symbolic Construction of Community*, Chichester: Ellis Horwood.

Cohen, P. (1972), 'Subcultural Conflict and Working Class Community', *Working Papers in Cultural Studies*, 2: 5–70.

Cohen, Sara (1991), *Rock Culture in Liverpool: Popular Music in the Making*, Oxford: Clarendon.

Cohen, Sara (1993), 'Ethnography and Popular Music Studies', *Popular Music*, 12(2): 123–137.

Cohen, Sara (1994), 'Identity, Place and the "Liverpool Sound"', in M. Stokes (ed.), *Ethnicity, Identity and Music*, Oxford: Berg.

Cohen, Stanley (1972), *Folk Devils and Moral Panics: The Creation of the Mods and Rockers*, London: MacGibbon & Lee.

Curtin, M. (1996), 'On Edge: Culture Industries in the Neo-Network Era', in R. Ohman (ed.), *Making and Selling Culture*, London: Wesleyan University Press.

Denzin, N. (1989), *Interpretive Interactionism*, London: Sage.

Dirlik, A. (1996), 'The Global in the Local', in R. Wilson and W. Dissanayake (eds), *Global/Local: Cultural Production and the Transnational Imaginary*, London: Duke University Press.

Dorfman, A. and Mattelart, A. (1991), *How to Read Donald Duck: Imperialist Ideology in the Disney Comic*, New York: International General.

Dyer, R. (1997), *White*, London: Routledge.

Eadie, J. (1996), 'Being Who We Are (and anyone else we want to be)', in S. Rose and C. Stevens (eds), *Bisexual Horizons: Politics, Histories, Lives*, London: Lawrence & Wishart.

Featherstone, M. (1991), *Consumer Culture and Postmodernism*, London: Sage.

Fernback, J. (1997), 'The Individual Within the Collective: Virtual Ideology and the Realisation of Collective Principles', in S. Jones (ed.), *Virtual Culture: Identity and Community in Cybersociety*, London: Sage.

Fernback, J. (1999), 'There is a There There: Notes Toward a Definition of Virtual Community', in S. Jones (ed.), *Doing Internet Research: Critical Issues and Methods for Examining the Net*, London: Sage.

Finnegan, R. (1989), *The Hidden Musicians*, Cambridge: Cambridge University Press.

Foster, P. (1996), 'Observational Research', in R. Sapsford and V. Jupp (eds), *Data Collection and Analysis*, London: Sage.

Frith, S. (1981), 'The Magic That Can Set You Free: The Ideology of Folk and the Myth of the Rock Community', *Popular Music*, 1: 159–68.

Frith, S. (1983), *Sound Effects, Youth, Leisure and the Politics of Rock 'n' Roll*, London: Constable.

Frith, S. and McRobbie, A. (1978), 'Rock and Sexuality', in S. Frith and S. Goodwin (eds), *On Record: Rock, Pop and the Written Word*, London: Routledge.

Gelder, K. and Thornton, S. (eds) (1997), *The Subcultures Reader*, London: Routledge.

Gillespie, M. (1995), *Television, Ethnicity and Cultural Change*, London: Routledge.

Goodwin, J. (1991), 'Popular Music and Postmodern Theory', *Cultural Studies*, 5(1): 174–190.

Gordon, M. (1947), 'The Concept of Subculture and its Application', in K. Gelder and S. Thornton (eds) (1997), *The Subcultures Reader*, London: Routledge.

Hall, S. and Jefferson, T. (eds) (1977), *Resistance Through Rituals: Youth Subcultures in Post-War Britain*, London: Hutchison.

Hannerz, U. (1996), *Transnational Connections: Culture, People, Places*, London: Routledge.

Harris, K. (2000), '"Roots"?: The Relationship Between the Global and The Local Within the Extreme Metal Scene', *Popular Music* 19(1): 13–30.

Harvey, D. (1989), *The Condition of Postmodernity: An Enquiry into the Logics of Social Change*, Oxford: Basil Blackwell.

Hebdige, D. (1977), 'The Meaning of Mod', in S. Hall and T. Jefferson (eds), *Resistance Through Rituals: Youth Subcultures in Post-War Britain*, London: Hutchinson.

Hebdige, D. (1979), *Subculture: The Meaning of Style*, London: Methuen.

Hebdige, D. (1988), *Hiding in the Light: On Images and Things*, London: Routledge.

Hetherington, K. (1992) 'Stonehenge and its Festival: Spaces of Consumption', in R. Shields (ed.), *Lifestyle Shopping: The Subject of Consumption*, London: Routledge.

Hetherington, K. (1998a), *Expressions of Identity: Space, Performance, Politics*, London: Sage.

Hetherington, K. (1998b), 'Vanloads of Uproarious Humanity: New Age Travellers and the Utopics of the Countryside', in T. Skelton and G. Valentine (eds), *Cool Places: Geographies of Youth Cultures*, London: Routledge.

Hill, K. and Hughes, J. (1998), *Cyberpolitics: Citizen Activism in the Age of the Internet*, Oxford: Rowman & Littlefield.

Hine, C. (2000), *Virtual Ethnography*, London: Sage.

Hollows, J. and Milestone, K. (1995), 'Inter City Soul: Transient Communities and Regional Identity in an Underground Urban Club Culture', Paper presented at British Sociological Association Annual Conference: 'Contested Cities', University of Leicester, 13–15 April.

Irwin, J. (1970), 'Notes on the Status of the Concept Subculture', in K. Gelder and S. Thornton (eds) (1997), *The Subcultures Reader*, London: Routledge.

Jameson, F. (1982), 'Postmodernism and Consumer Society', in H. Foster (ed.) (1985), *Postmodern Culture*, London: Pluto Press.

Jameson, F. (1991), *Postmodernism or the Cultural Logic of Late Capitalism*, London: Verso.

Jenkins, R. (1983), *Lads, Citizens and Ordinary Kids: Working Class Youth Life-Styles in Belfast*, London: Routledge & Kegan Paul.

Jones, S. (ed.) (1995), *Cybersociety: Computer Mediated Communication and Community*, London: Sage.

Jones, S. (1997), 'The Internet and its Social Landscape', in S. Jones (ed.), *Virtual Culture: Identity and Communication in Cybersociety*, London: Sage.

Jones, S. (ed.) (1997), *Virtual Culture: Identity and Communication in Cybersociety*, London: Sage.

Jones, S. (ed.) (1999), *Doing Internet Research: Critical Issues and Methods for Examining the Net*, London: Sage.

Jones, S. (ed.) (2000), *Cybersociety 2.0*, London: Sage.

Kendall, L. (1999), 'Recontextualising "Cyberspace": Methodological Considerations for On-Line Research', in S. Jones (ed), *Doing Internet Research: Critical Issues and Methods for Examining the Net*, London: Sage.

Kruse, H. (1993), 'Subcultural Identity in Alternative Music Culture', *Popular Music* 12(1): 31–43.

Lash, S. and Urry, J. (1987), *The End of Organised Capitalism*, Cambridge: Polity.

Leonard, M. (1997) '"Rebel girl, you are the queen of my world": Feminism, "subculture" and grrrl power', in S. Whiteley (ed.) *Sexing the Groove: Popular Music and Gender*, London: Routledge.

Leonard, M. (1998), 'Paper Planes: Travelling the New Grrrl Geographies', in T. Skelton and G. Valentine (eds), *Cool Places: Geographies of Youth Cultures*, London: Routledge.

Liebes, T. and Katz, E. (1993), *The Export of Meaning: Cross-Cultural Readings of Dallas*, 2nd edn, Cambridge: Polity.

Locher, D (1998), 'The Industrial Identity Crisis: The Failure of a Newly Forming Subculture to Identify Itself', in J. Epstein, *Youth Culture: Identity in a Postmodern World*, Oxford: Blackwell.

Lury, C. (1996), *Consumer Culture*, Cambridge, Polity.

MacDonald, D. (1957), 'A Theory of Mass Culture', in B. Rosenberg and D.White (eds) *Mass Culture*, Glencoe: Free Press.

Maffesoli, M. (1996), *The Time of the Tribes: The Decline of Individualism in Mass Society*, London: Sage.

Malbon, B. (1998), 'The Club: Consumption, Identity and the Spatial Practices of Every-Night Life', in T. Skelton and G. Valentine (eds), *Cool Places: Geographies of Youth Cultures*, London: Routledge.

Malbon, B. (1999), *Clubbing: Dancing, Ecstasy and Vitality*, London: Routledge.

Mann, C. and Stewart, F. (2000), *Internet Communication and Qualitative Research: A Handbook for Researching Online*, London: Sage.

Marcuse, H. (1964), *One Dimensional Man: The Ideology of Industrial Society*, London: Sphere.

McLaughlin, M., Osborne, K. and Ellison, N. (1997), 'Virtual Community in a Telepresence Environment', in S. Jones (ed.), *Virtual Community: Identity and Communication in Cybersociety*, London: Sage.

McRobbie, A. (1980), 'Settling Accounts with Subcultures: A Feminist Critique', in A. McRobbie (2000), *Feminism and Youth Culture*, 2nd edn, London: Macmillan.

McRobbie, A. (1989), 'Second Hand Dresses and the Role of the Rag Market', in A. McRobbie (ed.), *Zoot Suits and Second Hand Dresses: An Anthology of Fashion and Music*, London: Macmillan.

McRobbie, A. (1994), *Postmodernism and Popular Culture*, London: Routledge.

McRobbie, A. (1999), *In the Culture Society: Art, Fashion and Popular Music*, London: Routledge.

McRobbie, A. and Garber, J. (1977), 'Girls and Subcultures: An Exploration', in S. Hall and T. Jefferson (eds), *Resistance Through Rituals: Youth Subcultures in Post-War Britain*, London: Hutchinson.

Mercer, M. (1988), *Gothic Rock Black Book*, London: Omnibus Press.

Mercer, M. (1991), *Gothic Rock: All You Ever Wanted to Know But Were Too Gormless to Ask*, Birmingham: Pegasus.

Merton, R. (1972), 'Insiders and Outsiders: A Chapter in the Sociology of Knowledge', *American Journal of Sociology*, 78.

Meyer, M. (1994), *The Politics and Poetics of Camp*, London: Routledge.

Miyoshi, M. (1996), 'A Borderless World? From Colonialism to Transnationalism and the Decline of the Nation State', in R. Wilson and W. Dissanayake (eds), *Global/Local: Cultural Production and the Transnational Imaginary*, London: Duke University Press.

Muggleton, D. (1997), 'The Post-Subculturalist', in S. Redhead (ed.), *The Club Cultures Reader: Readings in Popular Cultural Studies*, Oxford: Blackwell.

Muggleton, D. (2000), *Inside Subculture: The Postmodern Meaning of Style*, Oxford: Berg.

Negus, K. (1992), *Producing Pop: Culture and Conflict in the Popular Music Industry*, London: Arnold.

Peet, R. (1982), 'International Capital, International Culture', in M. Taylor and N. Thrift (eds), *The Geography of the Multinationals*, London: Croom Helm.

Peet, R. (1989), 'The destruction of Regional Cultures', in R. Johnston and P. Taylor (eds), *A World in Crisis? Geographical Perspectives*, Oxford: Basil Blackwell.

Plummer, K. (1995), *Telling Sexual Stories*, London: Routledge.

Polhemous, T. (1997), 'In the Supermarket of Style', in S. Redhead (ed.), *The Club Cultures Reader*, Oxford: Blackwell.

Poster, M. (1995), *The Second Media Age*, Cambridge: Polity.

Redfield, R. (1955), *The Little Community: Viewpoints for the Study of a Human Whole*, Chicago: University of Chicago Press.

Redhead, S. (1993), 'The End of the End of Century Party', in S. Redhead, *Rave Off: Politics and Deviance in Contemporary Youth Culture*, Aldershot, Avebury.

Redhead, S. (ed.) (1997a), *The Club Cultures Reader: Readings in Popular Cultural Studies*, Oxford: Blackwell.

Redhead, S. (1997b), *Subcultures to Clubcultures – An Introduction to Popular Cultural Studies*, Oxford: Blackwell.

Reynolds, S. (1990), *Blissed Out*, London: Serpent's Tail.

Rhinegold, H. (1994), *The Virtual Community: Homesteading on the Electronic Frontier*, New York: HarperPerennial.

Richard, B. and Kruger, H. (1998), 'Ravers' Paradise. German Youth Cultures in the 1990s', in T. Skelton and G. Valentine (eds), *Cool Places: Geographies of Youth Cultures*, London: Routledge.

Sabin, R. and Triggs, T. (2000), *Below Critical Radar*, Hove: Slab-O-Concrete.

Sanderson, D. and Fortin, A. (2001), 'The Projection of Geographical Communities into Cyberspace', in S. Munt (ed.), *Technospaces: Inside New Media*, London: Continuum.

Schiller, H. (1985), 'Electronic Information Flows: New Basis for Global Domination', in P. Drummond and R. Paterson (eds), *Television in Transition*, London: British Film Institute.

Schiller, H. (1991) 'Not Yet the Post-Imperial Era', *Critical Studies in Mass Communication*, 8: 13–28.

Schiller, H. (1992), *Mass Communication and American Empire*, 2nd edn, Oxford: Westview, 1992.

Shank, B. (1994), *Dissonant Identities: The Rock 'n' Roll Scene in Austin, Texas*, Hanover: University Press of New England.

Sharf, B. (1999), 'Beyond Netiquette: The Ethics of Doing Naturalistic Discourse Research on the Internet', in S. Jones, *Doing Internet Research: Critical Issues and Methods for Examining the Net*, London: Sage.

Shields, R. (1992a), 'Spaces for the Subject of Consumption', in R. Shields (ed.), *Lifestyle Shopping: The Subject of Consumption*, London: Routledge.

Shields, R. (1992b), 'The Individual, Consumption Cultures and the Fate of Community', in R. Shields (ed.) (1992), *Lifestyle Shopping: The Subject of Consumption*, London: Routledge.

Shuker, R. (1994), *Understanding Popular Music*, London: Routledge.

Shutz, A. (1964), *Studies in Social Theory*, The Hague: Martinus Nijhoff.

Shutz, A. (1970), *On Phenomenology and Social Relations*, Chicago: University of Chicago Press.

Skelton, T. and Valentine, G. (eds) (1998), *Cool Places: Geographies of Youth Cultures*, London: Routledge.

Slobin, M. (1993), *Subcultural Sounds: Micromusics of the West*, Hanover: University Press of New England.

Smith, M. and Kollock, P. (1999), *Communities in Cyberspace*, London: Routledge.

Song, M. and Parker, D. (1995), 'Commonality, Difference and the Dynamics of Discourse in In-Depth Interviewing', *Sociology* 29(2): 241–56.

Stratton, J. (1985), 'On the Importance of Subcultural Origins', in K. Gelder and S. Thornton (eds) (1997), *The Subcultures Reader*, London: Routledge.

Straw, W. (1991), 'Systems of Articulation, Logics of Change: Communities and Scenes in Popular Music', *Cultural Studies*, 5(3): 368–88.

Straw, W. (1997), 'Organised Disorder – The Changing Space of the Record Shop', in S. Redhead (ed.), *The Clubcultures Reader: Readings in Popular Cultural Studies*, Oxford: Blackwell, 1997.

Strinati, D. (1995), *An Introduction to Theories of Popular Culture*, London: Routledge.

Thornton, S. (1995), *Club Cultures: Music, Media and Subcultural Capital*, Cambridge: Polity.

Thornton, S. and McRobbie, A. (1995), 'Rethinking Moral Panic for Multi-Mediated Social Worlds', in A. McRobbie (2000), *Feminism and Youth Culture*, 2nd edn, London: Macmillan.

Tomlinson, J. (1991), *Cultural Imperialism: A Critical Introduction*, London: Pinter.

Tonnies, F. (1955), *Community and Association*, London: Routledge & Kegan Paul.

Triggs, T. (2000), 'Liberated Spaces. Identity Politics and Anti-Consumerism', in R. Sabin and T. Triggs (eds), *Below Critical Radar. Fanzines and Comics from 1976 to Now*, Hove: Slab-O-Concrete.

Turkle, S. (1995), *Life on the Screen: Identity in the Age of the Internet*, London: Phoenix.

Wallis, R., and Malm, K. (1984), *Big Sounds From Small Peoples*, London: Constable.

Wallis, R. and Malm, K. (1992), *Media Policy and Music Activity*, London: Routledge.

Watson, N. (1997), 'Why We Argue About Virtual Community: A Case Study of the Phish.Net Fan Community', in S. Jones (ed.), *Virtual Culture: Internet and Communication in Cybersociety*, London: Sage.

Wellman, B. and Gulia, M. (1999), 'Virtual Communities as Communities', in M. Smith and P. Kollock (eds), *Communities in Cyberspace*, London: Routledge.

Whyte, W. (1943), *Street Corner Society: The Social Structure of an Italian Slum*, Chicago: University of Chicago Press.

Widdicombe, S. and Wooffitt, R. (1995), *The Language of Youth Subcultures: Social Identity in Action*, New York: Harvester Wheatsheaf.

Willis, P. (1978), *Profane Culture*. London: Routledge & Kegan Paul.

Willis, P. (1990), *Common Culture: Symbolic work at Play in the Everyday Cultures of the Young*, Milton Keynes: Open University Press.

Wilson, R. and Dissanayake, W. (eds) (1996), *Global/Local: Cultural Production and the Transnational Imaginary*, London: Duke University Press.

Young, J. (1971), *The Drug Takers: The Social Meaning of Drug Use*, London: Paladin.

Newspaper/Magazine References

Alford, L. (1993), 'Art of Darkness', *Observer Life*, 31/10/93: 10–11.

BRV Magazine (1998), 'Gig Dates', Issue 24: 5.

Collins, A. (1991), 'Ghoul's Out: Bluffers Guide to Goth', *New Musical Express*, 30/11/91: 22–23.

Dalton, S. (1998), 'Garbage: Version 2.0', Album Review (Mushroom), *New Musical Express*, 09/05/98.

Davidson, J. (1999), 'Go Goth Young Girl', *The Herald Magazine*, 30/09/99: 30–3.

Gilbert, J. (1996), 'Goths Vamp it Up in Drac-by-the-Sea', *Independent on Sunday*, 29/09/96: 4.

Malins, S. (1998), 'Black Arts: Goth. It Wore Dark Eyeliner, Invented Nine Inch Nails and Today Lives in Morecambe', Album Review (Nocturnal, Procreate), *Q Magazine*, 07/98: 124.

Matherson, L. and Simpson, G. (1997), 'Oh My Goth: Weird Picture Report', *Minx*, 07/97: 68–70.

Myres, B. (1997), 'Some Might Slay', *Melody Maker*, 11/10/97: 25.

Myres, B. (1998), 'Re-Release the Bats', *Melody Maker*, 12/12/98: 23.

New Musical Express, 01/05/99, front cover.

No. 1 Magazine, (1986), 'Glad to be Goth', 1986: 34–5 (based on information provided by respondent – unsure on precise date).

North, R., (1983), 'Positive Punk', *New Musical Express*, 02/83.

Oldham, J. (1996), 'Placebo: Placebo', Album Review, *New Musical Express*, 14/09/96.

O'Sullivan, K. (1999), 'Rock King of Evil the Kids Adore: The Hero', *The Mirror*, 22/04/99.

Owen, R. and Mitchell, J. (1997), 'The New Black', *The Big Issue*, 27/11/97: 31.

Paterson, R. (1997), 'Goth It', *Spectrum (Scotland on Sunday)*, 12/07/97: 5.

Salter, M. (1998), 'Dark, Satanic Thrills', *The Big Issue in the North*, 08/98: 22–3.

Seagal, V. (1998), 'Nocturnal', Album Review, *New Musical Express*, 06/06/98.

Thompson, D. and Greene, J. (1994), 'Undead Undead Undead: The History of the Gothic Movement', *Alternative Press*, 11/94.

Thompson, N. (1999), 'The Mission: London WC2 Astoria', Gig Review, *New Musical Express*, 01/12/99.

Tovey, S. (1999), 'Moonspell: From the Cocoon Unfolds the Butterfly', *Terrorizer*, 10/99: 32–3.

Tsarfin, Z. (1999), 'Typonegative: The Wire in the Blood', *Terrorizer*, 10/99: 38–9.

Udo, T. (1996), 'The Mission: Blue (Equator)', Album Review, *New Musical Express*, 29/07/96.

Wright, G. and Miller, S. (1999), 'A Clique Within a Clique, Obsessed with Guns, Death and Hitler', *The Guardian*, 22/04/99: 3.

Younge, G. and Ellison, M. (1999), ' Black Tuesday', *The Guardian*, 23/04/99: 2–3 (G2).

Web Site References

alt.gothic FAQ (accessed July 2000), www.darkwave.org.uk/faq/ag

Darkwave.org.uk (accessed 1999–2000), www.darkwave.org.uk

Faithful Dawn Homepage (accessed January 1999), www.ourworld.compuserve.com/
  homepages/outletpromotions

gothicland (accessed July 2000), www.gothicland.com

helix (accessed 1997–2000), www.pennangalan.co.uk/Helix

International Goth Club Listing (accessed August 2000), www.vamp.org/Gothic/
  clublist.html

net.goth map, (accessed 1999–2000), www.gothmap.org.uk

Scathe, P. (accessed August 2000), *A History of Goth*, www.scathe.demon.co.uk/
  histgoth.htm

uk.people.gothic FAQ (accessed July 2000), www.darkwave,org.uk/faq/ukpg

On-Line Discussion Group References

Amison, N. (November 1998), 'Dream Disciples', *Contaminatii mailing list*.

De Bie, C. (April 2000), 'Re: It Used to be About the Music Man', *Tainted mailing
  list*.

Harvey, P. (November 1999), 'Re: Toreador on Saturday', *Tainted mailing list*.

Hemming, L. (May 1999), 'Re: Skirts on Blokes', *Contaminatii mailing list*.

Hobberstad, M. (January 1999), 'Wendyhouse', *Contaminatii mailing list*.

Johnson, M. (January 1999), 'A New Black Rose Emporium in Camden', *uk.people.
  gothic*.

MurkyGoth (May 1999), 'Re: Torrie Info', *Contaminatii mailing list*.

Sneekybat (January 1999), 'The End of Necromantik (sop weep etc)', *uk.people.
  gothic*.

Tudway (April 1999), 'Re: US Killings rant rant rant', *uk.people.gothic*.

White, J. (January 1999), 'Re: Whitby', *Contaminatii mailing list*.

Wilson, G. (December 1998), 'Melody Maker Goth Feature', *uk.people.gothic*.

Miscellaneous References

McCullie, D. (1999), *Wendy House promotional stickers*.

Discography

Please note that what follows is **NOT** a general discography for the goth
scene. It merely contains selected examples of releases from artists which
have been referred to directly in the text or the endnotes.

Alien Sex Fiend (1983), *Ignore the Machine/The Girl at the End of My Gun*, Anagram.

All About Eve (1988), *All About Eve*, Mercury.

Apoptygma Berzerk (1996), *Seven*, CD, Tatra Productions.

Aqua (1997), *Barbie Girl*, CD, Universal Music.

Bauhaus (1979), *Bela Lugosi's Dead/Boys/Dark Entries*, Small Wonder.

The Birthday Party (1981), *Release the Bats/Blast Off*, 4 AD.

Bowie, David (1972), *Ziggy Stardust*, RCA.

Covenant (1998), *Europa*, Off Beat.

The Cult (1985), *Love*, Beggars Banquet.

The Cure (1981), *Faith*, Fiction.

The Cure (1987), *Kiss Me, Kiss Me, Kiss Me*, Fiction.

The Cure (1989), *Disintegration*, Fiction.

Dead Can Dance (1988), *The Serpent's Egg*, 4AD.

Die Laughing (1996), *Heaven in Decline*, Grave News.

Faith and the Muse (1999), *Evidence of Heaven*, Neue Asthetik Multimedia.

Faithful Dawn (1999), *You Are Here*, Dark Beat Records.

Fields of the Nephilim (1987), *Dawnrazor*, Situation Two.

Fields of the Nephilim (1990), *Elizium*, Beggars Banquet.

Front Line Assembly (1996), *Plasticity*, Off Beat.

Funhouse (1996), *Never Again*, M&A Musicart.

Garbage (1995), *Garbage*, Mushroom Records.

The Horatii (1999), *Succour Punch*, Resurrection Records.

Joy Division (1980), *Love Will Tear Us Apart/These Days*, Factory.

Manuskript (1999), *Devil's Advocate*, Resurrection Records.

Marilyn Manson (1996), *Antichrist Superstar*, Nothing/Interscope.

Merry Thoughts (1993), *Millennium Done: Empire Songs*, Dion Fortune Records.

The Mission (1986), *Serpent's Kiss/Wake*, Chapter 22.

The Mission (1990), *Butterfly on a Wheel/The Grip of Disease*, Mercury.

Nekromantik (1998), *Fairy Catcher*, Dark Beat Records.

Nine Inch Nails (1994), *Closer*, Island Records.

Nosferatu (1993), *Rise*, Possession Records.

Placebo (1998), *Without You I'm Nothing*, Elevator.

Play Dead (1982), *Propaganda/Propaganda (mix)*, Jungle.

Sex Gang Children (1982), *Beasts*, Illuminated.

Shampoo (1995), *Trouble*, Food Ltd.

Siouxsie and the Banshees (1981), *Ju Ju*, Polydor.

Siouxsie and the Banshees (1988), *Peepshow*, Wonderland/Polydor.

Siouxsie and the Banshees (1992), *Twice Upon a Time*, Polydor.

Sisters of Mercy (1985), *First and Last and Always*, Merciful Release/WEA.

Sisters of Mercy (1987), *Floodland*, Merciful Release/WEA.

Sisters of Mercy (1993), *Greatest Hits Volume One: A Slight Case of Over Bombing*, Warner Music UK.

Specimen (1983), *Kiss Kiss, Bang Bang*, Jungle Records.

Suspiria (1997), *Drama*, Nightbreed Recordings.

Synthetic (1999), *MIDI Slave*, Resurrection Records.

Type O Negative (1996), *October Rust*, Roadrunner.

UK Decay (1981), *For Madmen Only*, Fresh.

Various Artists (1992), *Gothic Rock*, Jungle Records.

Various Artists (1995), *Gothic Rock 2*, Jungle Records.

Various Artists (1998), *Nocturnal*, Procreate.

Various Artists (1997), *Hex Files Vol. 1*, Credo Records.

Various Artists (1997), *Hex Files Vol. 2*, Credo Records.

Virgin Prunes (1982), *If I Die, I Die*, Rough Trade.

VNV Nation (1998), *The Solitary EP*, Off Beat.

Index

Printed in the United Kingdom
by Lightning Source UK Ltd.
102772UKS00001B/223-384